SELECTED CASES IN STRATEGIC MARKETING

for the University of Phoenix
SECOND EDITION

LINDA E. SWAYNE
PETER M. GINTER

SIMON & SCHUSTER CUSTOM PUBLISHING

Printed in the United States of America

10 9 8 7 6 5 4 3

ISBN 0-536-58813-9
BA 97025

SIMON & SCHUSTER CUSTOM PUBLISHING
160 Gould Street/Needham Heights, MA 02194
Simon & Schuster Education Group

CONTENTS

CASE 7   Pan Am Attempts Survival in the 1990s   125

CASE 23   HEALTHSOUTH Rehabilitation Corporation   438

CASE 26   Carolco Pictures   514

CASE 37   Lotus Development Corporation: Maintaining Leadership in the Competitive Electronic Spreadsheet Industry   695

CASE 1   Gatorade Defends Its No. 1 Position   1

CASE 9   Wal-Mart Stores: Strategies for Market Dominance   169

CASE 21   Verbatim Challenges 3M for Market Leadership   385

CASE 34   American Greetings Faces New Challenges in the 1990s   646

CASE 22   Anheuser-Busch Dominates in the 1990s   404

CASE 25   Harley-Davidson   485

CASE 29   Rubbermaid   567

CASE 33   Sun Microsystems: Competing in a High-Tech Industry   629

——————————————— CASE 7 ———————————————

PAN AM ATTEMPTS SURVIVAL IN THE 1990s

INTRODUCTION

In September 1991, the new president of Pan Am sat in his office, contemplating the lights of New York City as he attempted to calm himself before heading home. Delta and Pan Am had finally reached an accord that would allow Pan Am to survive, something few industry analysts had predicted. Delta agreed to purchase all of Pan Am's European routes, the East Coast shuttle, and related equipment, leaving Pan Am with a much smaller route structure confined to Central and South America. The president knew that many critics viewed this as merely postponing the inevitable; Pan Am, they said, could no longer compete. Better to let it go quietly rather than prolong the agony. The president could not accept that. "Pan Am's long and glorious history must count for something," he

This case was prepared by Kent N. Gourdin as a basis for class discussion rather than to illustrate either effective or ineffective handling of an administrative situation. Used with permission from Kent N. Gourdin.

thought. "The challenge will be to bring Pan Am back to profitability—to survive this brutally competitive industry."

A HISTORY OF PAN AM

Pan American Airways was formed by Juan Trippe in 1927 to carry mail between Florida and Cuba utilizing three Fokker trimotor aircraft. Trippe led the company until 1968, and it was his vision that guided the firm's development into the world-spanning airline it eventually became. Pan Am was a company of firsts: first to fly across the Pacific, first across the Atlantic, and first to successfully fly commercial jets. Furthermore, Pan Am was the only carrier to ever offer around-the-world service, with one daily flight traveling eastbound from New York while another flew west.

The magnitude of Trippe's accomplishments cannot be overemphasized. Prior to World War II, airlines were responsible for building their own infrastructure. Thus, Pan Am's Pacific expansion began with the arrival of ships carrying equipment and construction workers at places such as Honolulu, Midway Island, Wake Island, and Guam. The company's resources were then utilized to build and staff the airports, communications systems, and passenger support facilities that today are provided by the government. Pan Am repeated this pattern in Latin America, Alaska, and across the Atlantic. In addition, Trippe traveled around the world negotiating his own air rights with foreign countries.

Following World War II, Pan Am continued its domination of international commercial aviation, and came to symbolize U.S. supremacy in that area. Though other U.S. carriers began flying overseas as well, none enjoyed the comprehensive route network or long-standing reputation of Pan Am. Its world-spanning coverage reached its zenith in 1984 and is shown in Exhibit 7.1.

Management historically placed a great deal of emphasis on the physical aspects of the business. Pan Am pioneered in-flight dining and entertainment in the 1930s. It was the first customer for both the Boeing 707 in the late 1950s and the Boeing 747 10 years later. Trippe placed large initial orders for these revolutionary wide-body aircraft before they were even off the drawing board, thus ensuring that Pan Am would be the first airline to operate them. Indeed, the airline's commitment to technical excellence combined with its extensive international route structure made it the only choice for travel to or from the United States. In other words, you flew Pan Am or you did not go.

The second by-product of the company's international domination was that it had virtually no domestic route structure to feed traffic into its overseas routes. Congress had historically been supportive of Pan Am's worldwide growth, viewing the carrier as an instrument of national policy. This support took the form of subsidies and lucrative international route awards with little or no U.S. competi-

EXHIBIT 7.1   Pan Am Points Served, 1984

United States

Austin
Boston
Charlotte
Chicago
Cincinnati
Cleveland
Dallas/Fort Worth
Detroit
Honolulu
Houston
Indianapolis
Kansas City
Los Angeles
Miami
Minneapolis/St. Paul
Nashville
New Orleans
New York
Orlando
Philadelphia
Pittsburgh
Raleigh/Durham
St. Louis
San Antonio
Seattle/Tacoma
Tampa/St. Petersburg
Washington, D.C.

Atlantic/Caribbean Islands

Antigua
Bahamas: Freeport
   Nassau
Barbados
Bermuda
Guadeloupe
Martinique
St. Kitts
St. Lucia
St. Maarten
Trinidad
U.S. Virgin Islands
   St. Croix
   St. Thomas

Mexico and Central America

Guatemala City
Mexico City

South America

Buenos Aires
Caracas
Maracaibo
Montevideo
Rio de Janeiro
Santiago
Sao Paulo

Europe

Amsterdam
Athens
Belgrade
Bucharest
Budapest
Dubrovnik
Frankfurt
Geneva
Hamburg
Istanbul
London
Munich
Nice
Nuremberg
Paris
Rome
Stuttgart
Vienna
Warsaw
Zagreb
Zurich

Middle East

Dhahran
Dubai

Africa

Dakar
Johannesburg
Lagos
Monrovia
Nairobi

Orient/Asia

Bangkok
Beijing
Bombay
Delhi
Hong Kong
Karachi
Manila
Osaka
Seoul
Shanghai
Singapore
Taipei
Tokyo

South Pacific

Auckland
Melbourne
Sydney

Source: Pan Am Corporation, *Annual Report*, 1984, p. 2.

tion. However, that attitude changed dramatically in the late 1940s, when Congress began awarding overseas routes to other U.S. airlines such as TWA, Braniff, and Northwest. Indeed, this signaled the beginning of an "anti–Pan Am" sentiment in the government that would haunt the future development of the carrier. The government became so concerned about the size of Pan Am that Congress consistently refused to allow the airline to expand domestically for fear that it would become an overpowering competitor for other U.S. carriers. Thus, as other airlines grew and gradually expanded overseas, Pan Am was precluded from responding in kind domestically.[1]

As was the case with most other U.S. airlines, Pan Am was highly profitable during the 1960s, but its fortunes changed in the 1970s. Just after it introduced the first 747 jumbo jets in 1969, international travel promptly declined, the value of the dollar fell, and the price of oil skyrocketed. (Another by-product of the airline's international route structure was that Pan Am bought the majority of its fuel at overseas locations, where the cost was much greater than in the United States.) After turning a profit in 1977 and 1978, Pan Am again attempted to resolve its lack of a domestic route structure. Two months prior to the passing of the Airline Deregulation Act in 1978, Pan Am applied to merge with National Airlines.

The merger proved unexpectedly challenging for several reasons. First, the company got into a bidding war with Eastern Airlines and Texas International that resulted in Pan Am paying $50 per share for National's stock ($430 million total) versus the $30 per share initially offered.[2] Second, after finally taking over in January 1980, Pan Am raised the pay of National employees to Pan Am's higher wage scales almost immediately. Third, Pan Am failed to integrate the two operations smoothly. Finally, they failed to build the domestic network they were seeking.[3] The most distressing part of all, though, was that the deregulation of the U.S. airline industry just two months later permitted Pan Am to expand at its discretion; the company need not have put itself through the National agony at all.

The explosive growth of airline competition resulting from deregulation, together with Pan Am's on-going trouble, combined with various other environmental factors to produce ever-growing losses. Draconian actions were taken (1980—sale of the headquarters building in midtown Manhattan for $400 million; 1981—sale of the Intercontinental Hotel chain for $500 million; 1985—sale of Pan Am's entire Pacific division to United Airlines for $750 million), but to no avail. A terrorist bomb destroyed one of the airline's 747s over Lockerbie, Scotland, in December 1988, killing all aboard and costing the carrier $350 million in lost revenue and increased expenses. With the outbreak of war in the Middle East in 1990, Pan Am's fate was sealed. Foreign travel virtually stopped, and passengers that *did* fly avoided Pan Am studiously, concerned that it was a tempting terrorist

---

[1] Richard L. Stern, "The End of an Empire," *Forbes*, February 4, 1991, p. 76.
[2] "Pan Am's Flight to a New Hangar," *Newsweek*, August 6, 1979, p. 63.
[3] *Wall Street Journal*, July 12, 1991, p. A5.

target. In a final effort to survive, the airline sold most of its London routes along with its highly prized Heathrow hub, to United for $400 million. However, on January 8, 1991, Pan Am filed for protection from its creditors under Chapter 11 of the Federal Bankruptcy Code, which permits a company to continue operating while it attempts to reorganize. Financial data on Pan Am and its three largest U.S. competitors are presented in Exhibits 7.2 and 7.3.

EXHIBIT 7.2   Selected Financial Data, 1981–1990

	American	Delta	Pan Am	United
Operating Revenues (Millions of Dollars)				
1990	$10,639	$8,673	$3,969	$10,501
1989	9,961	8,648	3,612	9,742
1988	8,551	7,393	3,592	8,796
1987	7,124	6,094	3,121	7,863
1986	5,856	4,497	2,733	6,688
1985	5,860	4,738	3,156	4,920
1984	5,088	4,497	3,382	6,097
1983	4,532	3,905	3,529	5,287
1982	3,978	3,632	3,471	4,614
1981	3,911	3,644	3,586	4,470
Operating Expenses (Millions of Dollars)				
1990	10,249	8,518	4,250	10,284
1989	9,230	7,972	3,930	9,185
1988	7,749	6,868	3,698	8,129
1987	6,651	5,659	3,292	7,712
1986	5,465	4,271	3,106	6,698
1985	5,353	4,507	3,364	5,248
1984	4,748	4,209	3,517	5,547
1983	4,282	3,962	3,516	5,134
1982	3,996	3,718	3,844	4,682
1981	3,868	3,558	3,963	4,617
Operating Margin (Operating Revenue/Expenses)				
1990	103.8	101.8	.934	102.1
1989	107.9	108.5	.919	106.1
1988	110.3	107.6	.971	108.3
1987	107.1	107.7	.948	102.0
1986	107.2	105.3	.880	.999
1985	109.5	105.1	.938	.938
1984	107.2	106.8	.970	110.0
1983	106.8	.986	100.0	103.0
1982	.995	.977	.900	.985
1981	101.1	102.4	.900	.968

Source: *Standard and Poors Industry Surveys:* January 6, 1986, pp. A31, A32; April 28, 1988, pp. A33, A34; June 20, 1991, pp. A37, A38.

EXHIBIT 7.3   Net Operating Income and Net Income Figures (In thousands)

	American	Delta	Pan Am	United
Net Operating Income				
1990	$8,082	$ − 31,525	$ − 8,231	$112,051
1989	22,967	− 87	− 201,266	154,983
1988	7,528	84,110	75,832	206,367
1987	− 9,198	51,637	88,891	54,800
1986	14,025	12,774	− 89,526	− 61,021
1985	506,484	231,207	− 207,577	− 328,004
1984	339,065	287,344	− 135,216	550,006
1983	249,517	− 57,207	13,131	152,362
1982	− 18,247	− 85,948	− 372,736	− 68,549
1981	43,356	86,505	− 377,431	− 146,729
Net Income				
1990	$3,255	$ − 15,423	$ − 166,868	$101,823
1989	9,135	18,571	− 165,535	100,752
1988	− 416	58,972	70,411	163,739
1987	− 10,686	32,229	112,854	11,737
1986	6,893	8,571	− 157,461	− 36,884
1985	322,640	156,775	37,474	− 88,223
1984	208,606	258,641	64,080	235,856
1983	217,874	37,892	356,915	119,716
1982	− 14,476	− 17,058	—5,331	− 17,358
1981	47,440	91,640	− 18,875	− 104,893

Source: *Standard and Poors Industry Surveys,* January 6, 1986, pp. A31, A32; April 28, 1988, pp. A33, A34; June 20, 1991, pp. A37, A38.

AIRLINE DEREGULATION

In 1938, the U.S. government began regulating the domestic airline industry. For the next 40 years, the Civil Aeronautics Board (CAB), which was created for the express purpose of monitoring the economic aspects of commercial aviation, had the final authority regarding rates, routes, and services provided by the airlines. Economic regulation occurred for several reasons. First, Congress was concerned that uncontrolled competition would weaken the airlines and negatively impact the U.S. air transportation system. Second, transportation was, at the time, viewed as a service that should be made available to everyone. Since carriers would, if left alone, provide transportation only over profitable routes, Congress utilized the regulatory process to "force" them to serve unprofitable routes as well.

This was accomplished by limiting the number of airlines permitted to serve profitable routes. In exchange for this quasi monopoly, carriers were required to serve nonprofitable routes as a public service. Fares were, to a large degree, fixed, so that price competition was virtually unknown. Seeking CAB permission to fly a new route or alter fares was a difficult and time-consuming process for a carrier that, as often as not, ended in failure for the applicant, so the whole system was extremely stable. In essence, consumers chose their airline based upon which one flew to the destination of choice, and they paid the published fare.

This equilibrium was destroyed in October 1978 when Congress passed the Airline Deregulation Act, which freed the airlines from economic regulation, a move that signified the government's willingness to let market forces guide the allocation of transportation resources. If a route was not profitable, the carrier could stop service; generally new routes could be added at will. Carriers were given more freedom in setting rates; price became a function of demand and could be actively utilized as a marketing tool. Deregulation put the business of air transportation back into the hands of the managers, who became free to decide which routes they would serve and what fares they would charge. Managers had to bear the burden of their mistakes as deregulation also implied the freedom to fail, something that had been quite difficult under the sheltering umbrella of economic regulation.

Impact of Deregulation on the U.S. Airline Industry

In the late 1970s and early 1980s, there were numerous new airlines challenging the established carriers. Some (People Express, New York Air) offered low prices and minimal services; others (Presidential Air, Air One) adopted a high-service/high-price strategy. In fact, the number of scheduled carriers grew from 36 just prior to deregulation to a peak of 229 in 1984.[4] Although this number included companies of all sizes, this discussion focuses only on the larger, more well known airlines. In 1984, there were approximately 24 of these. By 1991, this number dwindled to roughly 13 as a result of mergers, acquisitions, and outright failures.[5] As shown in Exhibit 7.4, six of the survivors were operating under conditions of bankruptcy or default. Of great concern, however, was the fact that the five strongest airlines controlled approximately 75 percent of the market,[6] with American, Delta, and United accounting for 14.6, 13.1, and 11.5 percent, respectively.[7]

Despite this consolidation, however, opportunities continued to attract new entrants. By mid-1991, 17 requests for new operating certificates had been received by the Department of Transportation, despite a recession and a general downturn in air travel. Companies such as Air Reno, U.S.–Africa Airways, and Miami Air all hoped to succeed by exploiting niche markets of little interest to the major airlines.[8]

[4] Robert M. Kane and Allan D. Vose, *Air Transportation* (Dubuque, IA: Kendall/Hunt, 1987), pp. 11–24.
[5] Michael Oneal, Wendy Zellner, and Seth Payne, "Fly the Lucrative Skies of United American Delta," *Business Week*, October 14, 1991, p. 91.
[6] Ibid., p. 90.
[7] "Few Carriers Win Battle for Survival," *USA Today*, August 5, 1991, p. 1B.
[8] Edward L. McKenna, "More Entrant Airlines Seeking U.S. Approval, Defying Tight Market," *Aviation Week and Space Technology*, November 18, 1991, pp. 24–25.

EXHIBIT 7.4   Major Scheduled Airlines, 1984 and 1991

1984	1991
Air Cal[a]	Alaskan
Air Florida[b]	American
Alaskan	America West[j]
American	Continental[j]
America West	Delta
Continental	Midway[j]
Delta	Northwest
Eastern[c]	Pan Am[j]
Empire[d]	Southwest
Frontier[e]	Trump Shuttle[j]
Midway	TWA[j]
New York Air[c]	United
Northwest	USAir
Ozark[f]	
Pacific Southwest[g]	
Pan Am	
People Express[c]	
Piedmont[g]	
Republic[h]	
Southwest	
TWA	
United	
USAir	
Western[i]	

[a] Merged with American.
[b] Merged with Midway.
[c] Merged with, or absorbed by
Continental.
[d] Merged with Piedmont.
[e] Merged with Delta.
[f] Merged with People Express.
[g] Merged with TWA.
[h] Merged with USAir.
[i] Merged with Delta

[j] Operating in bankruptcy or default.

Source: "Fly the Lucrative Skies of United American Delta," *Business Week*, October 14, 1991,
p. 91.

Hub-and-Spoke Systems

Airlines adopted hub-and-spoke systems in an attempt to increase service and decrease costs. Passengers were brought from outlying cities (spokes) into the hub (large central airports), where they changed planes and proceeded to their destinations. For example, travelers flying from Knoxville, Tennessee, to Los

Angeles on USAir, would board a plane in Knoxville, fly to USAir's Charlotte hub, change planes, and complete their trip to the West Coast. This system allowed the carrier to offer more frequent service utilizing smaller aircraft. Unfortunately, it also meant that nonstop flights became less common, unless passengers were originating or terminating their trip at a hub.

One result of this route structure was that carriers were able to completely dominate the traffic into or out of their respective hubs, effectively limiting competition from new carriers. This occurred because the dominant airline (or airlines) leased all of the airport's gate space, thereby denying access to other carriers. Furthermore, the sheer number of flights operated at the hub by the dominant carrier made utilizing another airline simply less attractive to the passenger, since doing so meant making a stop at *their* hub versus going nonstop. USAir, for example, operated about 470 daily flights to or from Charlotte, North Carolina, accounting for approximately 94 percent of the total scheduled traffic at that airport in 1991. Exhibit 7.5 depicts the hubs maintained by U.S. air carriers as of late 1991.

EXHIBIT 7.5   **Major U.S. Airlines and Hub Locations**

Airline	Location of Hub Airports		
American	Dallas-Fort Worth Raleigh-Durham San Juan	San Jose, Calif. Miami	Chicago (O'Hare) Nashville
United	Chicago (O'Hare) Washington, D.C. (Dulles)	Denver Tokyo	San Francisco London
Delta	Atlanta Salt Lake City New York (JFK)	Cincinnati Los Angeles Frankfurt	Dallas-Fort Worth Orlando
Northwest	Detroit Washington, D.C. (National)	Memphis	Minneapolis
USAir	Pittsburgh Philadelphia	Charlotte	Baltimore
Continental	Denver Newark	Cleveland	Houston
TWA	New York	St. Louis	Paris (deGaulle)
Pan Am	Miami		
America West	Phoenix	Honolulu	Las Vegas
Southwest	Dallas	Houston	Phoenix
Alaska	Anchorage	Portland	Seattle
Midway	Chicago (Midway)		

Source: "Dogfight in the Skies," *USA Today*, August 5, 1991, pp. 2B, 3B.

Productivity

Deregulation forced airline companies to become more productive, both from the standpoint of increasing their output (moving more people) and lowering their input (controlling their costs). The computerized reservation system (CRS) emerged as a powerful tool for doing both. Many of the large carriers developed these highly sophisticated programs, which allowed travel agents and other service agencies to immediately present prospective travelers with all of the flight options available for their desired routing. American's SABRE system and United's APOLLO accounted for about 68 percent of the market, while SYSTEM ONE (Continental), WORLDSPAN (Delta/Northwest/TWA), and several foreign networks (GALILEO and AMADEUS in Europe, ABACUS in Asia, GEMINI in Canada) competed for the rest.[9] Typically, the host airline's flights were presented first, so that the agent might have to scroll through multiple screens in order to examine flights offered by competing carriers. Airlines that did not maintain their own CRS paid a fee to be listed on those belonging to other carriers.

A CRS could provide a significant competitive advantage to an airline. First, they were extremely costly to develop; second, in addition to air travel, the CRS could also be used to book hotel, rental car, and transportation services via other modes (i.e., rail); third, travel agents tended to subscribe only to one CRS; and, finally, with the multitude of ticket prices available, they provided travel agents and users virtually the only means of quoting reliable fare information. In short, computer reservation systems became such a powerful competitive weapon that the U.S. government was considering action that would force those airlines, such as American, United, and Delta, that owned large CRSs to either divest themselves of those assets or render them unbiased in their treatment of other carriers.

Airlines also adopted a very sophisticated pricing system. Commonly referred to as yield management, carriers were able to price based on the passengers' demand elasticity for air transportation. On any given plane, people may have paid any one of 12 to 15 different fares for the same basic service: movement from point A to point B. For example, passengers who were willing to book, and pay for, a flight far in advance and incur restrictions on their travel (no changes, cancellations, and so on) could often obtain a low fare. On the other hand, a person who needed to fly immediately, and who could not live with travel limitations, paid a much higher price. What made this pricing system work was the tremendous analytical capacity of the CRS, which provided management the utilization history on each flight so that fares could be tailored to extract the maximum revenue based on demand patterns. Obviously, what these efforts were intended to do was to fill the airplane, as an empty seat represented revenue that was lost forever. To that same end, management also became skilled at getting more people into each plane. Knee room was gradually reduced, as was the extent to which each seat could recline. Seats themselves were thinner and aisles

---

[9] *Standard and Poors Industrial Surveys 1991* (New York: Standard and Poors, 1991), p. A36.

narrower, all for the purpose of increasing the passenger-carrying capability of the aircraft.

Management also became adept at cutting costs (reducing input). As was mentioned previously, the hub-and-spoke system was initially devised as a way to lower costs and improve passenger loads. Airlines were utilizing aircraft that were extremely reliable, that were fuel efficient, and that in many cases only required the use of two cockpit crew members. Lower labor rates in general were negotiated, surplus jobs eliminated, and passenger services brought more into line with customer needs.

In light of the above discussion, one key point emerged with respect to deregulation's impact on the airline industry: Bigger seemed to be better. Rightly or wrongly, the key to success, at least in the United States, were computer reservations systems, hub domination, yield management, and cost control. This was not to say, however, that there were no longer opportunities available to smaller carriers. The entrepreneurial spirit still seemed to live in the airline industry, be it in the form of geographic markets that were underserved, or customer segments whose needs could not be met by the large carriers.

THE DELTA DEAL

The situation at Pan Am continued to worsen during 1991. By late summer, the carrier's continued viability was seriously in doubt. Several potential buyers began negotiations to purchase pieces of the ailing company, and in August Delta Airlines presented the bid that was ultimately accepted by Pan Am's management. They agreed to pay $416 million for Pan Am's New York–based transatlantic operations, the Pan Am Shuttle, and related aircraft, spares, and fixed assets. In addition, Pan Am would remain as an operating airline. The "new" Pan Am would be owned jointly by Delta (45 percent) and Pan Am's creditors (55 percent) including its major employee groups.[10] Delta would spend approximately $455 million more to turn Pan Am into a smaller Miami-based carrier primarily serving Latin America, the Caribbean, and one route each connecting Frankfurt and Paris with Miami.[11] The points served by the smaller Pan Am are shown in Exhibit 7.6.

There was little doubt that Pan Am would be a radically different company. Historically the Latin American division had been the firm's most lucrative, generating an operating profit of $46.9 million in the first quarter of 1991.[12] These routes supported a higher-than-usual percentage of first-class and business travelers, resulting in larger revenues per passenger-mile. In addition, many Latin

[10] James T. McKenna, "Delta Wins Pan Am Bidding, Gains on Larger Competitors," *Aviation Week and Space Technology*, August 19, 1991, p. 19.

[11] Ibid., p. 18.

[12] Alison Leigh Cowan, "The New Pan Am Rumbas Ahead," *New York Times*, August 19, 1991, p. C2.

EXHIBIT 7.6   Points Served by Pan Am, November 1, 1991

United States	Caribbean
Atlanta	Hamilton
Boston	Barbados
Chicago	Grand Cayman
Dallas/Fort Worth	Grand Turk
Detroit	Kingston
Houston	Montego Bay
Los Angeles	Nassau
Miami	Port-au-Prince
Newark	Port-of-Spain
New Orleans	Providenciales
New York	Puerto Plata
Orlando	San Juan
San Francisco	Santo Domingo
Tampa/St. Petersburg/Clearwater	St. Croix
Washington, D.C.	St. Maarten
	St. Thomas

Western Europe	Mexico
London	Cancun
Paris	Mexico City

Central America	South America
Guatemala City	Buenos Aires
Panama City	Caracas
San Jose	Maracaibo
	Montevideo
	Recife
	Rio de Janeiro
	Santiago
	Sao Paulo

Source: *Wall Street Journal*, October 18, 1991, pp. A8–A9.

American countries had erected protectionist barriers intended to shield their respective airlines from rigorous competition. Thus, in contrast to the 30 or 40 carriers competing over the North Atlantic, only 3 dominated in Latin America: Pan Am, Varig Brazilian Airlines, and American. However, Pan Am had only 7,000 U.S. employees versus the 26,000 it had at the start of 1991. In addition, its aircraft fleet dropped from 152 to approximately 50. Finally, massive organizational changes were required to cope with the new situation.[13]

[13] McKenna, "Delta Wins Pan Am Bidding," p. 21.

INTERNATIONAL COMMERCIAL AVIATION

The world of commercial air travel was extremely complex. Although the United States had an air transport system made up of privately held airlines, the rest of the world did not. In fact, most other international air carriers were either owned or controlled to some degree by their governments, which often adopted extremely protectionist policies designed to favor those companies vis à vis competing airlines. In addition, foreign airlines were often willing to operate at a loss just to "show the flag" for their home country, something U.S. firms were not able to do.

International aviation rights were negotiated between governments and were, for all practical purposes, treaties between the nations involved. Known as bilateral agreements, these accords were very specific regarding (among other things) service frequency and destinations, carriers providing that service, and occasionally even the equipment each airline could operate. If circumstances relative to the bilateral agreement changed (i.e., a new carrier wanted to provide service, or additional destinations were desired), the countries involved had to accede to the new conditions before they could take effect. Thus, Delta, despite having purchased Pan Am's right to fly to Germany from New York, could not start service until the Germans agreed. In some instances, the entire bilateral agreement had to be renegotiated, a time-consuming and often heated process conducted by the State Department.

When the United States deregulated its airline industry, the rest of the world did not. At the heart of that move was the encouragement of competition, which the United States did in the international arena by adopting very liberal bilateral agreements that encouraged foreign airlines to begin, or increase, their service to the United States. Of course, by definition, there were always a minimum of two carriers serving each route: one from each country. Unfortunately, the U.S. market was often much more lucrative for the foreign carrier than the foreign market was for the U.S. airline. Although there were signs that other countries (Canada, Australia, Brazil, members of the European Community) were slowly moving toward an "open skies" policy similar to that found in the United States, the facts were that air rights were closely guarded national assets that were awarded only after laborious diplomatic procedures wherein each nation negotiated to achieve the maximum benefit for itself.

Unfortunately, 1990 and 1991 were disastrous years for the airline industry in general. The combined effects of the Persian Gulf War (high fuel costs, fears of terrorism, and so forth), a worldwide economic slowdown, and low fares resulted in U.S. carriers losing over $3 billion in 1990, with similar results anticipated in 1991.[14] In fact, world airline traffic declined 4.1 percent in 1991, the first drop

[14] James Ott, "Airline Officials Fear Forecasts of Recovery Were Too Upbeat," *Aviation Week and Space Technology*, September 30, 1991, p. 30.

since the 1940s.[15] The result was a much smaller industry dominated by three major airlines.

There were signs, however, that the worst might be over. Fuel prices declined and stabilized after soaring to a high of $1.40 per gallon in late 1990.[16] (An increase of 1 cent per gallon cost U.S. carriers an extra $160 million annually.)[17] Certain markets showed significant growth in 1990 as well. Demand for travel over Pacific routes increased more than 20 percent over 1989, while Latin American services grew by 9.5 percent. Even traffic on the North Atlantic, the world's most heavily traveled air corridor, expanded 7.2 percent. In addition, the weak value of the dollar made travel to the United States a bargain for many foreign tourists, thus increasing the demand for air travel to, from, and within the United States.[18]

It was clear, however, that the industry was continuing to change dramatically. Worldwide passenger traffic was generally expected to expand on average by 5.2 percent over the next 15 years, although the strongest growth was anticipated for Europe-Asia (12.6 percent), Intra-Asia (9.0 percent), and Transpacific (8.5 percent) routes.[19] Assuming foreign governments continued to move toward airline deregulation, international competition between carriers would increase as more destinations opened to both U.S. and overseas airlines. In addition, if the U.S. experience was any indication, consolidations could be expected among the world's airlines as weaker carriers were taken over by stronger ones or simply failed.

Several companies, perhaps in anticipation of more competition, were attempting to establish nonowner partnerships with other carriers in order to form multinational groups of independent firms that would coordinate activities such as scheduling, marketing, and training. British Airways, KLM Royal Dutch Airlines, and Northwest Airlines were discussing just such an arrangement, as were Lufthansa and USAir.[20] Furthermore, the U.S. Department of Transportation had recently decided that foreign airlines could own as much as 49 percent of the shares of a U.S. carrier, further encouraging the development of global air transport systems.[21] Scandinavian Airline System (SAS) already owned 17 percent of Continental, while Ansett Airlines of Australia owned 20 percent of America West and KLM owned 49 percent of Northwest.[22]

Companies attempting to survive and prosper in an increasingly competitive global airline industry found that they would also have to become more adept at

---

[15] "World Airline Traffic Declined 4.1% in 1991," *Wall Street Journal*, January 2, 1991, p. A6.

[16] *Standard and Poors Industrial Survey*, p. A33.

[17] *1991 U.S. Industrial Outlook* (Washington, D.C.: U.S. Department of Commerce), pp. 41–43.

[18] Ibid.

[19] *Standard and Poors, Industry Survey*, p. A-27.

[20] James Ott, "European Airlines Eye Mergers to Match Global Competition," *Aviation Week and Space Technology*, November 25, 1991, p. 39.

[21] *Standard and Poors, Industry Survey*, p. A.33.

[22] Asra Q. Nomani and Laurie McGinley, "Airlines of the World Scramble for Routes in Industry Shakeout," *Wall Street Journal*, July 23, 1991, p. A8.

meeting customer needs as well as controlling costs. The temptation was to price for market share rather than profit; that is, to utilize low fares that did not cover costs. Fare increases were difficult to sustain when a competitor was offering lower prices, especially when passengers had become so price sensitive. The other difficulty was that many of an international carrier's revenues and costs could be impacted by events beyond management's control. The negative effects of the worldwide recession and the Persian Gulf War have already been discussed, as has the volatility of fuel prices. Similarly, governmental influences continued to impact managerial decision making even in a deregulated environment. Such issues as ticket taxes, noise requirements, and air traffic control could directly affect both the airline's costs and the quality of its service, yet managers had no direct control over these events. The competitive (some would say impossible) challenge, then, was to meet the passenger's price and service expectations and at the same time keep costs as low as possible.

MARKETING AIRLINE SERVICES

Historically, airlines were extremely "product" oriented; that is, they did not pay too much attention to their customers' needs and wants. Rather, managers relied on reputation and technological superiority (i.e., flying the newest airplanes) to draw passengers. In many cases, because of regulations, passengers had little choice among carriers depending on where they wanted to go. This was especially true for international travel on a U.S. airline. All of that changed dramatically in 1978 when Congress ushered in the era of deregulation. Competition from new and established domestic and foreign carriers offered alternatives for airline passengers dissatisfied with air service. Managers had to satisfy passengers or risk losing them. In short, for the first time airlines were faced with having to market their services.

Service

The airlines were challenged with the difficult task of differentiating what is, in many cases, a generic service: movement from point A to point B at a certain time. As a result of deregulation, any number of competitors could (at least theoretically) provide that service, so a carrier had to seek other ways of distinguishing itself from another airline. This might take the form of something tangible like operating the newest aircraft, offering roomier seating, better in-flight meals and entertainment, or a unique interior decor. These tended to be expensive (which raised costs) and could, in the case of seating options, lower the aircraft's revenue potential. Alternatively, intangible attributes could be stressed. Prompt baggage handling, responsiveness to customer complaints or suggestions, and attentiveness to passenger needs both on the ground and in the air were examples of service traits that could be turned into significant competitive advantages.

Price

Initially following deregulation, price was the key marketing variable, at least domestically. During the late 1970s and early 1980s, fares dropped dramatically as carriers sought to fill up airplanes with first-time air travelers. Airlines like Midway, which started service in 1979, and People Express, which followed in 1981, entered the industry as no-frills alternatives to the established carriers. These new entrants offered extremely low fares, although passengers had to accept fewer, or pay additional charges for, amenities such as meals and baggage checking. The success of this low-price approach was phenomenal: People Express became the success story of deregulation. It quickly became clear, however, that pricing strategies were easily imitated and offered little long-term competitive advantage. Strong carriers were able to match the low fares *and* provide services passengers had come to expect. But the fundamental truth that emerged from the initial use of low fares was that, even with a full airplane, the company was often losing money. People Express failed in the mid-1980s, while several other no-frills carriers were bought out by full-service airlines. Thus, while pricing was still a key part of an airline's marketing mix, it became less attractive as a means of differentiating one company from another.

Price was less useful in the marketing strategy of international carriers. Often, fare levels were established in the bilateral agreement specifying how the air service between two countries would be conducted. Any deviation from that agreement had to be agreed to by the governments involved, thus allowing managers little control over the prices they could charge.

Promotion

Airlines adopted several unique promotional activities to attract and keep customers. Frequent-flier programs rewarded continued patronage with premiums, free tickets, and other benefits based on the accumulation of miles on a specific airline. Often, airlines had reciprocal agreements with other carriers that allowed passengers from one frequent-traveler program to accumulate miles on the other airline. Typically, it cost nothing to join a frequent-flier club; the whole idea was to tie passengers to one airline by making it worth their while to fly that carrier all the time. Indeed, some passengers were willing to go out of their way (figuratively and literally) to stay on a particular airline just to accumulate the frequent-flier mileage. Foreign carriers were slower to adopt frequent-flier programs as a marketing tool on a wide scale, although mileage accrued through a U.S. carrier's plan could often be redeemed for flights on a foreign airline.

Carriers often maintained executive clubs at various airports that offered members a quiet alternative to the noisy, congested terminal area. Work space might be provided, along with complimentary beverages, food, and other services. Passengers paid a yearly fee and, in addition to the amenities mentioned earlier, also received a fair degree of exclusivity for their money.

Management also had to come up with an appropriate promotional mix to present their service offering to prospective customers. Here again, international carriers faced unique challenges, since media and message decisions were different for each country the carrier served. Indeed, promotional opportunities could be extremely limited in those markets that lacked commercial media such as television, radio, and newspapers.

Place

Airlines distributed their services in two ways. First, they sold directly to the passenger; that is, the customer arrived at the airport, bought a ticket, and departed. Alternatively, an intermediary in the form of a travel agent could be used. Many airlines spent enormous sums of money to develop their own computerized reservation systems, which were then utilized by travel agencies. Airlines other than the host, although their flights could be listed on the system, often felt they were at a disadvantage by virtue of their placement in the data base. In fact, foreign carriers had been known to use their reservation systems as a means of discriminating against their U.S. competitors.

THE COMPETITION

Whereas Pan Am once competed with many airlines, the smaller Pan Am had to compete with just two major carriers for South American traffic.

Varig Brazilian Airlines

Varig began operations on February 3, 1928, utilizing a single Dornier Wal aircraft over the Porto Alegre–Rio Grande route. In 1961, Varig became the largest airline in South America and in 1965 significantly expanded its international coverage when it was awarded the European routes of Panair do Brazil. Privately owned, the carrier offered extensive domestic and regional services as well as long-haul international routes to Europe, South Africa, Japan, Mexico, and the United States from its primary hub in Rio de Janeiro.[23] Varig's international destinations are presented in Exhibit 7.7.

American Airlines

American was organized on May 13, 1934, as a successor to American Airways, which was formed on January 25, 1930, to consolidate the services of numerous predecessor companies dating back to 1926.[24] Over the years, the carrier introduced innovations such as supersaver fares, frequent-flier programs, and lower wage scales to increase revenue and hold down costs.[25] Based on 1990 fiscal year revenues, American was the largest airline in the world.[26] Headquar-

[23] Gunter G. Endres, *World Airline Fleets 1987–1988* (London: Browcom, 1988), p. 246.
[24] Ibid., p. 133.
[25] Doug Carroll, "Few Carriers Win Battle for Survival," *USA Today*, August 5, 1991, p. 2B.
[26] James Ott, "Future of Global Environment Dictates Airlines' Agenda," *Aviation Week and Space Technology*, November 25; 1991, p. 49.

EXHIBIT 7.7   Varig Brazilian Airlines Points Served on International Routes, 1991[a]

South America	Africa	Europe
Asuncion	Capetown	Amsterdam
Belem	Johannesburg	Barcelona
Boa Vista	Lagos	Copenhagen
Bogota	Luanda	Frankfurt
Buenos Aires		Lisbon
Caracas	**North America**	London
Cayenne		Madrid
Florianopolis	Chicago	Milano
Foz Do Iguacu	Los Angeles	Oporto
Georgetown	Miami	Paris
Guayaquil	New York	Rome
Iquitos	San Francisco	Zurich
La Paz	Toronto	
Lima		
Macapa	**Asia**	
Manaus		
Montevideo	Tokyo	
Paramaribo		
Porto Alegre	**Central America**	
Quito		
Recife	Mexico City	
Rio de Janeiro	Panama City	
Salvador	San Jose	
Santa Cruz de La Sierra		
Santiago		
Sao Paulo		
Tabatinga		
Tefe		

[a] International routes are supported by an extensive domestic network connecting approximately 50 cities and towns within Brazil.

Source: Varig Brazilian Airlines Timetable, August 19, 1991.

tered in Fort Worth, Texas, the carrier operated seven major hubs in the United States, and provided services to 33 countries and the Caribbean. American's international destinations are depicted in Exhibit 7.8.

In comparing the three carriers over competitive routes, there were several similarities as well as a few notable differences. First, all offered essentially the same basic service between the United States and South America. All flew daily nonstop flights, and all operated wide-body aircraft such as the Boeing 747, DC10/MD11, Boeing 767, and Airbus A300. Two or three class services (first and economy; or first, executive or business, and economy) were provided, with first-

EXHIBIT 7.8   American Airlines Points Served on International Routes, 1991[a]

North America	South America	Asia
Anchorage	Asuncion	Hong Kong
Bermuda	Barranquilla	Tokyo
Boston	Bogota	
Calgary	Buenos Aires	**South Pacific**
Chicago	Cali	
Dallas/Fort Worth	Caracas	Auckland
Edmonton	Guayaquil	Sydney
Fairbanks	La Paz	
Honolulu	Lima	**Caribbean**
Kahului	Quito	
Los Angeles	Rio de Janeiro	Anguilla
Miami	Santa Cruz	Antigua
Montreal	Santiago	Aquadilla
Nashville	Sao Paulo	Aruba
New York		Barbados
Newark	**Europe**	Casa de Campo/La Romana
Raleigh/Durham		Fort-de-France
San Francisco	Brussels	Freeport
San Jose	Budapest	Governor's Harbour
Seattle/Tacoma	Duesseldorf	Grand Cayman
Toronto	Frankfurt	Grenada
Vancouver	Glasgow	Kingston
	London	Marsh Harbour
	Madrid	Mayaguez
Central America	Manchester	Montego Bay
	Milan	Nassau
Acapulco	Munich	Pointe-a-Pitre
Belize City	Paris	Ponce
Cancun	Stockholm	Port-au-Prince
Guadalajara	Zurich	Port-of-Spain
Guatemala City		Puerto Plata
Managua		St. Croix
Mexico City		St. Thomas
Monterrey		St. Kitts/Nevis
Panama City		St. Maarten
Puerto Vallarta		St. Lucia
San Jose		San Juan
San Pedro Sula		Santo Domingo
San Salvador		Tortola
Tegucigalpa		Treasure Cay
		Virgin Gorda

[a] International routes are supported by a domestic route network connecting over 200 points within the United States.

Source: American Airlines Passenger Schedule and Cargo Service Guide, World Edition, October 1, 1991.

class passengers enjoying sleeperette-type (lounger) seating on all three airlines. Fares were determined as a part of the agreement between respective countries establishing air service and thus were largely uncontrollable by management. Finally, promotional activities for all three included various forms of media advertising and tended to differ little in content across companies. Local and national newspaper ads tended to predominate, together with selected use of popular magazines and television.

On the other hand, Pan Am's aircraft fleet was significantly older than that operated by American and Varig (Exhibit 7.9 compares the aircraft fleet of Pan Am, American, and Varig). Indeed, Pan Am still operated some of the oldest B747s in commercial service. Both American and Pan Am offered passengers the opportunity to participate in frequent-flier programs. In addition, both maintained exclusive clubs at many of the airports they served, which passengers could utilize for an annual membership fee. Varig offered neither of these services. However, an airline survey conducted in 1990 found that U.S. travelers overwhelmingly preferred foreign air carriers. In fact, out of 27 airlines identified, not one based in the U.S. made the top 10. Asian and European carriers filled those

EXHIBIT 7.9   Passenger Jets in Service as of November 1, 1991 (By airline and type)

Aircraft Type	Pan Am	American	Delta	Varig
Boeing				
727	29	164	153	9
737	—	12	72	36
747[a]	8	2	—	8
757	—	37	69	—
767[a]	—	45	46	10
McDonnell-Douglas				
DC-9	—	—	30	—
DC-10[a]	—	59	—	10
MD-11[a]	—	3	2	—
MD-80/88	—	234	85	—
Lockheed				
L1011[a]	—	—	49	—
Airbus				
A300/310[a]	13	26	21	—
Fokker				
F100	—	—	—	—
Total	50	582	527	73

[a] Wide-body aircraft.

Source: Compiled from Alison Leigh Cowan, "The New Pan Am Rumbas Ahead," *New York Times,* August 19, 1991, p. C2; Report of Annual Meeting of AMR's Stockholders, 1991, p. 14; James Ott, "D-Day Due for Delta Takeover of Most Pan Am Operations," *Aviation Week and Space Technology,* October 14, 1991, p. 44; and Varig System Timetable, August 15, 1991, p. 8.

top spots with one exception: Varig. American was the highest ranked U.S. airline at number 11, while Pan Am was far down the list.[27]

THE CHALLENGE

As the Pan Am president slipped on his coat and headed for the elevator, he wondered how best to take advantage of this new beginning. Being the pragmatist that he was, he knew that Pan Am was still skating on extremely thin ice. "Our fleet is old, our reputation is tarnished, and our employees dispirited. If we fail this time, there will be no reprieve," he thought. "If we've learned one thing, it's that we can build on past glories, but we cannot rest on them. We have to figure out a way to entice the return of our old customers and capture new ones despite the bad press. We *will* succeed in the highly competitive and turbulent international aviation industry of the 1990s."

[27] Asra Q. Nomani, "U.S. Airlines Come up Short in Survey," *Wall Street Journal*, September 7, 1990, p. B6.

_____ CASE 23 _____

HEALTHSOUTH Rehabilitation Corporation

HEALTHSOUTH Rehabilitation Corporation (HRC) was by all measures one of the most successful business ventures in modern health care. Its growth was nothing less than phenomenal. Yet growth involved its own challenge. As Richard M. Scrushy, chairman, chief executive officer, and president of HEALTHSOUTH Rehabilitation Corporation, read the first quarter 1991 earnings release (Exhibit 23.1) and reflected on the company's first seven years of growth he wondered about HRC's future.

With 19 consecutive quarters of earnings growth, HEALTHSOUTH had been the darling of Wall Street. The medical rehabilitation niche within the health care industry had been as successful as originally believed. The company had achieved and exceeded all of the objectives of its original business plan.

Scrushy realized that in order to sustain growth, continued hard work was even more necessary than during the start-up period. He also knew that some key strategic decisions would have to be made:

- Should the company continue to focus on the rehabilitation business?
- Should the company concentrate more on one business segment?
- Should the company diversify further into the acute-care hospital business?
- What pitfalls lie ahead?
- Can success continue?
- Where should we go from here?

BEGINNING OF SUCCESS

The company was organized in 1983 as AMCARE but in 1985 changed its name to HEALTHSOUTH Rehabilitation Corporation. HEALTHSOUTH was founded by a group of health care professionals, led by Scrushy, who were formerly with LifeMark Corporation, a large publicly held, for-profit health care

This case was prepared by W. Jack Duncan, Peter M. Ginter, and Michael D. Martin as a basis for class discussion rather than to illustrate either effective or ineffective handling of an administrative situation. Used with permission from W. Jack Duncan.

EXHIBIT 23.1   HEALTHSOUTH News Release

NEWS RELEASE

For Immediate Release
April 16, 1991

HEALTHSOUTH's Net Income for First Quarter Up 64 Percent

Birmingham, AL—HEALTHSOUTH Rehabilitation Corporation (NYSE:HRC) reported today that it generated a net income of $4,230,000 on net revenues of $50,574,000 for the quarter ended March 31, 1991. This represents a 64 percent increase as compared to the net income generated in the first quarter, 1990. Net revenues were 17 percent greater in this quarter than those experienced in the same period prior year. Primary earnings per share for the quarter were 31 cents, an increase of 29 percent as compared to last year. On a fully diluted basis, earnings per share for this quarter were 28 cents, a seven cent increase as compared to last year.

"During the first quarter," said Richard M. Scrushy, Chairman of the Board, President and CEO, "we opened four new outpatient centers, bringing the total number of operating locations to 55. The construction of our Kingsport, Tennessee, rehabiliation hospital is on schedule and is expected to contribute to our operating results in the third quarter."

HEALTHSOUTH Rehabilitation Corporation, a leading provider of comprehensive medical rehabilitation services in the United States, currently operates 55 locations in 22 states.

Summary of Operating Results
(unaudited, in thousands except per share data)

	Three Months Ended March 31,	
	1990	*1991*
Net Revenues	$43,308	$50,574
Net Income	2,573	4,230
Weighted Average Common and Common Equivalent Shares Outstanding	10,826	13,709
Earnings Per Share		
Primary	$.24	$.31
Fully Diluted	$.21	$.28

services chain that was acquired by American Medical International (AMI) in 1984.

In 1982, Richard Scrushy indicated how he first recognized the potential for rehabilitation services: "I saw the Tax Equity and Fiscal Responsibility Act (TEFRA) guidelines and the upcoming implementation of Medicare's prospective payment system (PPS) as creating a need for outpatient rehabilitation services. It was rather clear that lengths of stay in general hospitals would decrease and that patients would be discharged more quickly than in the past. It became obvious to me that these changes would create a need for a transition between the hospital and the patient's home." Medicare provided financial incentives for outpatient rehabilitation services by giving comprehensive outpatient rehabilitation facilities (CORFs) an exemption from prospective payment systems and allowed the services of these facilities to continue to be reimbursed on a retrospective, cost-based basis (reimbursement paid after patient care based on the cost of care).

Mr. Scrushy anticipated the impact of the upcoming reimbursement changes: "I also saw that LifeMark would suffer significant reductions in profitability as the use of the then lucrative ancillary inpatient services was discouraged under the new reimbursement guidelines. I discussed my concerns about the upcoming changes in Medicare with LifeMark management and proposed that we develop a chain of outpatient rehabilitation centers. I saw that the centers I proposed were LifeMark's chance to preserve its profitability under PPS, and when they rejected my proposal, I saw cutbacks and a low rate of advancement in the future."

Mr. Scrushy repeated his proposal for AMI's management when it acquired LifeMark, but AMI could not implement the program immediately after a major acquisition. Scrushy resigned his position to move to Birmingham, Alabama, a city with an international reputation in health care, and there founded HEALTH-SOUTH Rehabilitation Corporation in conjunction with three colleagues from LifeMark.

Early Development

Initially organized as an Alabama corporation and subsequently reorganized as a Delaware corporation, HRC began operations in January 1984. Its initial focus was on the establishment of a national network of outpatient rehabilitation facilities and a rehabilitation equipment business. In September 1984, HRC opened its first outpatient rehabilitation facility in Little Rock, Arkansas, followed by another one in Birmingham, Alabama in December 1984. Within five years, HRC was operating 29 outpatient facilities located in 17 states throughout the southeastern United States. In the first nine months of 1990, it opened eight more outpatient facilities and its growth was impressive as illustrated in Exhibit 23.2.

In June 1985, HRC started providing inpatient rehabilitation services with the acquisition of an 88-bed facility in Florence, South Carolina. During the next five years, the company established 11 more inpatient facilities in 9 states, with a 12th under development. Although the rehabilitation equipment business portion of the corporation had grown rapidly, in August 1989, most of it was sold to National Orthopedic and Rehabilitation Services in order to concentrate resources on HRC's core business. As of April 1991, HRC was a publicly traded for-profit health care services company that operated 43 outpatient and 11 inpatient facilities in 24 states. Its stock was listed on the New York Stock Exchange.

EXHIBIT 23.2 Quarterly Number of Outpatient Visits and Inpatient Days

		Outpatient			Inpatient[a]			
	Facilities	Visits (000s)	Visits/ Facility	Licensed Beds	Available Beds	Inpatient Days	Average Daily Census	Occupancy[b]
1986 Q1	7	17.5	2,500	88	83	2,747	30	36.4%
Q2	8	27.5	3,438	88	83	3,164	35	41.9%
Q3	8	32.8	4,100	268	201	7,525	83	31.7%
Q4	9	35.0	3,889	358	351	17,129	188	53.6%
Total	8	112.8	14,100	358	351	30,565	84	23.9%
1987 Q1	11	38.0	3,455	358	351	20,543	228	64.3%
Q2	12	48.0	4,000	358	351	19,334	212	60.5%
Q3	12	53.8	4,467	618	457	20,722	228	49.8%
Q4	13	60.0	4,615	618	457	23,201	255	55.8%
Total	12	199.8	16,633	488	404	83,800	230	57.0%
1988 Q1	16	69.0	4,313	678	497	26,100	287	57.7%
Q2	17	78.0	4,588	830	597	28,578	314	52.6%
Q3	20	85.5	4,275	858	623	26,720	318	50.7%
Q4	21	88.7	4,129	858	623	30,511	335	53.5%
Total	19	319.2	17,254	805	585	113,909	313	53.5%
1989 Q1	22	92.2	4,191	960	707	35,617	391	55.4%
Q2	23	104.2	4,530	960	707	38,533	423	59.9%
Q3	28	111.7	3,989	960	707	39,214	431	61.0%
Q4	30	123.0	4,100	960	727	49,928	472	64.9%
Total	26	431.1	16,742	960	712	158,292	429	60.3%
1990 Q1	31	124.5	4,017	960	727	44,135	485	66.7%
Q2	33	140.7	4,265	1,020	787	45,500	500	63.5%
Q3	35	150.9	4,310	1,020	787	48,865	515	65.4%
Q4	37	166.1	4,490	1,020	787	48,230	530	67.3%
Total	34	600.0	17,647	1,005	772	184,730	508	65.7%
1991 Total	45	800.0	17,778	1,140	907	219,000	600	66.2%

[a]Does not include HEALTHSOUTH Medical Center.
[b]Calculated as average daily census divided by available beds. Available beds at some facilities differs from licensed beds.
Source: Company information and Alex. Brown & Sons estimates.

South Highlands Hospital Becomes HEALTHSOUTH
Medical Center

A key development in HRC's growth strategy was the acquisition, in December 1989, of the 219-bed South Highlands Hospital in Birmingham, Alabama. Renamed HEALTHSOUTH Medical Center (HMC), this hospital developed into a flagship facility.

South Highlands was a marginally profitable facility but due to restricted financing capabilities, was unable to meet the needs of its physicians, particularly Drs. James Andrews and William Clancy, both world-renowned orthopedic surgeons. As Mr. Scrushy noted:

> My immediate concern was to maintain the referral base that Drs. Andrews and Clancy provided. HRC had benefitted from the rehabilitation referrals stemming from the extensive orthopedic surgery performed at South Highlands. The surgeons needed a major expansion at South Highlands to practice at maximum effectiveness and Drs. Andrews and Clancy would seek the facilities they needed elsewhere if something wasn't done. On the surface our acquisition of South Highlands was defensive.

The purchase of South Highlands Hospital for approximately $27 million was far from a defensive move. HRC immediately began construction of a $30 million addition to the hospital. Even during construction, referrals continued to flow from HMC to other HRC facilities. The construction created interest in the medical community, which in turn, created business. The emergency facility at HMC eliminated the necessity of delaying evaluation and treatment of athletic injuries that could be quickly transferred to the facility through HRC's extensive linkages with 396 high school and college athletic programs. A brief overview of selected events in HRC's history is summarized in Exhibit 23.3.

INDUSTRY OVERVIEW

Medical rehabilitation involves the treatment of physical limitations through which therapists seek to improve their patients' functional independence, relieve pain, and ameliorate any permanent disabilities. Patients using medical rehabilitation services include the handicapped and those recovering from automobile, sports, and other accidents; strokes; neurological injuries; surgery; fractures; disabilities associated with diseases; and conditions such as multiple sclerosis, cerebral palsy, arthritis, and heart disease.

Rehabilitation Services

Medical rehabilitation provider services include inpatient rehabilitation in dedicated free-standing hospitals and in distinct units of acute-care hospitals; comprehensive outpatient rehabilitation facilities, specialty rehabilitation pro-

EXHIBIT 23.3   Key Events in HEALTHSOUTH'S History

1984 • Company started by Richard Scrushy and others
       • Raised $1 million from CitiBank Venture Capital
       • Opened two outpatient centers

1985 • Acquired first inpatient facility
       • Opened four new outpatient facilities

1986 • Initial public offering raised $15 million
       • Acquired two inpatient facilities
       • Opened three outpatient centers

1987 • Secondary stock offering raised $24 million
       • Acquired two inpatient centers
       • Opened four outpatient centers

1988 • Developed and acquired three inpatient facilities
       • Opened eight outpatient centers

1989 • Issued $52 million of subordinated convertible debentures
       • Listed stock on New York Stock Exchange
       • Developed two inpatient facilities
       • Acquired South Highlands Hospital (HEALTHSOUTH Medical Center)
       • Opened eight outpatient facilities
       • Listed as the 11th fastest-growing company by *Inc.* magazine
       • Listed as the 41st largest percentage gainer on the New York Stock Exchange by *Fortune* magazine
       • Divested equipment businesses

1990 • Developed one inpatient facility
       • Opened 10 outpatient facilities
       • Listed as the 35th largest percentage gainer on the New York Stock Exchange by *Fortune* magazine
       • Secondary stock offering raised $49 million

grams, such as traumatic brain injury and spinal cord injury; pediatric; occupational and industrial rehabilitation; and rehabilitation agencies. For a summary of types of providers see Exhibit 23.4.

The availability of comprehensive rehabilitation services was limited in the United States. Provision of rehabilitation services by outpatient departments of acute-care hospitals was fragmented because services were provided through several departments, and private practice therapists rarely provided a full-range of comprehensive rehabilitation services. Often, patients requiring multidisciplinary services would be treated by different therapists in different locations, which would result in uncoordinated care.

Comprehensive inpatient rehabilitation services were provided by free-standing rehabilitation hospitals, distinct units in acute-care hospitals, and skilled nursing facilities. As of September 1990, there were 136 dedicated rehabilitation hospitals and 628 distinct inpatient rehabilitation units in acute-care hospitals as shown in Exhibit 23.5.

EXHIBIT 23.4 Rehabilitation Industry Segments, 1989 (Estimated)

Industry Segment	Capacity		Revenues		Payer Mix		
	Facilities	Beds	(In billions)	Per Day or Visit	Private[a]	Medicare	Medicaid and Other Government
Acute-Care Hospitals							
Inpatient Units	625	15,000	$2.4	$700–900	30%	55%	15%
Outpatient Departments	2,270	n/a	$1.1	$85–110	60	25	15
Free-Standing							
Rehabilitation Hospitals	120	13,200	$2.3	$550–750	45	45	10
Traumatic Brain Injury Programs[b]	450	12,000	$3.0	$115–1,300	40	n/a	60[c]
Outpatient Rehabilitation							
CORFs[d]	170	n/a	$0.2	$85–110	40	40	20
Other Facility-Based	200	n/a	$0.1	$85–110	40	40	20
Other[e]	1,000++	n/a	$0.5	$75–100	25	60	15
Total			$9.6				

[a]Includes workers' compensation, self-pay, Blue Cross/Blue Shield, commercial insurers, managed care.
[b]Includes acute and extended rehabilitation as well as transitional living programs.
[c]Contracted rates between provider and government programs, typically 10–15 percent discount from charges.
[d]Medicare-certified comprehensive outpatient rehabilitation facilities.
[e]Highly fragmented market including 1,000 Medicare certified agencies plus many private practitioners.
n/a = not applicable.
Source: American Hospital Association; National Association of Rehabilitation Facilities; National Head Injury Foundation.

Analysts with Goldman Sachs believed that the rehabilitation services segment of the health care industry in the United States would grow at a rate of 15 to 20 percent through 1993. A number of factors would influence this growth.

Increased Need for Services.   The incidence of major disability increases with age. Improvements in medical care enabled more people with severe disabilities to live longer. Data compiled by the National Center for Health Statistics showed that in 1989 there were 35 million people in the United States (one out of every seven people) with some form of disability. The National Association of Insurance Commissioners pointed out that 7 out of 10 workers will suffer a long-term disability between the ages of 35 and 65.

Economic Benefits of Services.   Purchasers and providers of health care services, such as insurance companies, health maintenance organizations (HMOs), businesses, and industry are seeking economical, high-quality alternatives to traditional health care services. Rehabilitation services, whether outpatient or inpatient, represent such an alternative. Often early participation in a disabled person's rehabilitation may prevent a short-term problem from becoming a longterm disability. Moreover, by returning the individual to the work force, the

EXHIBIT 23.5   HEALTHSOUTH's National Network

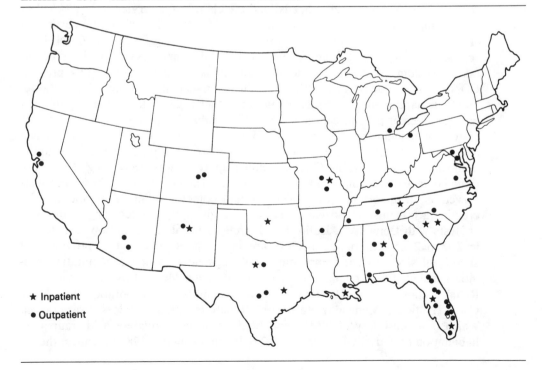

★ Inpatient

● Outpatient

number of disability benefit payments is reduced, thus decreasing long-term disability costs. Independent studies by companies such as Northwestern Life have shown that of every $1 spent on rehabilitation a savings of $30 occurs in disability payments.

Favorable Payment Policies for Services.   As noted previously, inpatient rehabilitation services, organized as either dedicated rehabilitation hospitals or distinct units, were eligible for exemptions from Medicare's prospective payment system. Outpatient rehabilitation services, which are organized as comprehensive outpatient rehabilitation facilities or rehabilitation agencies, were eligible to participate in the Medicare program under cost-based reimbursement programs. Inpatient and outpatient rehabilitation services were typically covered for payment by the major medical portion of commercial health insurance policies.

Competition

HRC's operating units were located in 36 primary markets in 24 states (refer to Exhibit 23.5). The competition faced in each of these markets was similar although unique based on the number of health care providers in a specific metropolitan area. The primary competitive factors in the rehabilitation services business were quality of services; projected patient outcomes; responsiveness to the needs of the patients, community, and physicians; ability to tailor programs and services to meet specific needs; and the charges for services.

Competition was faced every time HEALTHSOUTH initiated a certificate of need (CON) project or sought to acquire an existing facility or CON. This competition would arise from national or regional companies or from local hospitals filing competing applications or who opposed the proposed CON project. CONS were unique to the health care industry in that states having CON requirements demanded that hospitals, clinics, or other organizations wanting to open new facilities or purchase expensive and specialized equipment convince a regulatory or planning agency that such facilities or equipment were really needed and would not merely move patients from one provider to another. Although the number of states requiring CON or similar approval was decreasing, HRC continued to face this requirement in several states. The necessity for these approvals served as an important barrier to entry and potentially limited competition by creating a franchise to provide services to a given area. According to industry analysts with Donaldson, Lufin, and Jenrett, medical rehabilitation represented less than 2 percent of the health care industry. Relatively few providers of significant size existed; competition was fragmented. Major rehabilitation providers included four public companies (Continental Medical Systems, Greenery Rehabilitation Group, HEALTHSOUTH Rehabilitation Corporation, and Nova Care), National Medical Enterprises' Rehab Hospital Services Corporation, which is a subsidiary of NME, and MediCo, a new privately held trauma rehabilitation provider. Of a total of $8.2 billion in estimated 1988 revenues, the six largest providers represented less than 20 percent of total rehabilitation provider revenues. Consolidation was likely to occur because of the stronger entities' access to capital, strong clinical programs, and sophisticated management systems. However, major companies in this industry tended to compete only indirectly with one another because they targeted different market niches and/or different geographic markets.

Reimbursement

Reimbursement for services provided by HRC could be divided into two distinct categories: private pay and Medicare. The percentage of each varied by business segment and facility. Private pay represented 90 percent of all outpatient business and 50 percent of all inpatient business, or 62 percent of total revenues.

Private Pay.   Approximately 80 percent of the population under the age of 65 had medical insurance coverage. The extent of the coverage varied by location. Generally, charges for inpatient and outpatient rehabilitation were reimbursed 100 percent. Insurers preferred established programs that could demonstrate functional outcomes. The private-pay segment included general medical insurance, workers' compensation, health maintenance organizations, preferred provider organizations, and other managed-care plans.

Medicare.   Industry sources estimated that Medicare spent approximately $1.9 billion on inpatient medical rehabilitation during 1988. These sources also estimated that Medicare represented 45 percent of free-standing general rehabilitation inpatient stays and revenues, 55 percent of acute-care hospital rehabilitation unit stays and revenues, and 40 percent of CORF revenues.

Since 1983, the federal government employed a prospective payment system (PPS) as a means of controlling general acute-care hospital costs for the Medicare program. In the past, the Medicare program provided reimbursement for the reasonable direct and indirect costs of the services furnished by hospitals to beneficiaries, plus an allowed return on equity for proprietary hospitals. As a result of the Social Security Act Amendments of 1983, Congress adopted a prospective payment system to cover the routine and ancillary operating costs of most Medicare inpatient hospital services.

Under PPS, the secretary of Health and Human Services established fixed payment amounts per discharge based on diagnosis-related groups (DRGs). With limited exceptions, a hospital's payment for Medicare inpatients was limited to the DRG rate, regardless of the number of services provided to the patient or the length of the patient's hospital stay. Under PPS, a hospital could retain the difference, if any, between its DRG rate and the operating costs incurred in furnishing inpatient services, and was at risk for any operating costs that exceeded its DRG rate. HMC was generally subject to PPS with respect to Medicare inpatient services.

In 1992, Medicare paid certain distinct units, free-standing rehabilitation facilities, and certified outpatient units on the basis of "reasonable costs" incurred during a base year (the year prior to being excluded from Medicare's prospective payment system or the first year of operation) adjusted by a market basket index. However, many rehabilitation providers faced an increase in rates that was less than that of their actual costs. In addition, many Medicare intermediaries such as Blue Cross had an incomplete understanding of rehabilitation services and, therefore, might deny claims inappropriately.

Regulation

The health care industry was subject to regulation by federal, state, and local governments. The various levels of regulatory activity affected organizations by controlling growth, requiring licensure or certification of facilities, regulating the use of properties, and controlling the reimbursement for services provided. In some states, regulations controlled the growth of health care facilities.

Capital expenditures for the construction of new facilities, addition of beds, or acquisition of existing facilities could be reviewable by state regulators under a statutory scheme (usually referred to as a CON program). States with CON requirements placed limits on the construction and acquisition of health care facilities as well as the expansion of existing facilities and services.

Licensure and certification were separate, but related, regulatory activities. The former was usually a state or local requirement, and the latter was a federal requirement. In almost all instances, licensure and certification would follow specific standards and requirements set forth in readily available public documents. Compliance with the requirements was monitored by annual on-site inspections by representatives of various government agencies.

In order to receive Medicare reimbursement, each facility had to meet the applicable conditions of participation set forth by the U.S. Department of Health and Human Services relating to the type of facility, equipment, personnel and standards of medical care, as well as compliance with all state and local laws and regulations. In addition, Medicare regulations generally required entry into such facilities through physician referral.

HEALTHSOUTH TODAY

When patients were referred to one of HEALTHSOUTH's rehabilitation facilities, they underwent an initial evaluation and assessment process that resulted in the development of a rehabilitation care plan designed specifically for each patient. Depending upon the patient's disability, this evaluation process could involve the services of a single discipline (such as physical therapy for a knee injury) or of several disciplines (such as physical and speech therapy in the case of a complicated stroke patient). HRC developed numerous rehabilitation programs, including stroke, head injury, spinal cord injury, neuromuscular, sports, and work injury, that combined specific services to address the needs of patients with similar disabilities. When a patient entered one of these programs, the professional staff tailored the program to meet the needs of the patient. In this way, all of the facility's patients, regardless of the severity and complexity of their disabilities, could receive the level and intensity of those services necessary for them to be restored to as productive, active, and independent a lifestyle as possible.

The professional staff at each facility consisted of licensed or credentialed health care practitioners. The staff, together with the patient, his or her family, and the referring physician, formed the "team" that assisted the patient in attaining the rehabilitation goals. This interdisciplinary approach permitted the delivery of coordinated, integrated patient care.

Outpatient Rehabilitation Services

HEALTHSOUTH operated the largest group of affiliated proprietary CORFs in the United States. Comprehensive outpatient rehabilitation facilities played an important role in the health care industry by offering quality care at a reasonable price. The continuing emphasis on reducing health care costs, as evidenced by PPS, reduced the length of stay for patients in acute-care facilities. Some critics even suggested patients did not receive the intensity of services that may be necessary for them to achieve a full recovery from their diseases, disorders, or traumatic conditions. CORFs satisfied the increasing needs for outpatient services because of their ability to provide hospital-level services at the intensity and frequency needed.

HEALTHSOUTH had comparative advantages over most small therapy centers. HRC possessed state of the art equipment as well as experience in operations. HEALTHSOUTH's experience in operating its many outpatient centers offered:

- An efficient design that aided in the delivery of rehabilitation services in terms of quality and cost.
- Efficient management of the business office function—accounting, billing, managing, staffing, and so on.
- The ability to provide a full spectrum of comprehensive rehabilitation services.
- The ability to draw referrals from a large mass of sources due to its lack of affiliation with one specific group.

Inpatient Services

HEALTHSOUTH was one of the largest independent providers of inpatient rehabilitation services in the United States. HRC's inpatient rehabilitation facilities provided high-quality comprehensive services to patients who required intensive institutional rehabilitation care. These patients were typically experiencing physical disabilities due to various conditions such as head injury, spinal cord injury, stroke, certain orthopedic problems, or neuromuscular disease. Except for the St. Louis facility that exclusively provided head injury rehabilitation services, these inpatient facilities provided the same professional health care services as the company's outpatient facilities, but on a more intensive level. In addition, such facilities provided therapeutic recreation and 24-hour nursing care. An interdisciplinary team approach, similar to that used in the outpatient facilities, was employed with each patient to address rehabilitation needs.

HEALTHSOUTH MEDICAL CENTER

HMC was a world-class orthopedic surgery and sports medicine complex. It was an acute care hospital reimbursed under the prospective payment system. The key to the hospital's success was the affiliation with a group of renowned orthopedic surgeons. These surgeons treated famous patients such as Bo Jackson, the king and the prince of Saudi Arabia, Jane Fonda, golfers Jack Nicklaus and Greg Norman, Charles Barkley of the Philadelphia 76ers, and Troy Aikman of the Dallas Cowboys. The prestige and publicity of these patients enhanced the demand for local Birmingham services, HEALTHSOUTH's main business. One patient's father stated, "If HEALTHSOUTH was good enough for Charles Barkley, then it's good enough for my son" (a high school football player who suffered a knee injury). The group of surgeons had 8 to 10 "fellows" or physicians who spent a year studying under the group before returning to their practices. This provided a network for future business and additional outpatient and inpatient development for HEALTHSOUTH. Since acquiring HMC in 1989, the prominence of the affiliation with this network of physician "fellows" led to several new acquisitions and many more opportunities.

Rehabilitation Management

HEALTHSOUTH Rehabilitation Corporation provided, as an extension of its outpatient and inpatient rehabilitation services, one or more of its clinical services to outside client facilities on a contractual basis. These contract opportunities represented a limited investment and capital risk and were only a small portion of the company's total revenues.

FUNCTIONAL CONSIDERATIONS

HRC's management was comprised of a group of young energetic professionals. The average age was 38 years. See HRC's organization chart in Exhibit 23.6.

The corporate climate was characterized by a sense of urgency and was instilled in all of HEALTHSOUTH's employees directed by the chairman, chief executive officer, and president—Richard Scrushy. He founded HEALTH-

EXHIBIT 23.6 HEALTHSOUTH's Organization Chart

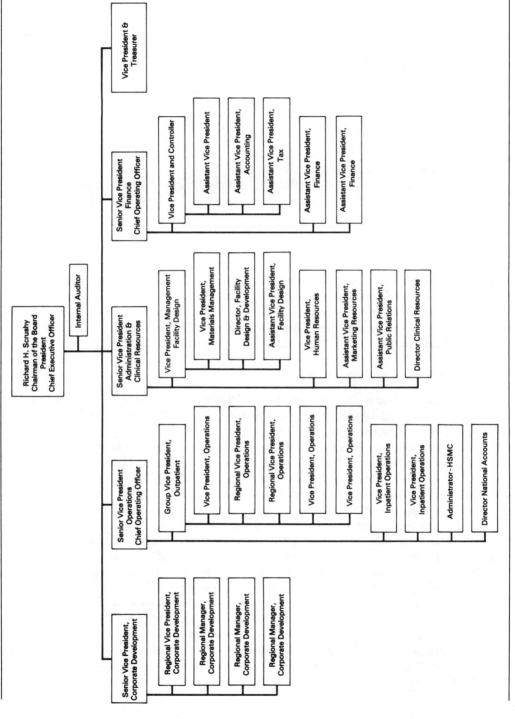

SOUTH at the age of 32. As with many entrepreneurs, he was a visionary and had the ability to make things happen. He worked virtually 365 days a year, 16 to 20 hours a day for the first five years, waiting until 1989 before taking his first vacation. His pace remained furious, working over 75 hours a week.

As a result of Scrushy's "hands-on" style, HRC was run; it did not drift. One of the company's most effective tools was a weekly statistical report, which was compiled every Thursday and distributed on Friday. The report included weekly statistics and trends such as payer mix, census, and revenue. It was reviewed over the weekend; if there was a negative trend, it was corrected. Thus, any problem was short-lived. In this manner the management team was focused on real and developing problems.

Another tool was effective communications. Every Monday morning at 7 A.M. there was a meeting of the company's officers, which included personnel from operations, development, finance, and administration. In this meeting each employee made a presentation detailing what he or she accomplished in the previous week and what was planned for the current week. Questions were answered and problems resolved. One additional benefit was that each employee was held accountable for his or her actions. While this could be perceived to be overkill, it was believed to be necessary and helpful to the participants. At one time the meetings were stopped for about six weeks. After the company experienced a slight dip in performances and coordination, the meetings were immediately reinstated.

Staffing and Compensation

Unlike many other health care companies, HEALTHSOUTH did not experience staffing shortages. Clinicians were in short supply, but HRC was able to recruit and maintain excellent personnel. The ability to offer a challenging environment was a key factor. A HEALTHSOUTH inpatient facility in a metropolitan location typically competed favorably against other hospitals and nursing homes for the skills of new therapists. HEALTHSOUTH's outpatient facilities offered an attractive alternative to the clinician by offering 8-hour workdays with weekends and holidays off.

All of the company's employees were competitively compensated. One compensation tool used was employee incentive stock options, which were granted to key corporate and clinical personnel. The options required a vesting period of four years with 25 percent of the amount being vested annually. If the employee left for another job, the options were lost. With the tremendous success of the company, the stock options created "golden handcuffs." Many employees had options that could be exercised at prices under $10 a share. In August 1991, the stock was trading for $30 per share. Additionally, during August the company created an employee stock ownership plan whereby eligible employees received HRC stock at a rate of about 100 shares per $20,000 of compensation.

Development

A key element of HEALTHSOUTH's growth was its ability to develop and acquire new facilities. The company had a development team led by three individuals who were with HRC from the beginning. Each was responsible for the development of facilities in a particular business segment. Before seeking to develop or acquire an inpatient or outpatient facility, a number of factors had to be considered, including population, number of orthopedic surgeons and physical therapists, industry concentrations, reimbursement, competition, and availability of staff.

HEALTHSOUTH had a stated goal to develop or acquire two new inpatient facilities and 8 to 10 outpatient centers per year. The acquisition of another acute-care hospital specializing in orthopedic surgery (to be patterned after HEALTHSOUTH Medical Center) was a possibility but was not a part of the stated plan.

Outpatient Development. HEALTHSOUTH's outpatient units were usually acquired. The company targeted existing centers that were seeing 50 or more patients per day for purchase. New centers were set up as limited partnerships, typically with the former owners (physicians and therapists) maintaining a limited partnership interest. Ownership provided an incentive to continue referring patients to the center and the limited partners shared in the cash flow. Additionally, HEALTHSOUTH brought in other physicians and groups as partners and would give up 40 percent ownership in the facility. Interestingly, on the average, only 40 percent of the visits came from referrals of partners.

The cost of acquiring and opening a center ranged from $300,000 to $800,000. This included equipment and buildings of $200,000 to $350,000 and acquisition costs of $100,000 to $450,000. All centers were leased except one, allowing for lower capital requirements. The company was evaluating all of its leases and could possibly move toward acquiring buildings where existing facilities were proven and met financial requirements.

Inpatient Development. Inpatient facilities were usually developed. They were customarily located in regulated environments requiring a CON. The company targeted a number of markets for rehabilitation hospitals; however, HEALTHSOUTH's competition was usually seeking the same markets. HEALTHSOUTH never lost a CON battle for two reasons. First, the quality of care provided by existing HEALTHSOUTH facilities was excellent. Second, the lower cost of the facility led to lower health care costs.

HEALTHSOUTH's inpatient facilities were typically located on or near the campus of an acute-care hospital that served as a trauma center. This provided a steady stream of patients when trauma victims were discharged from the hospital. Additionally, physical therapy could be conducted by HEALTHSOUTH for the hospital on an inpatient and outpatient basis. Typically, HEALTHSOUTH's inpatient facilities cost from $6 to $10 million compared to its competitors' costs of $10 to $12 million.

The development of additional acute-care hospitals stressing orthopedics similar to HMC was a future possibility. A potential acute-care hospital acquisition had to possess an orthopedic concentration. The cost of an acute-care hospital meeting HEALTHSOUTH's criteria ranged from $20 to $50 million depending on its size and types of equipment.

Marketing

The company's marketing efforts were similar for each business segment. The demand was controlled by physicians, workers' compensation managers, insurance companies, and other intermediaries. Administrators and clinicians were involved in the marketing effort. The company hired a number of individuals who were formerly case managers with local intermediaries, such as insurance companies and HMOs.

HRC recently entered into contracts to be the exclusive provider for rehabilitation services directly to industry. Firms such as General Motors were excellent targets, since they had many employees in various markets that HEALTHSOUTH served. In such cases, significant new business could be generated and in return HEALTHSOUTH could afford to discount its charges.

HEALTHSOUTH established a national marketing effort with training programs, national account managers, case managers, and a carefully developed plan. The objective was to put into place a consistent sales methodology throughout HEALTHSOUTH and take advantage of its national system of rehabilitation facilities. This national coverage enabled HEALTHSOUTH to provide services for national as well as regional companies.

HEALTHSOUTH's pricing was usually lower than that of competition. The company's daily inpatient charges were sometimes as much as $100 to $400 less per day than competition due to its lower cost of capital and facilities. However, pricing was not used as a major selling point but rather a bonus. HEALTHSOUTH focused mainly on quality of services and outcomes as the best marketing tool.

Financial Structure

HEALTHSOUTH's growth was funded through a mix of equity and debt. The company raised $13 million in venture capital before going public in 1986. Because of the company's start-up nature in its early years, commercial banks were reluctant to lend significant funds for development. After the company's initial public offering, commercial bankers were more responsive to financing growth plans. HRC continued to use a conservative mix of equity and debt and believed its cost of capital was the lowest in the health care industry. A decision to give up ownership was an easy one. The founders understood that a smaller percentage ownership of a larger company would be worth more and would not carry as much risk.

Earnings increases were significant, with compounded earnings growth of 416 percent from 1986 to 1990. About 75 percent of HRC's revenues were generated primarily through inpatient services. Typically, a mature inpatient facility generated $10 to $15 million annually in revenues, an outpatient center generated $2 to $3.5 million annually, and an acute-care facility generated $40 to $60 million. The operating margin on inpatient business ranged from 15 to 25 percent and outpatient margins were 20 to 30 percent. The return on assets of a given facility ranged from 10 to 30 percent with an average of 17 percent for all facilities. HRC financial statements are provided in Exhibits 23.7 through 23.11. Revenue summaries are shown in Exhibits 23.12 and 23.13.

EXHIBIT 23.7   Consolidated Balance Sheets (In thousands)

	December 31,	
	1989	*1990*
Assets		
Current Assets		
Cash and Marketable Securities	$ 31,830	$ 71,201
Accounts Receivable—Net of Allowances for Doubtful Accounts and Contractual Adjustments of $13,020,000 in 1989 and $20,093,000 in 1990	47,771	48,988
Inventories, Prepaid Expenses and Other Current Assets	7,213	7,626
Total Current Assets	86,814	127,815
Other Assets	8,613	9,848
Property, Plant and Equipment—Net	94,081	126,732
Intangible Assets—Net	29,622	36,785
Total Assets	$219,130	$301,180
Liabilities and Stockholders' Equity		
Current Liabilities		
Accounts Payable	$ 5,866	$ 7,342
Salaries and Wages Payable	3,414	3,972
Accrued Interest Payable and Other Liabilities	3,978	4,522
Current Portion of Long-Term Debt and Leases	1,637	1,394
Total Current Liabilities	14,895	17,230
Long-Term Debt and Leases	132,748	149,801
Other Long-Term Liabilities	3,870	5,172
Minority Interests—Limited Partnerships	1,742	1,076
Stockholders' Equity		
Preferred Stock, $.10 Par Value—1,500,000 Shares Authorized; Issued and Outstanding—None	--	--
Common Stock, $.01 Par Value—25,000,000 Shares Authorized; 10,290,000 and 12,713,000 Shares Issued at December 31, 1989, and 1990, Respectively	103	127
Additional Paid-in Capital	49,777	100,443
Retained Earnings	15,995	27,331
Total Stockholders' Equity	65,875	127,901
Total Liabilities and Stockholders' Equity	$219,130	$301,180

EXHIBIT 23.8   Consolidated Statements of Income (In thousands except per share data)

	Year Ended December 31,		
	1988	1989	1990
Net Revenues	$77,493	$118,862	$180,482
Operating Expenses	59,312	90,068	135,822
Provision for Doubtful Accounts	1,415	2,512	5,120
Depreciation and Amortization	4,088	7,110	11,056
Interest Expense	3,822	8,121	11,547
Interest Income	(942)	(1,954)	(4,136)
	67,695	105,857	159,409
Income before Minority Interests and Income Taxes	9,798	13,005	21,073
Minority Interests	857	495	924
	8,941	12,510	20,149
Provision for Income Taxes	3,208	4,363	7,226
Net Income	$ 5,733	$ 8,147	$ 12,923
Weighted Average Common and Common Equivalent Shares Outstanding	10,392	10,707	12,139
Net Income per Common and Common Equivalent Share	$ .55	$ .76	$ 1.06
Net Income per Common Share—Assuming Full Dilution	$ .55	$ .73	$ .96

WHERE DOES HEALTHSOUTH GO FROM HERE?

Richard Scrushy was reviewing company projections to plan for the continued success of HEALTHSOUTH Rehabilitation Corporation. Money managers continued to reward the company for its historical and expected performance with the stock trading at a price earnings ratio of 30 to 1.

Recently, Craig Dickson, an analyst with Rauscher, Pierce, Refsnes, had posed a question concerning HEALTHSOUTH's ability to continue the trend. Scrushy reflected on all the questions he had asked himself earlier and wondered if the rate of success could continue. "What will I need to do to make it happen? Are there things we should be doing differently? How can I ensure that HEALTHSOUTH does not outgrow its resources—either capital or management? Does the market provide sufficient opportunity to grow at 20 to 30 percent per year? What external factors do we face? What should we do to ensure that medical rehabilitation continues to be favorably reimbursed? What is the real number of facilities needed and how many acquisition targets are there?"

Scrushy focused on answering the questions. He knew that he could formulate a plan to ensure HEALTHSOUTH's success. In fact, in a probing interview in *Rehabilitation Today* (May 1991), Mr. Scrushy was careful to state that he would consider any acquisition where he believed "value could be added" and dismissed the possibility that the company's "regional name" implied that his aspirations were regional. Clearly, he was willing to go anywhere, anytime he believed opportunities existed.

EXHIBIT 23.9 Consolidated Statements of Stockholders' Equity (In thousands)

	Common Stock	Additional Paid-In Capital	Retained Earnings	Treasury Stock	Total Stockholders' Equity
			Years Ended December 31,		
Balance at January 1, 1988	$100.2	$48,400.0	$2,783.8	$ (.3)	$ 51,283.7
Proceeds from Issuance of 16,969 Common Shares	.2	279.8	—	—	280.0
Proceeds from Exercise of Options	.6	176.2	—	—	176.8
Purchase of Limited Partnership Units	—	—	(191.4)	—	(191.4)
Purchase of Treasury Stock (1,550 Shares)	—	—	—	(.1)	(.1)
Net Income	—	—	5,733.4	—	5,733.4
Balance at December 31, 1988	101.0	48,856.0	8,325.8	(.4)	57,282.4
Proceeds from Exercise of Options	2.0	953.1	—	—	955.1
Purchase of Treasury Stock (1,250 Shares)	—	—	—	(15.8)	(15.3)
Treasury Stock Used in the Exercise of Options	(.1)	(9.5)	—	9.6	—
Common Stock Exchanged in the Exercise of Options	—	(22.7)	—	—	(22.7)
Sale of Treasury Stock	—	—	—	6.1	6.1
Purchase of Limited Partnership Units	—	—	(477.8)	—	(477.8)
Net Income	—	—	8,147.3	—	8,147.3
Balance at December 31, 1989	102.9	49,776.9	15,995.3	0	65,875.1
Proceeds from Issuance of 48,196 Common Shares	.5	1,096.0	—	—	1,096.5
Proceeds from Issuance of 2,221,182 Common Shares	22.2	48,476.6	—	—	48,498.8
Proceeds from Exercise of Options	1.5	1,115.8	—	—	1,117.3
Common Shares Exchanged in the Exercise of Options	—	(22.6)	—	—	(22.6)
Purchase of Limited Partnership Units	—	—	(1,587.3)	—	(1,587.3)
Net Income	—	—	12,923.2	—	12,923.2
Balance at December 31, 1990	$127.1	$100,442.7	$27,331.2	0	$127,901.0

EXHIBIT 23.10   Consolidated Statements of Cash Flows (In thousands)

	Years Ended December 31,		
	1988	*1989*	*1990*
Operating Activities			
Net Income	$5,733	$8,147	$12,923
Adjustments to Reconcile Net Income to Net Cash (Used)			
Provided by Operating Activities			
Depreciation and Amortization	4,088	7,110	11,056
Income Applicable to Minority Interests of Limited			
Partnerships	857	495	924
Provision for Deferred Income Taxes	1,410	606	1,788
Provision for Deferred Revenue from Contractual Agencies	597	(101)	(230)
Changes in Operating Assets and Liabilities, Net of Effects of			
Acquisitions:			
Increase in Accounts Receivable	(11,906)	(15,806)	(183)
Increase in Inventories, Prepaid Expenses and Other			
Current Assets	(2,295)	(738)	(390)
Increase in Accounts Payable and Accrued Expenses	198	3,854	2,255
Net Cash (Used) Provided by Operating Activities	$(1,318)	$3,567	$28,143
Investing Activities			
Purchase of Property, Plant, and Equipment	$(16,934)	$(19,992)	$(37,548)
Additions to Intangible Assets, Net of Effects of			
Acquisitions	(7,323)	(8,908)	(9,051)
Assets Obtained through Acquisition, Net of Liabilities			
Assumed	(5,592)	(30,110)	(5,239)
Additions to Notes Receivable	(116)	(586)	(1,553)
Reduction in Notes Receivable	0	144	394
Proceeds Received on Maturity of Long-Term Marketable			
Securities	2,124	1,849	1,659
Investment in Long-Term Marketable Securities	(1,864)	(3,239)	(7,522)
Deposits Placed in Escrow Related to Acquisitions	(288)	288	0
Net Cash Used by Investing Activities	$(29,993)	$(60,554)	$(58,860)

EXHIBIT 23.10 (continued)

	1988	1989	1990
		(In thousands)	
Financing Activities			
Proceeds from Borrowings	$41,460	$104,246	$57,243
Principal Payments on Debt and Leases	(15,129)	(34,169)	(40,531)
Proceeds from Exercise of Options	177	923	1,095
Common Stock Issued on Acquisition	—	—	1,096
Proceeds from Issuance of Common Stock	—	—	48,499
Purchase of Treasury Stock	—	(15)	—
Sale or Transfer of Treasury Stock	—	16	—
Proceeds from Investment by Minority Interests	423	998	247
Purchase of Limited Partnership Interests	(365)	(733)	(1,460)
Payment of Cash Distributions to Limited Partners	(1,370)	(1,547)	(1,964)
Net Cash Provided by Financing Activities	25,196	69,719	64,225
(Decrease) Increase in Cash and Cash Equivalents	(6,115)	12,732	33,508
Cash and Cash Equivalents at Beginning of Year	21,959	15,844	28,576
Cash and Cash Equivalents at End of Year	$15,844	$28,576	$62,084
Supplemental Disclosures of Cash Flow Information			
Cash Paid During the Year for:			
Interest	$4,589	$7,657	$13,062
Income Taxes	2,375	3,617	5,008

Noncash Investing and Financing Activities:

Common stock was issued in 1988 for satisfaction of $280,000 due on a purchase agreement.

Assets related to three of the company's rehabilitation equipment businesses, having a net book value of $5,783,000, were sold during 1989. The consideration for the assets consisted of a note receivable, an interest in the purchaser's company, and the assumption of certain liabilities.

EXHIBIT 23.11   HEALTHSOUTH Rehabilitation Corporation Quarterly Revenues (In millions)

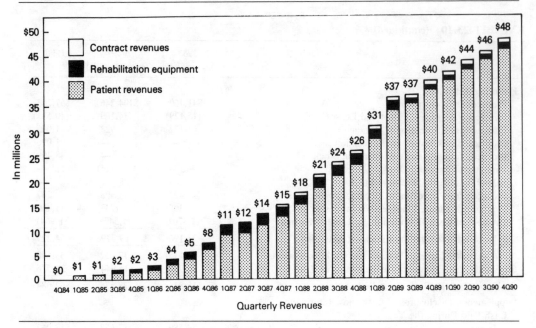

Source: HEALTHSOUTH Rehabilitation Corporation.

EXHIBIT 23.12   HEALTHSOUTH Rehabilitation Corporation Quarterly Gross Patient Revenues (In millions)

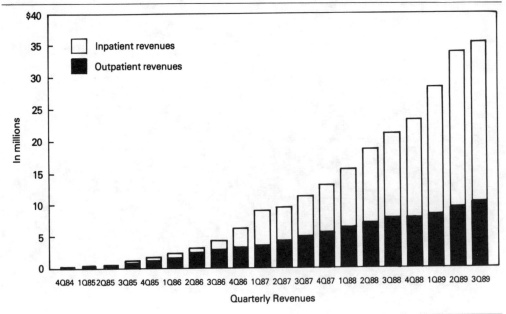

Source: HEALTHSOUTH Rehabilitation Corporation.

CASE 26

Carolco Pictures

PROLOGUE

"Gentlemen, place your bets."

Mario F. Kassar, chairman of Carolco Pictures, pushed a stack of thousand-dollar chips forward. He turned toward a nearby waitress and ordered another bottle of Tattinger Compte de Champagne, 1981. He was in his element at the casino in Monte Carlo, and as usual the forthcoming bottle would be gratis. He was a favorite of the casino and would often vacation there to relax after the premiere of a Carolco production. The casino was expecting an active night, for, in recreational pursuits as in business, Mario Kassar spent freely. On this occasion Mario Kassar was celebrating the premiere of the most expensive movie ever made.

Terminator 2: Judgment Day had a production cost of $90 million. Did the movie's foreboding title allude to a coming apocalypse for Carolco? Indeed, the auditors had felt compelled to include a statement in the annual report addressing their concerns over the company's viability as an ongoing entity. The production had left Carolco in an ominous financial position. Cash strapped, the company had a negative cash flow from operations from 1988 to 1991. In addition to reporting a $6.3 million loss, the company had to seek concessions from its debt holders.[1]

None of that mattered to Kassar, for he was in the casino to unwind and escape such concerns. Here he could more easily control the outcome and receive instant gratification for his efforts. He motioned toward his evening companion to place all of his bet on one number. "Let her roll," he announced as the roulette wheel began to spin. "I need a winner."

This case was prepared by James Breshnahan, Karen Keniff, Mark Mitchell, and Dan Twing under the supervision of Sexton Adams and Adelaide Griffin as a basis for class discussion rather than to illustrate either effective or ineffective handling of an administrative situation. Copyright © 1991 by Sexton Adams and Adelaide Griffin. Used with permission from Sexton Adams.

[1] "Carolco Needs a Hero, and the Terminator May Prove to Be It," *Wall Street Journal* (southwest ed.) July 9, 1991, p. A1.

HISTORY

Mario F. Kassar first met Andrew Vajna at the Cannes Film Festival in 1975. Andrew Vajna was born in Hungary, raised in Los Angeles, and made his first fortune in Hong Kong manufacturing wigs and later blue jeans. In the early 1970s Vajna bought two Hong Kong movie theaters, which led him to become a film licensing agent in the Far East. Mario Kassar, born in Beirut and raised in Rome, became a sales agent for movies at age 18, specializing in the Middle East.[2] They formed a movie distribution company soon after meeting and ventured into film production in the early 1980s. The original purpose of the partnership was to obtain better terms by buying rights to movies for both the Far East and the Middle East.

Kassar and Vajna incorporated Carolco Pictures in Delaware in April 1986. They set up desks facing each other and together picked and produced most of Carolco's movies. They "hit the jackpot" quickly after making *First Blood* and later *First Blood II* starring Sylvester Stallone. The two movies took in $420.5 million at the box office domestically and in foreign distribution.[3] Soon after going public, Peter Hoffman, a top entertainment and tax lawyer, was recruited to be president and chief executive officer. One of his first duties was to establish a tax haven for Carolco in the Netherlands.[4] Hoffman also acquired operations in video and television distribution and production to help maximize revenues from Carolco movies.

Carolco pursued a strategic agenda dissimilar to other independent movie producers. Rather than limiting risks by making numerous small-budget productions, Carolco's main strategy had been to make four or five "event" pictures a year with budgets of $20 million and up while selling distribution in advance to help cover costs.[5] Because of the risk involved, Carolco had not engaged in the domestic theatrical distribution of its films. Instead, the company entered into a distribution agreement with Tri-Star Pictures. The company usually reserved all domestic pay and free television, domestic home video, and foreign rights to its films.[6]

In 1989, Carolco released three low-budget, nonaction films, all of which scored poorly at the box office. The same year cochairman Andrew Vajna decided to break up the 13-year partnership. "Colleagues say a clash in the style of the two co-founders contributed to the split, with Mr. Vajna opposing the high spending and rapid growth. At the time, a company official said Mr. Vajna 'would prefer to have a bag of cash instead of the pressure and stress in building a large public company.'" Mr. Vajna indeed received his "bag of cash." Mario Kassar bought

---

[2] Alex Ben Block, "Is There Life beyond Rambo?" *Forbes*, June 1, 1987, pp. 88–92.
[3] "Carolco Needs a Hero," p. A10.
[4] Block, "Is There Life Beyond Rambo?" p. 92.
[5] "Carolco Needs a Hero," p. A1.
[6] *Standard and Poor's Stock Reports*, New York Stock Exchange, February 1991, p. 448.

11.2 million shares from his partner for $108 million in December 1989.[7] This gave Kassar 63 percent controlling interest in the company. Mario Kassar had the reputation within the industry as a gambler. Said David Goldman, an agent at International Creative Management, "He's a movie mogul in the style of Samuel Goldwyn."[8]

MANAGEMENT

When he cofounded Carolco Pictures, Mario Kassar stated three basic principles to the stockholders. These guidelines included:

1. To produce and distribute a limited number of "event" motion pictures; that is, movies with cast and production values that would give them major box office appeal both within and beyond the borders of the United States.
2. To finance these often expensive productions through "presales" of exhibition rights in various media in countries around the world, with nearly all the marketing costs borne by our subdistributors, not by Carolco.
3. To maximize returns from such rapidly growing "ancillary" markets as video and television, both pay and free, via the establishment of a distribution capability for these markets, either within Carolco or in a separate publicly owned subsidiary.[9]

These three basic principles on which Carolco was founded were the same principles that guided operations in 1991. Carolco's mission was: "To develop an integrated worldwide independent motion picture, television, and video company with important strategic relationships. This would create a company equal to any major in the quality, if not quantity, of its film release schedule."[10]

Kassar endeavored to establish relationships with the most talented and sought-after creative individuals in the film industry. Both directors and stars of Carolco's films included the most consistently popular box office attractions. Carolco had produced such box office hits as *First Blood, Rambo: First Blood Part II, Red Heat,* and *Total Recall.* The company also produced other major event films such as *Rambo III, Basic Instinct, Extreme Prejudice, Johnny Handsome, Air America, Narrow Margin,* and *LA Story.*

In conjunction with Kassar's style of seeking out the most creative and talented individuals, he spared no expense. Industry analysts cited Kassar's management style as the leading cause of Carolco's soaring overhead. Kassar received a salary of $1.5 million in 1990, as well as the use of a Carolco jet. Carolco paid $410,000 to install security devices in Kassar's Beverly Hills mansion in 1988 and an additional $259,000 in security services in 1990.[11]

7 "Carolco Needs a Hero," p. A10.
8 Ibid., p. A1.
9 Carolco Pictures, Inc. *Annual Report,* 1990, p. 2.
10 Ibid., p. 4.
11 "Carolco Needs a Hero," p. A1.

Directors and producers who contracted with Carolco enjoyed Kassar's liberal spending as well. "Mario Kassar does everything with a great deal of style, and he does it bigger and better than anyone else," according to David Goldman in a *Wall Street Journal* article. For example, in 1990, Carolco flew seventy of Hollywood's most famous to the Cannes Film Festival, transported them via a fleet of limousines accompanied by a police motorcade, to the Hotel du Cap, where they were lodged courtesy of Carolco. In addition, Kassar threw a gala aboard a yacht to promote Carolco's film. The party, complete with fireworks, was reported to be the most expensive in Cannes.[12]

Carolco was also setting spending precedents at home in Hollywood. In early 1990, Carolco paid scripter Joe Esterhas $3 million and producer Irwin Winkler $1 million for *Basic Instinct*. This was the highest amount ever paid for a spec script. Later that same year, Kassar set a new record by paying what was to be the highest amount ever to a writer on assignment. Kassar paid to Oscar-winning screen writer Barry Levinson of *Rain Man* fame $2 million to script an idea based on the supernatural thriller by T. M. Wright, *Manhattan Ghost Story*. One top agent remarked, "I've never heard of a deal where a writer is guaranteed $2 million for an idea."[13] In negotiations with Kassar, people rarely walked away feeling short-changed. When producer Brian Grazer's rights to *The Doors* were within hours of expiring, he contacted Kassar. After a 10-minute phone conversation, Kassar had agreed to do the movie and Grazer had a check within a few hours.[14]

Arnold Schwarzenegger, star of Carolco hit *Terminator 2: Judgment Day*, received approximately $15 million for the movie. According to *Entertainment Weekly*, Schwarzenegger spoke about 700 words. This cost Carolco approximately $21,429 per word. For example, Schwarzenegger's famous line from the movie, "Hasta la vista, baby," cost Carolco $85,716.[15]

Kassar's free spending did not set well with shareholders, however, and they complained that Kassar stacked the deck in his favor. In September 1990, Carolco agreed to purchase 3.4 million shares from Kassar at a price of $13 each when the market price was $7.25. In addition, during the 1988–1989 season, an $8 million loan was made to Kassar and Vajna with the stipulation that if Carolco's stock reached $11 per share before August 1989, the loan would be forgiven. The loan was forgiven when the stock reached the stipulated price in June 1989. A shareholders' suit was filed that charged Kassar with self-dealing. The suit stated that he used the company, which he controlled, to further his own interests. Further, the suit charged that the stipulated price of the stock was reached "due to the manipulative actions of Kassar and others." A judge froze 2.2 million shares of Carolco stock owned by Kassar and limited his ability to draw funds

[12] Ibid.

[13] Claudia Eller, "Scripter to Get $2 Million to Adapt 'Manhattan,'" *Variety*, October 8, 1990, p. 28.

[14] "Carolco Needs a Hero," p. A1.

[15] "News Summary—People," *Dallas Morning News*, July 15, 1991, p. A-2.

from the company pending further motions. Carolco has never paid dividends to its shareholders.[16]

OPERATIONS

Major Motion Picture Production

To produce its major event films, Carolco enlisted top producers, directors, writers, and stars. Some of Hollywood's most artistic, exciting, and commercially successful directors and producers worked on Carolco's films. These included Tim Burton, James Cameron, George Cosmatos, John Hughes, Robert Redford, Oliver Stone, and Paul Verhoeven. Big name stars were also part of Carolco productions including such names as Arnold Schwarzenegger, Sylvester Stallone, Michael Douglas, Lou Gosset Jr., Steve Martin, John Candy, Val Kilmer, and Jean-Claude Van Damme.

Carolco did not maintain a substantial staff of creative or technical personnel. Management believed that sufficient motion picture properties and creative and technical personnel (such as screenwriters, directors, and performers) were available in the market at acceptable prices, enabling the company to produce as many motion pictures as it planned or anticipated, at the level of commercial quality the company required. To ensure the availability of such personnel, Carolco had multiple-year production and development agreements with a number of prominent directors. Typically, under such agreements, the director submitted to Carolco on a "first-look" basis any project he or she wished to direct. In some cases, the director was obligated to direct one or two films for the company within a set period of time. Carolco provided office support and development funding for the director. In many cases, the director rendered services on outside projects controlled by other studios.[17]

As of April 1, 1991, Carolco employed approximately 295 people full time. Certain subsidiaries of Carolco were subject to the terms of collective bargaining agreements with the Writers Guild of America, Directors Guild of America, the Screen Actors Guild, and the International Alliance of Theatrical Stage Employees (concerning certain technical crafts such as director of photography, sound recording, and editing). A strike, job action, or labor disturbance by the members of any of these organizations could have had a tangible adverse effect on the production of a motion picture within the United States. Carolco believed its relationship with its employees was satisfactory.

Due to the level of talent and the grand scale of Carolco's major event productions, large budgets, usually over $25 million per film, were not uncommon. *Total Recall* cost $59 million to make.[18] *Terminator 2: Judgment Day* was

---

[16] "Carolco Needs a Hero," p. A1.

[17] Carolco Pictures, Inc., *Form 10-K*, 1990, pp. 1, 5.

[18] Claudia Eller and Don Groves, "Carolco Prexy Defends Its Talent Megadeals," *Variety*, October 29, 1990, p. 10.

rumored to cost $90 million.[19] Although some industry observers questioned the logic of such spending, Carolco continued to produce high-budget, high-tech action thrillers.

Besides making major event films, Carolco had several subsidiaries to perform such functions as production of moderate budget films, foreign leasing of theatrical productions, domestic and foreign distribution to television, merchandise licensing, operation of production studios, and home entertainment software distribution. These subsidiaries are shown in Exhibit 26.1.

EXHIBIT 26.1   Carolco Pictures Major Subsidiary Operations

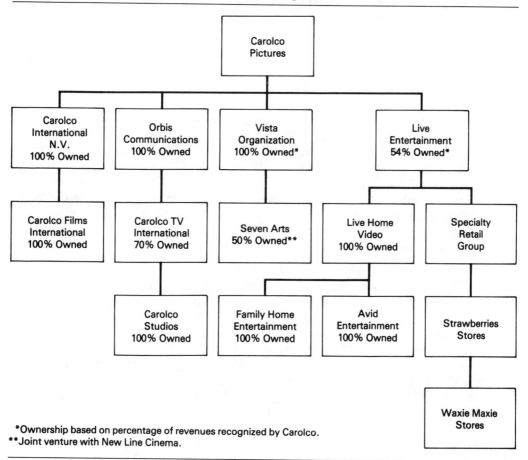

*Ownership based on percentage of revenues recognized by Carolco.
**Joint venture with New Line Cinema.

Source: Derived from Carolco Pictures *Annual Report* 1990 and *Form 10-K* 1990.

[19] "Carolco Needs a Hero," p. A1.

Moderate Budget Film Production

In 1989, Carolco purchased a one-third interest in the Vista Organization. Vista formed Seven Arts in 1990 as a joint venture with New Line Cinema. This venture was established to supplement the production of major event films. Seven Arts financed, produced, acquired, and distributed moderate budget motion pictures. This new division was formed to capitalize on Carolco's expertise in motion picture financing, strength in foreign distribution, and relationships with leading talent from around the world. Seven Arts' films were released theatrically in the United States through the joint venture with New Line Cinema. Seven Arts also made arrangements with LIVE Home Video (a partially owned subsidiary of Carolco) for domestic video release of its pictures, and with Carolco International for the foreign distribution of its pictures.

Foreign Leasing of Theatrical Productions

As the international appetite for American-made movies expanded into new markets, Carolco Pictures and its subsidiaries continued to be leading independent suppliers of major motion pictures throughout the world. At the international film festivals and markets held in Cannes, Milan, and Los Angeles, groups of Carolco's films were successfully sold to leading international distribution firms around the world. Carolco conducted foreign distribution through a wholly owned subsidiary, Carolco International N.V. (CINV), with offices and employees in Curacao, Zurich, and London. Although CINV's main activities involved the international leasing of Carolco-produced films, the division acquired foreign distribution rights for important films produced by other studios and producers.

Television Distribution

Although domestic theatrical distribution of Carolco major event films was accomplished through an agreement with Tri-Star Pictures, and Seven Arts films were distributed domestically through an arrangement with New Line Cinema, Carolco retained the rights to television distribution through its wholly owned subsidiary, Orbis Communications. Orbis Communications operated three main areas of business in 1990: domestic distribution of motion pictures for free and pay television; licensing of Carolco films and other programming in the international television market; and production and acquisition of television programming such as telefilms, miniseries, and game shows. Revenues from Orbis reached $42 million in 1990, almost double those of 1989.[20]

All foreign rights to Orbis' television products and television rights to Carolco's theatrical motion pictures were distributed to worldwide television outlets by Carolco Films International Ltd. (CFIL), a London-based wholly owned subsidiary of Carolco International N.V. During 1990, CFIL's priorities

---

[20] *Annual Report*, 1990, p. 5.

included licensing Carolco feature films in those territories where TV rights were available and marketing Orbis' catalog of television programming.

Although Orbis continued to make substantial progress in domestic syndication and international television licensing of Carolco's and others' films, Orbis' production activities consistently failed to reach management profit objectives. Television productions were not staying in syndication. For example, the game show *Joker's Wild* was not picked up for a second season. As a result, on April 11, 1991, Carolco signed an agreement with Multimedia to sell Orbis' production and development activities.

Merchandise Licensing

In operation since 1987, Carolco Licensing Division had evolved into a full-service licensing entity. In 1990, Carolco Licensing successfully exploited merchandising rights to *Total Recall* in a variety of categories. The *Total Recall* Nintendo game was a landmark for the video game industry, as the game was marketed in conjunction with the film's release. Carolco Licensing remained extremely active in publishing and 1990 saw the *Total Recall* novelization become a top seller. Through an expanding network of foreign licensing agents, Carolco Licensing coordinated the licensing of Carolco's properties worldwide, and was also responsible for the placement of products and corporate signage in Carolco films.

Production Studio Operations

In May 1990, a wholly owned subsidiary of Carolco merged with De Laurentiis Entertainment Group to form Carolco Television Inc. (CTI). CTI included a development library containing over 100 feature film projects and a full-service 32-acre production facility in Wilmington, North Carolina. The studio housed eight fully equipped sound stages with all necessary support facilities and services. The studio backlot had three blocks of city streets that were transformed to represent specific eras and locations. Carolco, as well as other companies, used these facilities for its productions.

Home Entertainment Software Distribution

Carolco distributed home entertainment software through its partially owned subsidiary, LIVE Entertainment. In 1990, Carolco recorded 54 percent of LIVE's net income in its earnings as a result of its ownership of approximately 47 percent of LIVE's outstanding common stock and 100 percent of its series A common stock. LIVE's operations were conducted through the following operating entities: video distribution through LIVE Home Video (LHV), rackjobbing through Lieberman Enterprises Incorporated (Lieberman), and entertainment software retailing through the Specialty Retail Group. As of July 22, 1991, Carolco's annual stockholders' meeting had been postponed to allow Carolco's board of directors to consider a proposal by LIVE to discuss a possible business combination of the two companies.[21]

LIVE Home Video

LIVE Home Video provided a broad selection of high-performance programming from Carolco Pictures, as well as such top film makers as IndieProd, Miramax Films, New Visions Pictures, Avenue Pictures, Gladden Entertainment, and Working Title Films, among others. Children's films were distributed through a division called Family Home Entertainment, and a newly formed division, Avid Entertainment, distributed midline home videos.

Lieberman Enterprises

Lieberman Enterprises was the nation's second largest supplier of prerecorded music, prerecorded videocassettes, and personal computer software (PCS) to mass merchandisers and specialty retailers in over 3,400 retail locations. Carolco was searching for sources of cash and, in an effort to allay its cash-poor standing, sold Lieberman Enterprises in 1991 for approximately $100 million.[22]

LIVE Specialty Retail Group

The LIVE Specialty Retail Group (LSRG) operated 144 retail stores in 11 states offering compact discs, audio cassettes, prerecorded videos, and accessories. The stores operated under the name of Strawberries in the Northeast, including New England, New York, Pennsylvania, and New Jersey, and under the name Waxie Maxie in the Mid-Atlantic area, including Maryland and Virginia.

MARKETING

Carolco's market niche was to produce big-star action films that had as much or more success abroad than in the United States. This meant it produced high-action movies starring popular actors with broad-based appeal to ensure that these films would perform very well both domestically and internationally. In fact, its high action films such as the *Rambo* series and *Total Recall* brought in more revenue abroad than domestically.

Once Carolco completed a motion picture, it would generally be distributed and made available for license in the steps illustrated in Exhibit 26.2.

During the late 1980s, revenues from licensing of rights to distribute motion pictures in ancillary (i.e., other than domestic theatrical) markets, particularly pay television and home video, had significantly increased. The company had obtained a substantial part of the advances and guarantees for its pictures from the license of distribution rights in these ancillary markets.

---

[21] Carolco Pictures Inc., *News Release*, June 10, 1991.
[22] "Carolco Needs a Hero," p. A1.

EXHIBIT 26.2   Timing of Carolco Distribution and License Procedures

Marketplace	Months after Initial Release	Approximate Period (Months)
Domestic Theatrical		6
Domestic Home Video	6	6
Domestic Pay Television	12–18	12–24
Domestic Network Television	30–36	30–36
Domestic Syndication Television	30–36	30–36
Foreign Theatrical		4–6
Foreign Video	6–12	6–18
Foreign Television	18–24	18–30

Source: Carolco Pictures Inc., *Form 10-K* 1990, p. 8.

Domestic Markets

Tri-Star handled domestic distribution of Carolco's feature products, which freed Carolco of the significant overhead and marketing costs that accompanied film distribution. Under the arrangement, Tri-Star paid the print and advertising costs, and after recouping those expenses, kept an average of 35 percent of Carolco's net profits.[23] Carolco did not want to distribute its own films domestically, since the demise of several other independent filmmakers was attributed to those costs.

Orbis Communication conducted Carolco's domestic distribution of motion pictures for free and pay television, production and acquisition of television programming, miniseries, and game shows. Orbis packaged and sold motion pictures to the U.S. broadcast market. In 1989, Carolco marketed its first motion picture package in domestic syndication under the "Carolco I" banner containing *First Blood, Angel Heart, The Terminator, Kiss of the Spider Woman*, and other motion pictures. In 1990, it sold "Carolco II," which included films such as *Rambo: First Blood Part II, Rambo III*, and *Hoosiers* to the USA Network for $25 million.[24] In December 1990, Carolco introduced "Carolco III," a package of 25 titles including such artistically successful pictures as *Platoon, The Last Emperor*, and *Red Heat*. As of April 15, 1990, this package had been sold to more than 60 percent of the U.S. broadcast markets, which resulted in over $21 million in revenue. Carolco continued to receive revenue from the earlier packages, and anticipated that an additional one or two motion picture packages would be marketed domestically in 1992 and 1993.

Also in 1990, under Carolco Television Productions (CTP), Orbis reintroduced the game show *Joker's Wild*, but it met with limited success. Orbis found greater success in the game show business with *The $100,000 Pyramid* before it sold CTP due to its inability to meet management's profit objectives.

---

[23] Geraldine Fabrikant, "Finding Success in Movie Niches," *New York Times*, April 4, 1990, p. C1(N).

[24] *Form 10-K*, 1990, p. 34.

Carolco distributed its own, as well as others', moderate-budget motion pictures domestically through its Seven Arts division. Seven Arts' films and videos were released domestically through a joint venture with New Line Cinema and LIVE Home Video, respectively. During 1990, Seven Arts released *Repossessed* and *King of New York*. In February 1991, Seven Arts released *Queens Logic*. Other films released later in 1991 included *Rambling Rose*, *The Dark Wind*, *Aces: Iron Eagle III*, and *Petleir*.

LIVE Entertainment (LIVE) was a leading distributor of home videos, which it marketed through LIVE Home Video and LIVE Specialty Retail Group. In 1990, LHV was the leading independent home video company and was fifth among all video software suppliers in the country. LHV had the second largest market share, falling just behind Disney in the sell-through video market. This market consisted of videos selling for less than $25, mainly from its Family Home Entertainment division sales. LHV's revenues from newly released rental titles rose by one-third in 1990 and sell-through revenues saw a fivefold increase, boosted in particular by two mega-hits: *Teenage Mutant Ninja Turtles: The Movie* and Carolco's *Total Recall*. LHV expanded in 1990 with Avid Entertainment, which offered titles generally priced under $15. Initial releases included such hits as *Eddie and the Cruisers II*, *Millennium*, and *Wired*. Strawberries and Waxie Maxie, LSRG's retail outlets, made them the leading music retailer in the greater Boston and Washington, D.C., areas and a strong retailer in Philadelphia, Baltimore, and upstate New York.

International Markets

In 1991, the international market for American-made movies had expanded and Carolco was a leading independent supplier of major motion pictures, videos, and related accessories throughout the world. In 1990, *Total Recall* met with great success overseas, bringing in $260 million as opposed to $118 million domestically.[25] The film's overseas success was mainly attributable to its star, Arnold Schwarzenegger, who was probably the biggest box office attraction of the world at the time.

Carolco's overseas marketing activities were conducted by Carolco International N.V. and included international leasing of Carolco produced action films, Seven Arts' films, and foreign distribution rights for important films produced by other studios. In 1990, foreign rights were acquired to three pictures from Universal Studios: *The Wizard*, *Opportunity Knocks*, and *Career Opportunities*. Carolco also acquired the foreign theatrical distribution rights to the 20th Century Fox production *Robin Hood*. Peter Hoffman speculated that Fox believed Carolco could generate more revenue through its distribution system than Fox could through its own channels.[26]

---

[25] Ibid., p. 25.
[26] Eller and Groves, "Carolco Prexy Defends Its Talent," p. 10.

During 1990, CINV signed distribution agreements with leading distributors including Guild Entertainment in the United Kingdom; Unirecord International S.A., in Spain; Pentafilm S.P.A., in Italy; and others in Europe, Japan, Australia, and Latin America. Foreign leasing amounted to 60 percent of Carolco's feature film revenues in 1990, and with the strong line up of releases scheduled for 1992, it was expected to continue to be a major profit center for the company.

To distribute Orbis' television products and Carolco's theatrical motion pictures worldwide, the firm used Carolco Films International. During 1990, CFIL sold $20 million in license fees through 150 licenses for Carolco feature films, telefilms and miniseries, and Orbis' catalog of television programming.[27]

Foreign sales were headed by Guy East, former international sales director for Goldcrest Film and Television. He commented on the prospects of Carolco in the foreign market: "There is every indication of huge growth in the foriegn area that Carolco wants to position itself to be part of."[28] East saw an expansion of the European market, with the advent of private television in France, Italy, and Spain, and from increased interest in construction of new screens. Additionally, the demise of several competitors, including PSO, Goldcrest, and Thorn EMI in Europe, gave Carolco opportunities to increase market share by capturing its competitors' lost distribution agreements. Executive vice president of foreign sales, Rocco Viglietta, stated, "The TV market overseas continues to grow particularly given the pending single Euro market in 1992 and the privatization of stations worldwide."[29]

As part of Carolco's international thrust, the company considered entering the home video market in the former Soviet Union through an arrangement with Sintez International in Moscow. Orbis' executive vice president, Ethan Podell, said, "We're very interested in exploiting opportunities in Eastern Europe and Russia." The Carolco exchange would have initially provided Sintez with TV documentaries, specials, and children's programming for the Russian market. Revenues were to be split between Sintez and Carolco and were required to remain in Russia where Orbis could use the rubles to finance productions in Russia.[30] A note of caution in this market was expressed by Viglietta, "People there are looking to be fed first . . . it will be sometime before the Eastern Bloc becomes capitalized and people get VCRs in their homes."[31]

Licensing

Many of Carolco's popular films created a great worldwide demand for action figures, books, games, and toys. Carolco's licensing division developed

[27] *Annual Report*, 1990, p. 27.

[28] James Greenberg, "Newly Formed Carolco Int'l Gets O'Seas Rights to Carpenter Pix," *Variety*, August 5, 1987, p. 28.

[29] "Carolco Presses on without Its Cofounder Vajna: Has 9-Title Package Ready," *Variety*, February 21, 1990, p. 88.

[30] "Carolco Says 'Da' to Pack," *Variety*, December 3, 1990, p. 19.

[31] Eller and Groves, "Carolco Prexy Defends Its Talent," p. 88.

into a full-service licensing entity. For example, *Total Recall* was a great success for Nintendo. Carolco also published the novel, which became a top seller. For *Terminator 2: Judgment Day*, Carolco licensing was also involved in heavy licensing activity of toys, Nintendo and computer software games, video and pinball arcade games, publishing, comic books, apparel, and collectible products. Also national promotions were planned during the release of the film including promotional tie-ins with Pepsi, Subway sandwich chain, and Hero Cologne by Faberge. Carolco Licensing was very successful in managing the licensing activities of Carolco's properties worldwide. For example, Rambo remained the number one action figure in Brazil and Argentina years after the series was released, and demand remained high for the toy in Europe and the South Pacific as well.

The licensing division was also responsible for product and corporate identity signage in Carolco films. The placement of products and logos in movies not only generated revenue for Carolco, but it also served as a base to build consumer promotion relationships with the client companies.

ECONOMIC ENVIRONMENT

In January 1991, reports from Washington regarding the nation's economic recession offered little encouragement. As real incomes were falling, consumer spending subsequently took a downturn. Consumer confidence fell approximately 12 percent in January to reach its lowest level in 10 years.[32] The nation fought a war with Iraq and consumer spending continued to decline. However, consumers were faced with rising inflation and increasing federal income and payroll taxes. This "double whammy" affected the typical family, consisting of two full-time wage earners with two dependent children, by lowering their real after tax net income.[33]

The movie business historically fared well in bad, even disastrous, economic times. Economist Albert Kapusinki's study of the years 1928–1975 showed that approximately 70 percent of the time the film industry thrived in economic troughs. In each of the three major recessions from 1971 to 1991, the strong countercyclical nature of the film industry triumphed.[34]

The recession of the early 1990s found the film industry competing in a diverse media spectrum. Viewers had the option to choose from a widening range of film entertainment as well as basic cable television to pay-per-view movies and events. Also in the arena was a fully matured home video business. "The argu-

---

[32] James C. Cooper and Kathleen Madigan, "The Consumer Is Blue, Broke, and Burdened with Debt," *Business Week*, February 11, 1991, p. 17.

[33] Gene Koretz, "A Double Whammy for Double-Income Families," *Business Week*, December 31, 1990, p. 32.

[34] Paul Nogolows, "Will B.O. Prove Recession-Proof This Time Out?" *Variety*, December 10, 1990, p. 1.

ment has been made that people are going to go out to the video store and rent a cassette and bring it home rather than going out to the movie theater and having a pizza and getting a babysitter, and I would agree with that," said analyst Chris Dixon of Kidder, Peabody & Co.[35] Dixon also noted that the film industry was driven by demand and revenues will continue to be at rates above normal in the consumer sector. Strength in the overseas theatrical market and increased penetration of television households in Europe were accredited for these revenues.[36]

COMPETITION

Carolco competed in the motion picture production and distribution industry. This industry was divided between two groups of competitors, major film production companies and independent film companies. Major film production companies included such common names as:

- Warner Brothers
- 20th Century Fox
- MGM/United Artists
- Orion
- Paramount
- Walt Disney-Buena Vista
- Others

Independent film companies included:

- Carolco
- Nelson Entertainment
- Samuel Goldwyn
- Miramax
- New Line/Seven Arts
- Castle Rock
- Cinergi Productions (formed by Carolco cofounder Vajna)

During the 1970s and 1980s, the number of films produced by independents increased from 133 in 1970[37] to a peak of 380 in 1987.[38] As shown in Exhibit 26.3, U.S. new film releases by independents increased between 1985 and 1987, while U.S. new film releases by majors decreased. During the period 1988 to 1990, the

[35] Ibid., p. 3.
[36] Ibid.
[37] Todd McCarthy, "Whopping Year For U.S. Independents," *Variety*, June 22, 1988, p. 22.
[38] Lawrence Cohn, "Fewer New Pix in '90, but More by Majors," *Variety*, December 24, 1990, p. 8.

EXHIBIT 26.3   New U.S. Feature Film Releases

	1985	1986	1987	1988	1989	1990
Film Source						
Majors	150	144	135	161	159	164
Independents	304	333	380	352	287	253

Source: Lawrence Cohn, "Fewer New Pix In '90, But More by Majors," *Variety*, December 24, 1990, p. 8.

majors released more films while independents released less, illustrating the direct competition for market share between the two groups.

Carolco's positioning between the two groups—by releasing major event films, distributing videos and television programming, and offering packages of movie titles, all worldwide—helped to hedge its position, protecting the organization from the cyclical swings in market share between the two segments.

Carolco's worldwide distribution network was beneficial as earnings from the domestic film market only covered the costs of making films. For example, the approximate aggregate investment by domestic producers in summer 1991 films, including ad costs, was $2 billion. However, the 1991 summer market size for the films was only approximately $2 billion. The summer season provided 40 percent of the total annual U.S. box office gross. Therefore, there were many pictures that did not receive a return on their investment from U.S. theatrical distribution and had to turn to ancillary markets around the world to make a profit. With so many pictures crammed into such a narrow corridor, it became intimidating for even the most stalwart veterans of the distribution wars. As one Hollywood CEO remarked, "No matter how you rationalize it, this exercise is basically suicidal. . . . By mid-summer you're going to see a succession of pictures yanked from the schedule."[39]

In 1991, industrywide domestic theatrical income accounted for only about 20 percent of the total revenue stream and rose to 35 percent including all foreign theatrical earnings. The rest of the pie consisted of worldwide video, television syndication, cable, satellites, and all other esoteric new markets. This meant that U.S. theatrical openings were helpful but not necessarily vital to a new film. If a movie did poorly in the United States, it could still be successful in foreign markets and from studio output deals with the Showtimes and the HBOs.

Since domestic markets failed to provide enough return on investment, offshore markets became vital to filmmakers. For many producers, foreign markets accounted for nearly half the gross of a hit film. Carolco claimed between 65 percent and 75 percent of its revenues from overseas. So vital were the foreign markets that independents were caught in a vice between major U.S. studios, which were intensifying their quest for a bigger share of the foreign market, and

[39] Peter Bart, "View from the War Room," *Variety*, May 27, 1991, p. 3.

the changing tastes of foreign viewers. Foreign audiences were becoming more sophisticated, switching from low-budget action, horror, and slam-bang adventures to movies with big budgets, big stars, and big production values. The independents were known for the low-budget films, but these movies were not selling overseas anymore. Sigrid Ann Davidson, a vice president at Skouras Pictures, said, "The most important thing is to acquire better-quality star vehicles, not necessarily stars of the quality of Meryl Streep, but actors who have value overseas. The days of selling a film with boobs, bullets, and happy endings are a fading memory."[40]

One problem facing all U.S. film companies was the development of quotas within the European Community. France, for example, set a local quota of 60 percent for all its filmed entertainment, and unless the independents associated with foreign firms in coproductions or had local offices, their opportunities in the expanding European market was limited. One independent, Nelson Entertainment, secured films from Columbia and Orion and was successful in distributing them in the foreign market. These types of arrangements allowed an independent to swing some heavy weight behind its name.[41]

Many independents accumulated catalogs of titles to sell to foreign operations. As Herb Fletcher, Crown International vice president for international sales, said, "We have the advantage of being able to sell groups of pictures to television," but even companies with large catalogs are discovering narrower buying patterns. For the independents operating on a shoe-string budget, the fear of being put out of business because they failed to keep up to date with changing global tastes became their number one concern.[42]

LITIGATION AND CONTINGENCIES

In September 1990, two similar lawsuits were initiated, one in a Delaware Court of Chancery, the other in a California Superior Court, by stockholders of Carolco. These suits were aimed at the directors of Carolco and specific lenders with whom the company had loans outstanding. The lawsuits, which sought unspecified compensatory damages, stemmed from alleged self-dealings and breach of various fiduciary duties in connection with an approval of a stock purchase by CINV (the company's wholly owned foreign affiliate) from New CINV (a Netherlands corporation that at that time owned 62 percent of Carolco's common stock). Under the terms of the previously negotiated agreement, CINV purchased 3,461,538 shares of Carolco's common stock from New CINV at a price of $13 per share. At the time the agreement was executed, the shares were trading at about $7.25 on the New York Stock Exchange.[43] Furthermore, New

---

[40] Elliot Tiegel, "Surviving as an Indie," *California Business*, August 1990, p. 18.
[41] Ibid., p. 19.
[42] Ibid., p. 67.
[43] Cohn, "Fewer New Pix in '90," p. 9.

CINV was deemed to be beneficially owned by Mario Kassar and certain trusts set up for the benefit of his family. CINV paid New CINV a total of $44,999,994 for the stock, which consisted of cash and the assumption of a significant amount of New CINV's liabilities. The breakdown of the $44,999,994 included (1) the assumption of obligations New CINV owed the company totalling $25,050,075, (2) the payment of a loan outstanding to Credit Lyannais Bank Nederland N.V. of $8,000,000, and (3) a promissory note payable to New CINV from CINV of $11,949,319.[44]

On December 24, 1990, a Los Angeles Superior Court judge imposed a freeze on 2.2 million shares of Carolco stock owned by Kassar. This freeze was made in lieu of the transaction between CINV and New CINV. Carolco claimed the transaction was approved by its board and that the transaction had received support from large stockholders that represented a majority of the shares now owned by Kassar and his family. The court, however, remained intent on imposing the order stating that, in its view, based on the evidence, there was a high probability that the plaintiffs would prevail in the litigation.[45]

Carolco and its predecessors paid little or no federal or state income taxes, as a significant amount of the company's total revenues were recognized from the foreign releases of its films through CINV, a Netherlands Antilles subsidiary of the company, which under the United States–Netherlands Antilles Tax Treaty was not subject to U.S. taxation (see explanation of CINV's tax situation under Financial Analysis below). Although the company anticipated that it would not pay substantial U.S. taxes in 1991, this tax position could have been adversely affected by the following:

1. The allocation of income and deductions between Carolco and CINV may have been subject to challenge by the Internal Revenue Service.
2. Carolco and its subsidiaries could have been deemed personal holding companies and the company's subsidiary could have been deemed a foreign personal holding company due to the substantial stock ownership potentially attributable to Kassar, thus requiring the company to pay dividends or a penalty tax on its income from motion pictures.
3. Even with the tax treaty in place, the Internal Revenue Service could have contended that some of CINV's income was directly subject to U.S. tax.

As of December 31, 1990, management stated that, in its opinion, none of the above-mentioned theories could have applied to Carolco's tax situation.[46]

---

[44] *Form 10-K*, 1990, p. 23.
[45] Cohn, "Fewer New Pix in '90," p. 9.
[46] *Form 10-K*, 1990, p. 33.

FINANCIAL ANALYSIS

The financial structure of Carolco included wholly owned and partly owned subsidiaries as well as wholly owned foreign affiliates. As previously mentioned, Carolco attempted to minimize the risks associated with the production and distribution of its major motion pictures through its distribution agreement with Tri-Star Pictures. Under this agreement Tri-Star was obligated to make certain advances to the company to cover Carolco's negative costs associated with the production of a motion picture, and to spend significant amounts on printing and advertising expenses associated with the marketing of the theatrical releases. For the year ending December 31, 1990, approximately one-fourth of the company's revenues were derived from the sale of both theatrical and nontheatrical rights of its major motion pictures to Tri-Star. The remaining three-fourths of Carolco's revenues were received through its affiliates and wholly owned subsidiaries.[47]

For the year ending December 31, 1990, approximately 15 percent of the company's revenues were derived from the domestic production and distribution of motion pictures to television through Orbis Communications. LIVE Entertainment was responsible for approximately 13 percent of Carolco's revenues for the year ending December 31, 1990.[48]

Carolco International N.V., a wholly owned foreign subsidiary, was responsible for the leasing of motion picture rights in foreign markets. CINV, as distinguished from other subsidiaries responsible for distribution, incurred only minimal distribution expenses and was responsible for only a small portion of general overhead expenses. However, because of the nature of the leasing transactions, CINV was responsible for a significant amount of Carolco's revenues (approximately 47 percent in 1990). Furthermore, under the United States–Netherlands Antilles Tax Treaty, none of the foreign source income from CINV was subject to U.S. taxation. Therefore, CINV's tax rates were significantly lower than U.S. statutory rates, resulting in substantial tax savings and deferrals for Carolco. As of December 31, 1990, CINV had accumulated approximately $153 million of earnings not subject to U.S. taxes.[49]

The breakdown of operating revenues by line of business for the year ending December 31, 1990, is included in Exhibit 26.4. Films released domestically contributed 23 percent of Carolco's revenue, while films released outside the United States contributed 35 percent. Video releases domestically represented 13 percent of revenue and TV releases domestically represented 15 percent. Revenues from distribution of TV and video releases outside the United States represented 10 percent. Other operating revenues from Canadian partnerships and unrelated foreign corporations, including interest from related parties, amounted to 4 percent.

[47] Ibid., p. 1.
[48] Ibid., p. 9.
[49] Ibid., p. 32.

EXHIBIT 26.4   **Breakdown of 1990 Revenues**

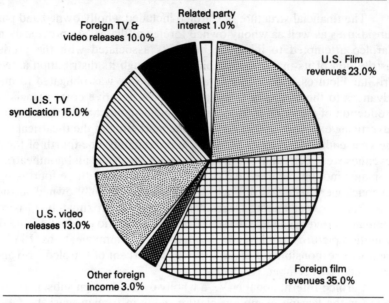

Foreign TV & video releases 10.0%

Related party interest 1.0%

U.S. Film revenues 23.0%

U.S. TV syndication 15.0%

U.S. video releases 13.0%

Other foreign income 3.0%

Foreign film revenues 35.0%

Source: Derived from Carolco Pictures, *Annual Report* 1990 and *Form 10-K* 1990.

The very nature of Carolco's business required huge amounts of working capital to fund the costs associated with the production of the films. A portion of these costs were borne by Tri-Star. However, in order to meet additional working capital requirements, the company and certain of its subsidiaries had to enter into agreements with two banks (BT/Chemical and CLBN) for revolving credit facilities. The amount of credit that both banks were committed to extend totaled $225 million. As of December 31, 1990, Carolco had a cumulative outstanding balance of approximately $156 million to BT/Chemical and CLBN. Substantially all of the company's assets were pledged under the credit agreements. Although the company was in compliance with its debt covenants at year end, the disclosures in the 1990 audit report indicated that the company might not be able to continue to conform to these covenants in 1991.[50] Therefore, the company submitted a Consent Solicitation Statement to the Securities and Exchange Commission, which sought to have the holders of the company's 14 percent senior notes approve a change in the financial covenants. On May 15, 1991, Carolco issued a press release stating that it had indeed received consent from the noteholders.[51] Among other things, the new amendments allowed the company to reduce its required cash flow coverage ratio from 1.5 to 1 to 1.2 to 1, and to restructure the

[50] Ibid., p. 14.
[51] Carolco Pictures Inc., *News Release*, June 5, 1991.

restrictions on liens which the company was permitted to incur. In return for these concessions, the company was required to make a one-time cash payment of $15 per $1,000 principal of notes, and to issue approximately 202,000 shares of its common stock to the noteholders.

In addition to the revolving line of credit with BT/Chemical and CLBN, the company had outstanding at December 31, 1990, approximately $76 million of 14 percent senior notes and $16 million in subordinated notes. Proceeds from the issuance of the senior notes were used to repay a large portion of the subordinated notes, as well as to fund additional working capital requirements.

Carolco also had an additional outstanding loan for $25 million from CLBN to finance the cash flow needs of Vista (the company's domestic group responsible for the Seven Arts joint venture). Vista was totally dependent on Carolco to finance its cash flow needs since its purchase on September 20, 1989. Although the company owned only one-third of the outstanding stock of Vista, it accounted for its investment as a purchase, since it funded all of Vista's cash needs and guaranteed Vista's loan from CLBN.

As shown in Exhibit 26.5, Carolco's debt load had increased significantly from 1988 to 1991. The majority of the debt was generated to provide the company with the needed capital to finance its major films as well as acquisitions. All costs associated with the production and filming of motion pictures were initially capitalized and subsequently written off as the films and made-for-television movies were released, based on management's expectations regarding the life of the films.

Operating revenues increased steadily from 1988 to 1991; however, operating and general and administrative expenses associated with these revenues rose sharply as well. Management attributed the large increases in general and administrative expenses in 1990 to an increase in the company's personnel in the legal and accounting areas, as well as increased distribution expenses. The company publicly stated that these increases would not continue.[52] However, the first-quarter results for the period ending March 31, 1991, showed a 46 percent increase in general and administrative costs over the first-quarter results for 1990.

Analysis of the company's cash flows from operations, shown in Exhibit 26.6, indicated large negative cash flows from 1988 to 1991. The negative cash flows forced the company to incur additional debt and issue equity capital in order to generate the cash needed to fund the company's on-going operations.[53] Management relied heavily on the success of its major motion picture releases in 1991 to provide the cash flow needed for operations.

Carolco's management stated that it was determined to build the equity base of the company during the 1990s through the formation of a series of strategic alliances with major worldwide entertainment and media companies. In 1990, three such alliances took place with the following companies: Canal+, an enter-

[52] Carolco Pictures Inc., *News Release*, May 16, 1991.
[53] "Carolco Needs a Hero," p. 1.

EXHIBIT 26.5   Selected Financial Information for Carolco Pictures, Inc. (In thousands)

	Year Ended December 31,			
	1987	1988	1989	1990
Operating Revenues				
Feature Films and Videocassettes	$ 54,477	$138,461	$115,113	$216,720
Television Syndication	42,790	19,597	21,552	42,130
Total Operating Revenues	97,267	158,058	136,665	258,850
Operating Expenses				
Film and TV Amortization	74,158	116,735	104,892	204,108
Total Operating Expenses	74,158	116,735	104,892	204,108
Gross Operating Profit	23,109	41,323	31,773	54,742
Gross Profit Percentage	24%	26%	23%	21%
Other Revenues				
Interest Income—Related Parties	2,452	1,696	858	2,148
Other Income—Foreign Affiliates	4,002	4,147	3,940	8,147
Other Expenses				
General and Administrative Expenses	12,907	14,122	19,879	32,942
Interest Expense	4,911	7,906	12,598	24,314
Income before Equity Income and Income Taxes	11,745	25,138	4,094	7,781
Equity in Income of Affiliates	2,682	11,197	10,862	13,340
Provisions for Income Taxes	95	831	920	3,823
Net Income Attributable to Common Stock	$ 14,332	$ 35,504	$ 14,036	$ 17,298
Balance Sheet Data				
Cash	$11,191	$8,094	$8,871	$12,552
Accounts Receivable	41,217	49,566	41,156	84,558
Film Costs, Net of Amortization	113,723	180,776	333,303	387,845
Total Assets	229,555	342,410	520,148	631,907
Long-Term Debt, Including Related Parties	80,582	136,788	274,368	294,934
Stockholders' Equity	$79,266	$118,894	$134,243	$191,077

Source: Carolco Pictures, Inc., *Form 10-K* 1990.

tainment company based in France; Technicolor, a U.S. film products company; and RCS Video, a media and publishing company in Italy. These companies purchased substantial amounts of Carolco stock during 1990, investing heavily in the long-term outlook of Carolco.[54]

Carolco had approximately 4,500 beneficial holders of common stock as of April 17, 1991. The amount of beneficial ownership that was attributable to officers and directors of the company constituted 79.2 percent of the common shares outstanding. Furthermore, Kassar was deemed to beneficially own up to

[54] *Annual Report*, 1990, p. 2.

EXHIBIT 26.6   Carolco Pictures Inc., and Subsidiaries Statements of Cash Flow (In thousands)

	Year Ended December 31,		
	1988	*1989*	*1990*
Net Cash Flow from Operating Activities			
Net Income	$35,504	$14,036	$17,298
Adjustment to Reconcile Net Income to Net Cash Provided (Used) by Operating Activities			
Amortization of Film Costs	96,287	80,091	175,601
Depreciation and Amortization	5,387	4,797	9,874
Equity in Income of Affiliates	(11,197)	(10,862)	(13,340)
Conversion of Video Guarantees to LIVE Series B Preferred Stock	(15,000)	(4,900)	—
(Increase) Decrease in Receivables	(8,949)	8,410	(35,753)
Increase (Decrease) in Payables, Accrued Liabilities, Accrued Residuals and Participations, Income Taxes Payable, and Other Assets	2,883	(24,418)	11,353
Increase in Film Costs and Rights	(163,340)	(232,618)	(224,540)
Payments on Contractual Obligations	(3,207)	(2,927)	(18,201)
Increase in Contractual Obligations	15,494	2,350	24,552
Increase (Decrease) in Advance Collections on Contracts	(8,214)	40,641)	4,225
Net Cash Used in Operating Activities	(54,352)	125,400	48,931
Cash Flow from Investing Activities			
Purchase of Property and Equipment	(11,746)	(3,065)	(2,420)
Sale of Marketable Securities	3,049	0	0
Investment in LIVE Entertainment, Inc.	(6,738)	805	(414)
Purchase of the Vista Organization, Ltd., the Vista Organization Partnership, L.P., and Carolco Television, Inc. Net of Cash Acquired	—	—	(21,003)
Net Cash Used in Investing Activities	(15,435)	(2,260)	(23,837)
Cash Flow from Financing Activities			
Proceeds from Debt	50,925	0	133,054
Payments on Debt	(71,913)	(1,077)	(106,166)
Increase in Borrowings from Banks	98,200	109,318	0
Borrowings from Vopic	0	30,000	0
Proceeds from Building Finance	12,900	0	0
Proceeds from Property and Equipment Financing	5,791	0	0
Decrease in Notes Payable to Related Parties	(4,000)	(941)	(17,003)
Increase in Receivables from Related Parties	(10,636)	(6,003)	(4,905)
Repurchase of Senior Subordinated Notes	(20,915)	(500)	(872)
Redemption of Warrants	—	—	(5,559)
Net Proceeds from Issuance of Preferred Stock—Series B	—	—	29,456
Net Proceeds from Issuance of Preferred Stock—Series C	—	—	56,559
Payment of Preferred Dividends	—	—	(971)
Proceeds from Sale of Stock	13,133	0	0
Repurchase of Common Stock	(1,379)	0	(45,385)
Increase in Debt Acquisition Costs	(3,089)	(4,037)	(2,221)
Exercise of Stock Options/Warrants	416	1,677	1,327

(Cont.)

EXHIBIT 26.6   (Cont.)

	Year Ended December 31,		
	1988	*1989*	*1990*
Issuance of Senior Notes and Common Stock in Connection with the Purchase of the Visa Organization, Ltd., and the Vista Organization, Partnership, L.P.	—	—	29,325
Net Cash Provided by Financing Activities	69,433	128,437	76,449
Increase (Decrease) in Cash	$ (354)	$ 777	$ 3,681
Supplemental Disclosure of Cash Flow Information			
Cash Paid During the Year for			
Interest (Net of Amount Capitalized)	$ 6,245	$ 23,167	$ 17,145
Income Taxes	$ 1,054	$ 637	$ 581

Source: Carolco Pictures Inc., *Annual Report,* 1990.

58.9 percent of the company, either directly or through entities that benefited Kassar or members of his family.[55]

Carolco's common stock traded on the New York Stock Exchange under the symbol CRS. Since January of 1989, the firm's stock had ranged from a high of $13.875 in the second quarter of 1990 to a low of $5.125 during the fourth quarter of 1990. Carolco's stock traded at $7.75 on July 23, 1991. Carolco never paid cash dividends on its common stock and intended to retain all future earnings to finance the expansion and development of its business. The consolidated balance sheet as of December 31, 1990, and the statement of operations for the year ending December 31, 1990, are included in Exhibits 26.7 and 26.8.

EPILOGUE

The champagne Mario Kassar ordered arrived perfectly chilled and in the hotel's signature crystal ice bucket. On the tray next to the bottle was an envelope bearing his name. Kassar ignored the envelope for the moment, as the roulette wheel began to slow and the ball began its descent. It bounced several times before settling to rest on black 2.

"Gentlemen, we have a winner."

Squarely positioned on the winning number was Kassar's stack of chips. With a sense of exhilaration, he reached for a flute from the tray at his side and, after inhaling the quintessential effervescence of its contents, emptied the flute in one celebratory flourish. As he set the stem back on the tray, his eyes fell upon the envelope. Kassar immediately knew its contents and ripped open the flap in

[55] *Form 10-K*, 1990, p. 42.

EXHIBIT 26.7   Carolco Pictures Inc. and Subsidiaries Consolidated Balance Sheets[a] (In thousands)

	December 31,	
	1989	1990
Assets		
Cash	$8,871	$12,552
Accounts Receivable, Net of Allowances of $2,545 (1989) and $5,821 (1990)	41,156	84,558
Accounts Receivable, Related Parties	10,839	5,933
Film Costs, Less Accumulated Amortization	333,303	387,845
Property and Equipment, at Cost, Less Accumulated Depreciation and Amortization	31,123	30,223
Investment in LIVE Entertainment Inc.	76,974	91,044
Other Assets	17,882	19,752
Total Assets	$520,148	$631,907
Liabilities and Stockholders' Equity		
Accounts Payable	$11,816	$16,775
Accrued Liabilities	26,717	26,159
Accrued Residuals and Participations	21,656	28,528
Income Taxes Current and Deferred	943	4,159
Debt	252,915	289,328
Advance Collections on Contracts	49,112	53,337
Contractual Obligations	1,293	7,644
Notes Payable, Related Parties	21,453	5,606
Total Liabilities	385,905	431,536
Commitments and Contingencies Due to Minority Shareholders	—	9,294
Stockholders' Equity		
Preferred Stock—$1.00 Par Value, 10,000,000 Shares Authorized: Series A Convertible Preferred Stock, 4,000,000 Shares Authorized, None Issued	—	—
Series B Convertible Preferred Stock, 30,000 Shares Authorized and Issued ($30,000,000 Aggregate Liquidation Preference)	—	30
Common Stock—$.01 Par Value, 100,000,000 Shares Authorized, 29,834,681 Shares Issued and Outstanding in 1989 and 30,281,075 Shares Issued and Outstanding, Including 3,475,538 Shares in Treasury in 1990	298	301
Additional Paid-In Capital	39,347	125,146
Treasury Stock	—	(45,385)
Retained Earnings	94,598	110,925
Total Stockholders' Equity	134,243	191,077
Total Liabilities and Stockholders' Equity	$520,148	$631,907

[a] A number of "Notes to Consolidated Financial Statements" have not been included in this exhibit. For a complete understanding of Carolco's financial situation refer to the *Annual Report*.

Source: Carolco Pictures Inc., *Annual Report* 1990.

EXHIBIT 26.8   **Carolco Pictures Inc., and Subsidiaries Consolidated Statements of Operations[a] (In thousands except per share data)**

	Year Ended December 31,		
	1988	1989	1990
Revenues			
Feature Films (Including $15,000 in 1988, $17,850 in 1989 and $27,625 in 1990 from a Related Party)	$138,461	$115,113	$216,720
Television Syndication	19,597	21,552	42,130
Interest Income from Related Parties	1,696	858	2,148
Other	4,147	3,940	8,147
Total Revenues	163,901	141,463	269,145
Cost and Expenses			
Amortization of Film and Television Costs, Residuals, and Profit Participation	116,735	104,892	204,108
Selling, General, and Administrative	14,122	19,879	32,942
Interest	7,906	12,598	24,314
Total Costs and Expenses	138,763	137,369	261,364
Income before Equity in Income of Affiliated Companies and Provision for Income Taxes	25,138	4,094	7,781
Equity in Income of Affiliated Companies	11,197	10,862	13,340
Income before Provisions for Income Taxes	36,335	14,956	21,121
Provision for Income Taxes	831	920	3,823
Net Income	$ 35,504	$ 14,036	$ 17,298
Preferred Dividends	0	0	971
Net Income Attributable to Common Stock	$ 35,504	$ 14,036	$ 16,327
Net Income per Share (Based on Weighted Average Shares and Common Share Equivalents Outstanding of 30,999,608 Shares (1988), 30,296,670 Shares (1989), and 30,015,720 Shares (1990))	$ 1.15	$ .46	$ .49

[a] A number of "Notes to Consolidated Financial Statements" have not been included in this exhibit. For a complete understanding of Carolco's financial situation refer to the *Annual Report*.

Source: Carolco Pictures Inc., *Annual Report* 1990.

anticipation. With a quick glance at the single sheet inside, he shouted, "Yes, indeed! We do have a winner."

The envelope contained the opening box office report for *Terminator 2*. The movie had opened to massive crowds, and the box office take had exceeded even Kassar's expectations. But as the euphoria of the moment subsided, Kassar reflected, "Would it be enough to save Carolco? Or, would it be 'Hasta la vista, Baby'?"

———————————— CASE 37 ————————————

Lotus Development Corporation: Maintaining Leadership in the Competitive Electronic Spreadsheet Industry

With sales of microcomputers increasing faster than sales of minicomputers and mainframes, sales of microcomputer software were growing at a fairly rapid rate. The growth rate for microcomputer software was a respectable 24 percent in 1987 compared with 23 percent in 1986. Growth increased 27 percent in 1988 but fell slightly to 18 percent in 1989.[1] The United States software industry was expected to achieve its historical growth rate of approximately 20 percent per year during the first half of the 1990s.[2]

This case was prepared by William C. House, University of Arkansas, as a basis for class discussion rather than to illustrate either effective or ineffective handling of an administrative situation. Used with permission from William C. House.

[1] U.S. Industrial Outlook, Department of Commerce, January 1988, pp. 30-7, January 1990, pp. 30–12.

[2] "Software Plays Hardball," *Time,* May 11, 1987, p. 52.

According to Dataquest, worldwide shipments of personal computer units increased from 15.2 million units in 1986 to 17.4 million units in 1987.[3] Worldwide shipments of personal computers increased 9 percent in 1990, slightly less than the growth rate in 1989.[4] Although shipments of computers were not increasing at previous levels, revenues of the top 50 independent software companies continued to escalate. Revenues increased from $3.6 billion in 1986 to $5.2 billion in 1987, $6.7 billion in 1988, $8.3 billion in 1989, and $10.7 billion in 1990.[5] The top 50 company sales revenues increased 42 percent in 1988, 25 percent in 1989, and 29 percent in 1990, compared to the previous year.

The microcomputer software industry had thousands of small independent suppliers with less than $1 million in annual sales. The Big Three (LOTUS, Ashton Tate, and Microsoft) held about 50 percent of the market as represented by revenues of the top 100 vendors. The gap between these three companies and other companies seemed to be widening as a transition was made from a cottage industry to one dominated by a very few suppliers. The top 12 companies produced 77 percent of total industry revenues, a sizable increase from about two-thirds of total industry revenues in 1985.[6]

Barriers to entry increased as the industry experienced intense competition, a high degree of product similarity, and product changes geared to hardware innovations. Brand-name recognition and increased marketing and product development/implementation costs discouraged the entry of competitors. Small companies did not have the market position, sales forces, or financial resources for advertising and sales promotion necessary to compete successfully with the larger companies.

The Big Three possessed broad user bases, strong customer loyalty, and large, well-developed research and development programs. These companies had sufficient resources to acquire competitors, to expand product bases, and to diversify into application areas not previously covered. The acquisition of Ashton-Tate by Borland and Samma Corporation by LOTUS were examples of the trend. Ashton-Tate identified price/performance, marketing and sales expertise, ease of use, product support, product line integration, and vendor financial strength as key factors in product success.[7] Although price competition was not as important as brand-name recognition and product improvements in product sales growth, an industry trend toward site licensing and volume discounts could make price more important in future years.

[3] Peter C. Wood, "Computers Current Analysis," *Standard & Poor's Industry Surveys*, May 26, 1988, p. C61.

[4] U.S. Industrial Outlook, Department of Commerce, January 1991, pp. 28-8.

[5] *Software Magazine*, Special Report, June 1989, 1990, 1991.

[6] William M. Bulkeley, "Software Industry Loses Start-Up Zest as Big Firms Increase Their Dominance," *Wall Street Journal*, August 27, 1991, p. B1.

[7] *Standard and Poor's Industry Surveys*, p. C61.

LOTUS COMPANY HISTORY

Mitchell Kapor, a disc jockey with an interest in transcendental meditation, developed LOTUS 1-2-3 in 1981 along with associate Todd Agulnick. At the time, Kapor was president of Cambridge-based Micro Finance Systems, a small New England software company. Several years earlier, Dan Bricklin, a Harvard University dropout, had developed and introduced the first electronic spreadsheet, VisiCalc, which was designed for the Apple II computer.

LOTUS grew astronomically from the time of its inception in 1983. In that first year, LOTUS had sales of $53,000 and a staff of several dozen people. It increased in size to the point that by 1987, revenues were just under $400 million, and the number of employees had increased to 2,400. Jim Manzi, a former newspaper reporter and a scholar in Greek and Latin joined the firm in 1984 as sales and marketing manager. Kapor, an informal, undisciplined entrepreneur, came to rely increasingly on Manzi, who joined the company with a reputation as a hard-headed businessman.

Kapor left the company in 1986 and Manzi became president. The brash, aggressive, and competitive former newspaper reporter very quickly made it clear that he expected LOTUS to continue to be the number one microcomputer software company in terms of size, sales, profits, and image. He was one of the highest-paid executives in the industry, receiving more than $26 million in salary and stock options in 1987. Stock analysts pointed out that LOTUS' current president, unlike the chief executives of other major companies such as Microsoft, Ashton-Tate, and Borland, had no prior software company experience.

In 1987, as sales and growth began to level off, Manzi issued orders to staff members to exercise close control over costs. After a series of negative articles appeared in a New England newspaper in response to published reports of Manzi's salary and a series of insider stock sales shortly before announcement of further delays in introducing an updated version of LOTUS 1-2-3, Manzi ordered company employees not to talk with the reporters from that newspaper. The order was later rescinded. LOTUS claimed that officer salaries were not out of line with those of other industry leaders and justified the stock sales as necessary to cover income taxes on stock options granted to key executives. Concurrently with these developments, a number of key executives left the company, and the stock price declined sharply.

Frank King, a 17-year IBM veteran involved in the development of the PC/2, became senior vice president of software products in the spring of 1988. Because of his computer experience and engineering background he gained greater credibility with the LOTUS staff than his predecessor. Outsiders said the more highly organized work environment contrasted with the informal, individualistic environment fostered by Kapor. However, morale appeared to be better and annual turnover declined to 15 percent compared with an industry average of 20 percent.

In November 1991, LOTUS announced that Frank King was being replaced by John Landry, previously executive vice president and chief technology officer at Dun & Bradstreet Software. Some insiders said the move was an indirect result of the delayed introduction of 1-2-3 for Windows, a product plagued with slow operating speed and numerous bugs. During Chairman Manzi's tenure, at least a dozen senior executives left the company. These moves developed into a typical pattern—an initial announcement of the new executive as a company "savior" followed by a hasty exit as disappointment and disenchantment occurred when the company failed to meet expectations.

Landry had considerable experience with mainframe software products and client-server architecture, a concept involved with linking personal computers with mainframe data bases. The enticement of Landry to LOTUS was widely touted as a harbinger of the company's seriousness concerning delivery of its networked computing strategy. Manzi indicated that the company's focus would be to produce and market an integrated set of desktop products for work-group computing including cc:Mail, Notes, and Agenda. Industry observers said that Landry had both mainframe and personal computer experience as well as familiarity with expert systems and object-oriented technology that would be valuable in moving LOTUS away from its heavy dependence on spreadsheet software.

PRODUCT DEVELOPMENT

LOTUS' goal was to be number one in the microcomputer software industry in terms of sales, profits, size, and reputation. It relied heavily on one product, LOTUS 1-2-3, although a personal information manager, Agenda, and a word processing package, AMI, were added to its product lines in the late 1980s. Most of the new products introduced since 1984 were add-ons or add-ins designed to speed up worksheet operation or to enhance such functions as data base management, word processing, and graphics display. In recent years, its sales and profits lagged behind those of its number one competitor, Microsoft.

Spreadsheet

LOTUS desired to improve 1-2-3 while still retaining the familiar look of the present version. Competitors such as Borland, Microsoft, and Computer Associates, offered improved programs with added features at the same price as 1-2-3 or, in some cases, at even lower prices. LOTUS indicated its intention to develop versions of 1-2-3 that would run on all types of computer hardware, including mainframes, minicomputers, and microcomputers. If this goal were to be achieved, it would allow sharing of worksheets, files, and terminals and reduce training costs. However, achieving this objective was likely to be difficult. For example, writing one program that would work satisfactorily on the 8088, 80286, and 80386 microprocessor-based hardware presented formidable challenges.

From its introduction in 1983, LOTUS sold more than 5 million copies of its 1-2-3 program and at one time had 70 to 80 percent of the IBM PC-compatible spreadsheet market. In 1991, its market share ranged between 50 to 60 percent, based on estimates from several sources. In its early years, the only serious competitors were Microsoft's Multiplan and Sorcim's (now Computer Associates) SuperCalc. V-P Planner (later withdrawn) was introduced in 1986 followed by Microsoft's Excel and Borland's Quattro in 1987. LOTUS sold 100,000 copies of 1-2-3 in its first year of operation and by 1992 sold that many copies in one month.

LOTUS 1-2-3 was designed as a relatively easy-to-use product to appeal to a broad user base. It was a familiar, proven package with established compatibility across company lines and within company divisions. Added power and utility came from LOTUS add-ins such as HAL (natural language interface), Freelance Plus (graphics), and Manuscript (word processing). In comparison with the products of its competitors, LOTUS had limited functions, poorer graphics, and a higher price in many cases. It lost sales because of its restrictive site licensing and copy protection not attached to other spreadsheets. A lack of LAN (local area network) support caused some users to switch to other spreadsheets such as SuperCalc.

Spreadsheet linking for 1-2-3 was cumbersome, and multiple spreadsheets could not be displayed on the same screen. Graphics capabilities were limited, and printing was often unwieldy and time-consuming. LOTUS' macro capability permitted customization of the spreadsheet program to fit many different situations, and many users have invested a large amount of time, money, and effort in developing macros and templates for use with 1-2-3. Fortunately for LOTUS, the investment in time by users inhibited switching to other products unless they were vastly superior to 1-2-3 and could clearly demonstrate file and macro compatibility.

To overcome some of its inherent limitations, LOTUS developed several add-ins to perform functions not available on its 2.0 or 2.1 version. Speedup increased the effective operating speed of LOTUS by only recalculating cells affected by the previous command or command sequence. LEARN gave LOTUS the capability of memorizing keystrokes for macro generation without the need to use a complex series of commands. HAL, a natural language interface, provided an easier-to-use command structure and permitted easier linking of multiple spreadsheets than was possible with the original product.

LOTUS announced that after prolonged delay, version 3.0 of 1-2-3 would be made available during the fourth quarter of 1988. At that time a further postponement was announced, moving the target date for version 3.0 to the second quarter of 1989. Version 3.0 was expected to add a number of performance features not possible with earlier versions of 1-2-3 such as the ability to link several worksheets, display up to three worksheets on the same screen, and capability to merge text and graphics in the same worksheet. Layered worksheets could be stored in main memory, faster recalculation of spreadsheet changes was implemented, and the revised spreadsheet program could be automatically reconfigured to work with either DOS or OS/2 operating systems.

With all the new features and an easier-to-use interface the look and feel of version 3.0, while retaining many of the features of 2.0, *appeared* to be considerably different from previous versions. With the new version requiring some retraining, existing users of 1-2-3 were reluctant to switch to the newer version in some instances and a few even considered adopting a competitor's spreadsheet. Another problem was that version 3.0 would not run efficiently unless the user had a 286 or 386 microprocessor-based computer. LOTUS originally claimed that the new version of 1-2-3 would perform satisfactorily on an 8088-based system if users had 640K of internal memory and a hard drive.

LOTUS was striving to develop 1-2-3 versions that would run on both micros and mainframes, on minicomputers, and in distributed and nondistributed environments. New versions of 1-2-3 were being written in C language instead of assembler to ensure a high degree of portability, but these versions required more memory than those originally written in assembly language. As part of its plan to push 1-2-3 as an operating environment, LOTUS announced a high-level language for developing customized applications called "extended applications facility."

LOTUS' STRATEGIES IN A MORE COMPETITIVE ENVIRONMENT

LOTUS' early success with its spreadsheet allowed it to set the industry standard and made it time-consuming and difficult for users to change even if competing companies offered software products with superior performance. In addition, high product development costs and the willingness of software developers to create LOTUS-compatible products acted as a barrier to entry into the market. Despite these barriers, the success of two competitors motivated LOTUS to sue both Paperback Software, developer of V-P Planner, and Borland (Quattro) for alleged copyright infringement. As a result, V-P Planner was withdrawn from the market, but the suit against Borland was still in the appeals process.

Improvements in computer technology and changes in user expectations finally necessitated a change in the original 1-2-3 program. LOTUS reluctantly split its core product into two categories—one version for older PCs (version 2.0) and another for 286/386 machines (version 3.0). The 3.0 version offered improved graphics output and recalculation and allowed users to take advantage of the extended memory capacity of 286/386 machines to create multiple spreadsheets. The 3.0 consolidation, advanced file linking, and data base connectivity features required more memory than was available in older machines and publishing facilities were lacking in quality compared to competitors' software products. Version 3.1 was designed to correct many of these problems, but early indications were that not many users were upgrading to 3.1.

LOTUS 1-2-3 version 2.2, introduced after 3.0 sales lagged during the introductory period, was outselling version 3.0 by a margin of three to one. Many

users were choosing not to upgrade, with current estimates indicat
about 40 percent of existing 1-2-3 users upgraded to new versions.
product line dilemma highlighted the difficulty that a dominant cor
experience in defending its market position in a changing environm(
was in the position of a cash cow, milking existing products withou
pects for future growth in those products (Exhibit 37.1 provides d
LOTUS product line). Some users felt that LOTUS made a mistake in
ing too much on sales to large companies; some evidence existed
customers in small businesses and users of home computers were s
competitors' products.

LOTUS' goal was to have 1-2-3 installed on a wide variety c
including micros, minis, and mainframes. A decline in market sl
LOTUS to seek new markets and to diversify into new products. Th
had two strategic alternatives. One was to engage in a price war with
Quattro, defending its turf with drastic price reductions and cut-throa
practices. It would have had to sacrifice substantial profits with unce
range returns, especially in the emerging Windows environment. A
proach was to diversify into other areas such as word processing, grou
text management, striving to obtain no more than 50 percent of its reve
nonspreadsheet products. LOTUS followed the latter approach to som(
acquiring the rights to the AMI Pro word processing package, and
Notes groupware and Agenda, a personal information manager. Hov
returns from this strategy had been modest so far.

**EXHIBIT 37.1   LOTUS' Breadwinners—Sales by Product
(In millions)**

	1990	1991[a]
1-2-3		
New Units Based on Intel Platforms	$442	$446
New Units Based on Other Platforms	22	45
Upgrades	40	65
AMI Word-Processor	0	21
cc: Mail	0	20
Notes	4	25
I/S and Consulting Services	31	37
Freelance	62	70
Other Products	29	23
Symphony	53	57
Total	$683	$809

[a] estimated.

Source: Sanford C. Berbstein & Company, *Computerworld*, November
29, 1991, p. 8.

Stand-Alone Competitive Spreadsheet Products

Paperback Software introduced V-P Planner as a LOTUS clone for $99 during the mid-1980s and Borland introduced a lower-priced LOTUS compatible for $195 in 1988 that had more features than 1-2-3, could access all LOTUS files and performed most LOTUS functions. In addition, Borland acquired the rights to Surpass from Sergio Rubenstein, the developer of WordStar. Surpass was a higher-priced LOTUS-compatible spreadsheet that sold for $495 and offered many advanced features. In 1987, Microsoft introduced an IBM-compatible version of its popular Macintosh spreadsheet Excel for $495 that had a graphic interface characterized by ease of use. During 1988, LOTUS expected to sell 1.2 million copies of 1-2-3, Borland estimated sales of 150,000 copies of Quattro, and industry analysts expected Excel sales to be at least 120,000 units. Sales of V-P Planner and SuperCalc were forecasted to level off or even decline.

LOTUS competitors such as Microsoft, Borland, and Computer Associates offered additional features and ease of use along with function and file compatibility at the same price or a lower price than 1-2-3. However, other spreadsheets had two disadvantages: they required user retraining and had to demonstrate 1-2-3 file compatibility. Because of the use of 1-2-3 over the years, history files had been developed and maintained. These files had to be accessible, thus compatibility had to be demonstrated before the alternative products became viable contenders.

Microsoft

Microsoft had two spreadsheet products: Multiplan and Excel. Multiplan was a solid but not spectacular software product with a slightly different formula and command structure from 1-2-3. It had data base capability with mouse support, and ran under M/S Windows as well as on networks. Multiplan had 1-2-3 file read/write capability and could import files from dBase and R:Base. Although the worksheet had no graphics capability, it could import graphs from Microsoft's Chart program.

Excel, a Microsoft worksheet program that proved to be popular for the Apple Macintosh, had a graphics interface and was more powerful than 1-2-3. It could operate on arrays, handle trend projection and optimization calculations, and display multiple spreadsheets on the same screen, linking them through the use of a mouse or by keystroke commands. The maximum spreadsheet size was two times that of LOTUS, and graphs could be printed from within the spreadsheet. The user selected from 42 different graph formats and numerous font, boldface, and italic sizes. Variable character heights, borders, shaded areas, and underlying areas were easy to implement. It was not copy protected and offered flexible site-licensing provisions.

Excel was designed for 286 or 386 personal computers with high-resolution graphics, at least 640k of internal memory, and a hard drive. It was fully compatible with 1-2-3 files and contained a help facility that automatically gave the Excel equivalent when a 1-2-3 sequence was entered. However, Excel was not keystroke compatible with 1-2-3 and was only 95 percent compatible with LOTUS macros. It had a macro translator that converted 1-2-3 macros into Excel macros. Some minimal recalculation was possible, and built-in auditing and data base capabilities were provided.

Microsoft emphasized high-resolution graphics interface, mouse applications, and an easy-to-use pull-down menu system in a package that could be run only on 286 and 386 machines. It expected Windows interface and OS/2 Presentation Manager with which its program was compatible to become an industry standard. Excel was written in C language, so portability was assured.

Borland—Quattro and Surpass

Quattro, at $195, was less expensive and offered more functions than 1-2-3. It provided selective recalculation, a greater variety of different types of graphs, and an impressive number of screen display and printing options. Graphs could be printed from within the spreadsheet, and the program took full advantage of EGA and VGA graphics adapters. Quattro offered full 1-2-3 file capability, improved macro development ability using a macro generator, and permitted extensive customization of applications. For debugging purposes, individual commands within a macro sequence could be executed one at a time. It required a minimum of 512k in internal memory and was not copy protected.

Surpass, at $495, appealed to users who had reached the limit of LOTUS 1-2-3 capabilities. A subset of Surpass could be used to implement all 1-2-3 key strokes, files, macros, and formulas, which made it unnecessary to completely retrain former 1-2-3 users. It handled multiple spreadsheets, aligned them in 3-D fashion, posted changes from one spreadsheet to others automatically, and referred to a spreadsheet without requiring that it be in main memory. Dynamic links between spreadsheets were provided, and a macro library contained command sequences that could be used on more than one spreadsheet. Multiple spreadsheets could be displayed on the screens, graphs could be displayed in 3-D format, and an undo command permitted easy correction of mistakes. A built-in file manager performed many common DOS functions.

Borland imitated LOTUS by writing Quattro in assembly language, making it as fast and as compact as possible. Unlike LOTUS, the company was opposed to using one product for multiple computer architectures. It preferred to develop a lower-priced package that would make the fullest possible use of a given type of machine. For users who wanted a higher-level LOTUS look-alike, the company offered Surpass with more features than 1-2-3 at a comparable price.

SuperCalc

SuperCalc, acquired by Computer Associates when it absorbed Sorcim in the mid-1980s, permitted use of larger spreadsheets than LOTUS (i.e., about 2,000 additional rows) and was not copy protected. The command structure differed somewhat from LOTUS, but a careful reading of menus allowed users to accomplish most of the functions possible with LOTUS. It could read and write 1-2-3 files and import or export VisiCalc, DIF, and ASCII files. Graphics and data base modules were included in the program, and as many as nine graphs per spreadsheet could be saved in memory. It permitted macro recording that offered more financial and logical functions than LOTUS. LAN support was also provided.

Version 5 of SuperCalc permitted faster retrieval of information from cells with similar names or codes than was previously possible. An optional 1-2-3 interface facilitated user transition from 1-2-3, and macros contained both 1-2-3 and SuperCalc commands. Enhanced presentation graphics, a toggle on and off minimum recalculation feature, and an undo command for ease of use in correcting errors were provided. In addition, macro debugging and built-in auditing capabilities were included. As a bonus feature with each SuperCalc purchase, a version of Sideways was provided at no additional cost. Computer Associates offered a volume discount and liberal site licensing for SuperCalc.

V-P Planner

V-P Planner, developed by Alex Osborne's Paperback Software, was a low-cost clone that cost $99 and used most LOTUS commands plus a few new ones. It would read and write dBase files, record macros, and open up to six windows. While work was being done on one spreadsheet, users could be printing another. V-P Planner could not run LOTUS add-ins, but some add-ons worked with this program (e.g., 1-2-3 Forecast, Ready-to-Run Accounting, Goal Seeker). V-P Planner had no built-in graphics capabilities but could develop graphs using the separate V-P Graph program. Another drawback was that unlike other spreadsheet companies, it charged users for technical support.

The notoriety from the LOTUS lawsuit charging copyright infringement based on the look-alike, feel-alike quality of V-P Planner hurt sales. However, it was obvious that V-P Planner was more than just a LOTUS clone. A new version, V-P Planner Plus carried a slightly higher price tag ($179.99) and provided twice as many financial and logical functions as LOTUS, permitted recalculation of selected calls, and was not copy protected. Graphics capabilities were only fair—definitely not in the same class as Quattro or Excel. An optional interface with pull-down menus made it easier to follow command sequences than what was possible with 1-2-3.

V-P Planner's data base capability permitted reading and writing dBase, V-P Info, and DIF files as well as viewing data in up to five dimensions. One obvious shortcoming of Paperback Software's marketing program was that it overstressed the value of V-P Planner as a low-cost LOTUS clone and did not emphasize its strong data base capability. In mid- 1990, LOTUS won its copyright infringement suit against Paperback Software, forcing the company to withdraw V-P Planner from circulation. By the end of 1991, the LOTUS clone was no longer a significant factor in the spreadsheet market.

Ashton-Tate

Ashton-Tate, which obtained 60 percent of its sales from dBase, its data base manager, was not an active player in the spreadsheet market, although it did have an integrated package named Framework. The competitive position of Ashton-Tate had eroded because its basic dBase III program would not work on the 386 machines, and it was facing intense competition in the data base market from Oracle, Borland, and others. The merger with Borland in 1990 raised questions about Ashton-Tate's future role in both the data base and integrated software markets. However, both LOTUS and Microsoft were moving into the data base market with add-ins or built-in capabilities as part of their spreadsheet programs suggesting that Borland would do the same.

Integrated Software

Integrated software packages combined several functions such as word processing, spreadsheet, data base management, and communications all into one package. The major advantage was that a user performed a number of computer-based functions with one program using a common command structure. Not having to switch from one program to another each time a different function was performed saved time and effort. The disadvantage was that normally a given integrated package emphasized one or two functions such as spreadsheet or data base management and provided only minimum capabilities for others (e.g., word processing, graphics). Some users were reluctant to pay the extra price for a package containing four or five functions when only one or two would be used continually.

Many users desired a "core" product to be used for data base, spreadsheet, word processing, memo writing, desk calculating, scheduling, and so on. However, the market for individual applications grew faster than that for integrated software packages. It was estimated that integrated package sales increased 4 percent in 1986 over 1985, while sales of individual applications increased at a rate of 31 percent. Exhibit 37.2 shows actual and estimated individual application package revenues compared with those of integrated software packages for 1985–89.

EXHIBIT 37.2   Revenues for Individual and Integrated Software Packages, 1985–1989 (In millions)

Year	Individual Applications	Integrated Packages
1985	$ 625	103
1986	820	107
1987	967[a]	120
1988	1,150[a]	130[a]
1989	1,350[a]	140[a]

[a] Estimated.

Source: Compiled from various issues of *PC Week*.

The major integrated software packages included LOTUS Symphony, which had a strong spreadsheet and a fair data base, and Ashton-Tate's Framework, which had a strong data base, good word processor, and a fair spreadsheet. In 1986, revenues from Symphony were estimated to be $36 million (36 percent market share); Framework generated $26 million (26 percent share). The other major players were Innovative Software's Smartware, which produced $14 million in revenues for a 14 percent share of the market, and the Enable Group's Enable package, which captured 3 percent of the market with $4 million in sales. More than 40 other competitors divided the remaining 22 percent.

At the lower end of the scale, Software Publishing Company (SPC) introduced First Choice in August 1986 and sold 70,000 units during the first six months of product life. It sold 25,000 copies of its separate Professional Plan spreadsheet during 1986. It was estimated that SPC sold 200,000 copies of First Choice at a list price of $195 through mid-1988. Version 2 of First Choice added graphics capabilities to other functions. After introducing its Better Working Eight in One program at $59.95 (containing outlining, word processing, spell checking, spreadsheet, data base, graphics, communications, and desktop organizing capabilities with a memo pad, address book, and calendar), Spinnaker bought the rights to First Choice.

Microsoft converted its Macintosh integrated package Works for use on the IBM-PC and compatibles. With a price comparable to First Choice, it was proving to be a strong competitor at the low end of the market. The recent acquisition of Alpha Four by LOTUS gave the company an entry into the low end of data base management with a system that had many of the characteristics of an integrated package.

THE COMPETITIVE ENVIRONMENT IN PERSONAL COMPUTER SOFTWARE

The demand for electronic spreadsheet software grew less rapidly than other types of software. Sales increases in recent years did not match those of earlier years. Exhibit 37.3 shows the actual and expected unit sales of electronic spreadsheets from 1986 to 1990, according to one industry source. After leveling off in 1988, electronic spreadsheet sales were expected to grow at a slow but steady pace during the rest of the decade. The impact of PS/2-based hardware on spreadsheet demand was less than expected, but the popularity of the Windows-based environment fueled increased demand for Windows-based spreadsheets.

Spreadsheets and word processing programs were the most widely installed applications and represented slower growth and mature markets. Data base managers had somewhat more potential with modest growth possibilities. Graphics, CAD/CAM, project management, and desktop publishing applications represented the fastest-growing markets with considerable room to develop without saturation. A Sierra Group poll of over 1,500 users found that 60 percent of users

EXHIBIT 37.3   Sales of Electronic Spreadsheets (In millions of units)

Year	Number
1986	1.20
1987	1.40
1988	1.50
1989	1.80
1990	2.00

Source: IDC Corporation, *Computerworld*, December 21, 1987.

EXHIBIT 37.4   Shipments of Applications Software Packages (In millions of units)

	1987	1988[a]	1992[a]
Word Processing	3.2	3.5	4.9
Spreadsheets	2.2	2.5	3.4
Communications	2.1	2.5	3.8
Graphics	1.4	1.8	3.3
Data Base Management	1.0	1.4	5.0

[a] Estimated.

Source: Dataquest, *Personal Computing*, October 1988.

surveyed planned to buy word processing packages, 54 percent planned to buy data base managers, 51 percent planned spreadsheet purchases, and 35 percent expected to buy graphics presentation packages.[8]

Exhibit 37.4 contains actual and estimated shipments of word processing, spreadsheet, graphics, communications, and data base management systems. Only modest sales growth had been expected during 1987 and 1988. For the period 1988 to 1992, spreadsheet sales were expected to increase at an average annual rate of 33 percent compared to 35 percent for word processing packages, 45 percent for graphics systems, 38 percent for communication packages, and 89 percent for data base managers.

IMPACT OF COMPETITION ON MARKET SHARE IN THE SPREADSHEET INDUSTRY

Fierce competition in the personal computer spreadsheet industry resulted in lower prices, inexpensive upgrades, and free add-ins during the late 1980s.. Dataquest (1991) reported that LOTUS' market share declined from 54 percent in

[8] Stephen Jones, "Software Applications," *Computerworld*, May 9, 1988, p. 126.

1989 to 47 percent in 1990.[9] During the same period, Borland increased its market share from 3 percent to approximately 14 percent using aggressive marketing tactics and Excel increased its market share from 12 percent to 14 percent. Borland sold its Quattro spreadsheet for $99 to any user offering proof of LOTUS ownership, and Microsoft was selling Excel for $129 direct from the firm. A Vista Market Research survey found that 80 percent of Quattro users previously used 1-2-3.[10] Although it had not lowered its prices significantly, LOTUS countered by including AMI Pro word processing system for $20 in the LOTUS package and offered upgrades to existing LOTUS users for as little as $49.

Dataquest (1991) predicted that in the 1990s, Quattro and Excel would gain market share at the expense of LOTUS, SuperCalc 5, and Lucid 3-D.[11] The existing base of LOTUS users held firm, but many 1-2-3 users disregarded price discounts and giveaways. The biggest barrier to switching to 1-2-3 alternatives was the cost of retraining users and resistance to change by users who were familiar and comfortable with the existing program. However, this situation could change as users switch from DOS to Windows environments.

Market share figures in the spreadsheet industry were only estimates and varied widely depending on the source. However, there seemed to be general agreement that LOTUS' market share declined from about two-thirds of the total market in the middle 1980s to approximately 50 percent in 1990. Estimated market shares are given for major spreadsheet competitors for 1989 and 1990 in Exhibit 37.5. Both Borland and Microsoft experienced sizable gains in market share during this period, while LOTUS and Computer Associates suffered moderate declines.

Prolonged delays in offering a 1-2-3 version for Windows caused LOTUS to lose some customers, and LOTUS 1-2-3 Windows was likely to spark fierce reactions in that environment from its principal competitors. Some experts predicted that LOTUS would obtain only about one-third of the Windows spread-

EXHIBIT 37.5   Market Shares for Major Spreadsheet Competitors, 1989 and 1990

Company	1989	1990
LOTUS	51.2%	49.6%
Borland	4.3	20.3
Microsoft	7.2	11.7
Computer Associates	11.7	8.0
Other	25.6	10.3
Total	100.0%	100.0%

Source: IDC Corporation and Info Corporation.

[9] John Schneidawind, "1-2-3 Upgrade, New Software Boosts Software Firm," *USA Today*, March 1991, pp. B1, B2.
[10] Mark Hendricks, "Spreadsheet Clash Improves User Choices," *PC World*, May 1991, p. 59.
[11] Schneidawind, "1-2-3 Upgrade," p. B2.

**EXHIBIT 37.6   Estimated Worldwide
1990 Spreadsheet Shipments (In millions)**

Company	Shipments
LOTUS	$1,700
Borland	600
Microsoft	400
Computer Associates	275
Other	340
Total	$3,315

Source: IDC, *Computerworld*, January 7, 1991.

sheet market. Preliminary evaluations of 1-2-3 Windows indicated that LOTUS' version was slower and less compatible with common Windows applications than Excel. Borland and Microsoft had price advantages over LOTUS in the spreadsheet market, as both competitors derived 25 percent or less of their revenue from spreadsheet programs and could afford to offer larger discounts than LOTUS, which obtained about 70 percent of its revenues from 1-2-3.

1-2-3 Windows was selling at moderate but not spectacular levels. Some corporate purchasers announced that they were delaying buying decisions. There were some reports of 1-2-3 users switching to Excel, which was designed for Windows and had superior graphics, consolidation functions, and embedded objects as opposed to the more bland 1-2-3 Windows. The new version was keystroke compatible with older 1-2-3 versions but was slower in performing calculations, largely because it was designed to work in both DOS and Windows environments. Exhibit 37.6 contains estimated 1990 shipments in dollars for the major spreadsheet competitors.

REVENUE AND INCOME GROWTH

LOTUS had to lower its long-term growth goals to reflect a loss of market share. Expected pretax profit margins were revised from 25 percent to 20 percent, revenue growth was expected to stabilize at 20 to 25 percent annually, and return on equity was forecasted to remain in the mid- to high 20s.[12] In 1989, revenue increased 19 percent to $556 million, and actual profit margins were 15 percent in 1987 and 17 percent in 1988. LOTUS initiated a hiring freeze and announced small-scale layoffs as Manzi maintained that slower growth in sales of personal computers was the principal factor in slower revenue growth at LOTUS. Indicated cutbacks in advertising and marketing could result in further loss of market share (Exhibit 37.7). The company work force of 3,100 was small by industry

[12] Patricia Keefe, "LOTUS Reshaping Long Term Goals," *Computerworld*, September 24, 1990, p. 96.

EXHIBIT 37.7   Advertising Expenditures for PC Software Companies, 1989 (In millions)

Company	Amount
Ashton-Tate	$ 6.10
Borland	4.56
Computer Associates	10.40
LOTUS	10.70
Microsoft	17.00
Novell	4.64
Oracle	9.80
Software Publishing Company	4.21

Source: *Computer Industry Almanac*, Brady, 1991.

standards with sales per employee of about $188,000 compared to an industry average of $175,000, but its operating costs were high compared to the industry average.[13]

LOTUS revenues increased 73 percent during the period from 1987 to 1990, but net income was down 26 percent during the same period. In contrast, Microsoft's revenues increased 342 percent and net income increased 571 percent during this period, while Computer Associates' revenues went up 436 percent and net income increased 725 percent. Exhibit 37.8 illustrates sales revenues for the years 1987 to 1990 for the eight major personal computer software companies. Exhibit 37.9 contains net income for the same companies during the 1987 to 1990 period.

EXHIBIT 37.8   Sales Revenues for Major PC Software Companies, 1987–1990 (In millions)

Company	1987	1988	1989	1990
Ashton-Tate	$ 211.0	$ 307.3	$ 265.3	$ 230.5
Borland	38.1	81.6	90.6	226.8
Computer Associates	309.0	709.1	1,030.0	1,348.2
LOTUS	396.0	468.5	556.7	684.5
Microsoft	346.0	590.8	830.5	1,183.4
Novell	—	—	421.9	497.6
Oracle	131.3	282.2	583.7	970.8
Software Publishing	38.6	73.1	103.5	140.6
Total	$1,470	$2,512.5	$3,854.5	$5,282.3
Industry Sales Growth	—	1.71	1.53	1.37

Source: *Business Week* R&D Scoreboard, 1990, 1991, 1992, and *Business Week* 1000 Companies, 1990, 1991, 1992.

[13] William Bulkeley, "LOTUS Replaces King as Head of Development," *Wall Street Journal*, November 22, 1991, p. C-15E.

EXHIBIT 37.9   Net Income for Major PC Software Companies, 1987–1990 (In millions)

Company	1987	1988	1989	1990
Ashton-Tate	$ 30.1	$ 73.5	$ (31.6)	$ (20.1)
Borland	1.3	3.8	(3.6)	41.9
Computer Associates	36.5	170.1	286.5	261.2
LOTUS	72.0	79.9	85.0	52.8
Microsoft	71.9	183.7	250.8	410.6
Novell	—	—	77.1	145.1
Oracle	15.6	65.0	120.2	172.7
Software Publishing	5.2	21.3	26.8	29.3
Total	$232.6	$1,182.3	$793.1	$1,093.5
Industry Income Growth	—	5.08	0.68	137.9

Source: *Business Week* R&D Scoreboard, 1988, 1989, and 1990, and *Business Week* 1000 Companies, 1988, 1989, and 1990.

Exhibit 37.10 shows total assets for the eight personal computer software companies for years 1987 to 1990. For the industry, assets increased from $1,556 million in 1987 to $5,459 million in 1990, or an increase of 351 percent compared to an increase of 359 percent in revenues and an increase of 470 percent in net income. LOTUS' assets increased 218 percent, revenues increased 173 percent, and net income declined to 73 percent of 1987 figures during the same period.

Exhibit 37.11 shows R&D outlays as a percentage of revenues and sales per employee for the eight personal computer software companies. R&D outlays compared to sales revenues for LOTUS declined during the period 1988 to 1990

EXHIBIT 37.10   Total Assets for Major PC Software Companies, for 1987 to 1990 (In millions)

Company	1987	1988	1989	1990
Ashton-Tate	$ 175	$ 293	$ 245	$ 246
Borland	28	54	53	87
Computer Associates	439	1,156	1,376	1,596
LOTUS	318	399	604	695
Microsoft	288	605	922	1,366
Novell	129	227	347	494
Oracle	144	321	584	855
Software Publishing	35	60	83	120
Total	$1,556	$3,115	$4,214	$5,459
Industry Growth	—	2.00	1.35	1.30

Source: *Business Week* 1000 Companies, 1988, 1989, and 1990; *Standard and Poor's Stock Reports*, Fall 1990.

EXHIBIT 37.11   R&D Outlays/Sales and Sales/Employee for PC Software Companies, 1988–1990

Company	R&D Investment/Sales			Sales/Employee		
	1988	1989	1990	1988	1989	1990
Ashton-Tate	17.2	25.9	17.2	$210.5	$185.5	$142.3
Borland	10.6	15.8	10.3	132.0	183.3	230.0
Computer Associates	11.5	13.0	13.2	158.7	164.2	201.2
LOTUS	17.9	17.0	16.1	187.4	198.6	195.6
Microsoft	11.8	13.7	15.3	211.5	199.0	210.0
Novell	—	10.1	11.9	—	199.5	205.7
Oracle	9.1	9.0	9.1	122.8	140.7	142.5
Software Publishing	16.1	15.7	16.1	188.5	217.4	214.0
Industry Average	13.5	15.0	13.6	$173.8	$186.0	$192.7

Source: *Business Week,* R&D Scoreboard 1989, 1990, and 1991.

while the industry average stabilized at around 13.5 percent. However, LOTUS' R&D ratio was still higher than the industry average. Industry average sales per employee steadily increased during this period; sales per employee for LOTUS also increased at about the same rate as the other companies in this industry segment.

REFERENCES

BULKELEY, WILLIAM. "After Years of Glory, LOTUS Is Stumbling in Software Market." *Wall Street Journal,* August 30, 1988, p. B1.

BULKELEY, WILLIAM. "LOTUS is Upgrading 1-2-3 Again; Move May Revive Sales, Earnings." *Wall Street Journal,* September 7, 1990, p. B2.

BULKELEY, WILLIAM. "LOTUS Effort to Please All with 1-2-3 Confuses Many." *Wall Street Journal,* July 20, 1990, p. B1.

BULKELEY, WILLIAM. "LOTUS Replaces King as Head of Development." *Wall Street Journal,* November 22, 1991, p. C-15E.

BRYAN, MARVIN. "How Spreadsheets Add Up." *Personal Computing,* September 1987, p. 202.

BURKE, STEVEN. "Borland's Attack on LOTUS Paid Off." *PC Week,* September 24, 1990, p. 160.

CURRAN, LAWRENCE. "Dueling Spreadsheets." *Electronics,* February 1991, p. 29.

DALY, JAMES. "Excel to Renew LOTUS Assault." *Computerworld,* January 7, 1991, pp. 1, 6.

DARROW, BARBARA, AND ED SCANNELL. "Manzi Admits That LOTUS Needs 1-2-3 for Windows." *Infoworld,* September 24, 1990, p. 51.

FERRANTI, MARC. "Version 2.2 Emerges as Sales Leader in LOTUS' 1-2-3 Family." *PC Week,* July 30, 1990, p. 5.

FERRANTI, MARC, AND BETH FREEDMAN. "At LOTUS, Landry Is In, King Is Out." *PC Week,* November 25, 1991, pp. 1, 6.

FISHER, SUSAN E. "1-2-3 for Windows Will Face Stiff Competition." *PC Week,* September 2, 1991, p. 99.

HAMMONS, KEITH. "Teaching Discipline to Six Year Old LOTUS." *Business Week,* July 4, 1988, p. 46.

HAMMONS, KEITH. "It's the Yawn of a New Age for LOTUS." *Business Week,* March 12, 1990, p. 42.

HENDRICKS, MARK. "Spreadsheet Clash Improves User Choices." *PC World,* May 1991, p. 59.

HOGAN, MIKE. "1-2-3 Opens Up Windows." *PC World,* July 1991, p. 15.

KEEFE, PATRICIA. "LOTUS Reshaping Long Term Goals." *Computerworld,* September 24, 1990, p. 96.

MARTIN, JAMES. "In Spreadsheet War, Excel Poses Serious Threat to 1-2-3." *PC Week,* November 27, 1989, p. 213.

MCWILLIAMS, GARY. "Another Year, Another Bitter Lesson for Jim Manzi." *Business Week,* December 9, 1991, p. 45.

RADDING, ALAN. "PC Spreadsheets." *Computerworld,* September 2, 1991, p. 59.

RADDING, ALAN. "Race of Power vs. Position." *Computerworld,* December 21, 1987, p. 117.

SCHNEIDAWIND, JOHN. "1-2-3 Upgrade, New Software Boosts Software Firm." *USA Today,* 1991, pp. B-1, B-2.

SCHWARTZ, JOHN. "LOTUS at War." *Personal Computing,* June 1989, p. 27.

WILKE, JOHN R. "LOTUS Fights to Regain Share with Discounts." *Wall Street Journal,* September 5, 1991, p. B1.

Gatorade Defends Its No. 1 Position

Gatorade, a subsidiary of the Quaker Oats Company, had an important objective for 1991: defend its dominant position in the sports drink market. Although Gatorade had achieved more than 90 percent market share, aggressive efforts by soft drink manufacturers and other companies to enter this profitable and growing market had generated a strong reaction from Quaker Oats. The company expected as many as four strong competitors by 1995. Its objective was to keep Gatorade synonymous with sports drinks well into the 21st century.

With current margins in the industry as high as 35 percent, projections of growth ranging to 30 percent for the next several years, and Gatorade sales estimated to be approximately $600 million, it was not surprising that established beverage producers as well as newcomers were eager to enter the sports drink market. However, Quaker Oats clearly recognized the marketing muscle of some of its challengers and had mounted defensive campaigns to specifically halt the erosion of its maket share.

In 1989, Quaker designed a marketing strategy to counter the expansion of 10-K. The campaign concentrated on protecting distribution and shelf space, communicating Gatorade's product superiority, eliminating any sports market segment voids, and eclipsing the visibility of 10-K in its home market of New Orleans. Gatorade sponsored the Louisiana High School football playoffs and ran an aggressive public relations campaign that included an effort to get Gatorade back on the sidelines of the New Orleans Saints.

Similarly, when Pepsi introduced Mountain Dew Sport (MDS) in test markets in 1989, Quaker again mobilized its forces to promote product superiority and to portray MDS as another "soda pop." Part of the strategy was to convince stores to shelve MDS with soft drinks where it would compete with other Pepsi products rather than with Gatorade. Ultimately, MDS was not well received and was withdrawn. Pepsi immediately followed MDS with another entry—AllSport, which was an indication of the appeal of the sports drink market. Quaker Oats executives knew that other companies would continue to challenge Gatorade's enviable market share. Gatorade was a brand worth protecting.

This case was prepared by Linda E. Swayne and Peter M. Ginter as a basis for class discussion rather than to illustrate either effective or ineffective handling of an administrative situation. Used with permission from Linda E. Swayne.

HISTORY

Gatorade was developed in the 1960s by Dr. Robert Cade (a kidney expert at the University of Florida) and a team of researchers studying heat exhaustion among the players on the University of Florida football team. By analyzing the content of the football players' perspiration, they devised a formula that would prevent severe dehydration brought about by fluid and mineral loss during physical exertion in high temperatures. In 1965, they tested the rehydration product on 10 players from the football team—the Florida Gators. The beverage became known, and was later trademarked, as Gatorade. During the 1966 season, the Gators used Gatorade on the sidelines of every game. That season they became known as the "second-half team" by consistently outplaying the competition in the final half of the game. Florida's coach noted the advantages of Gatorade as the players enjoyed increased efficiency and greater endurance. That year the Florida Gators won the Orange Bowl over Georgia Tech, after which Tech coach Bobby Dodd said, "We didn't have Gatorade. That made the difference." That statement was carried by *Sports Illustrated* and marked the beginning of Gatorade becoming the best-selling sports drink in the United States.

Stokely-Van Camp Grows the Brand

In May 1967, Stokely-Van Camp, a leading processor and marketer of fruits and vegetables, purchased the rights to Gatorade from Dr. Cade and began marketing it in the summer of 1968. Stokely's original objective was to promote Gatorade as not only a sports drink, but as a health food product. It was determined that it could be used as an electrolyte replacement for colds and flu, diarrhea and vomiting, and (although not publicized) as a cure for hangovers.

By May 1969, Gatorade was available throughout most of the United States (some areas of the Northeast did not have distribution). By September 1969, it was selling in every state except Alaska. Throughout the 1970s, as Americans became more interested in fitness, Gatorade sales increased accordingly.

Many competing products were introduced once it became apparent that Stokely had a very successful product. Most were unsuccessful; however, a few were able to compete in the institutional team sales market. Due to strong brand loyalty, no other sports drink could compete with Gatorade in the retail market in those early years. In addition, sports trainers continued to select Gatorade over all other thirst quenchers.

One very successful promotion used by Stokely was to provide participating National Basketball Association (NBA) and National Football League (NFL) teams with free coolers, squeeze bottles, and cups. When the team competed, the Gatorade coolers were visible to spectators and television audiences.

Quaker Oats Ownership

In the summer of 1983, Quaker Oats bought Stokely-Van Camp. Quaker Oats was a worldwide marketer of consumer grocery products. Acquiring

Gatorade proved to be a win/win situation by boosting Quaker Oats' sales and providing the product with needed financial backing. Quaker saw an opportunity to use its marketing prowess to widen distribution and to further increase penetration throughout the country. Marketing expenditures for Gatorade were doubled, and national promotion was stressed. The expected synergies have been realized, as Gatorade has posted an average compound growth rate of 28 percent since the 1983 acquisition. Sales have grown more than sixfold from approximately $100 million in 1983 to $600 million for fiscal 1990.

Quaker Oats Legacy.   The Quaker Mill Company was founded in 1877 in Ravenna, Ohio; however, its legacy as a marketing organization began under Henry Parson Crowell, who purchased the company in 1881. During his long tenure at Quaker, he continuously broke new ground in advertising and marketing. Quaker oatmeal was the first food product to be packaged in a cardboard container. It was the first to print recipes on the package, and it was the first to advertise nationally and then globally. Crowell put the Quaker name on billboards, buildings, trucks, and manufacturing plants to a greater extent than any one had previously attempted. He also made extensive use of the print media experimenting with emotional appeals including humor, sex, and love. All of this was done without the aid of advertising agencies because they did not yet exist. Crowell, however, was pragmatic and quickly turned the burden of advertising over to agencies after they came into existence in the early 1900s.

Crowell managed daily operations in conjunction with Robert Stuart, another major shareholder. Stuart was a perceptive businessman with an interest in diversification and expansion and an appreciation for Crowell's marketing genius. He instituted a strategy of acquiring promising products and using Quaker's marketing strengths to build the product's market share. Even today, this strategy continues and has built Quaker into a giant that offers dozens of food products globally and produced sales of $5 billion in 1990 (see Exhibit 1.1 for financial statements). Throughout the 20th century, Stuart's son and grandson maintained the company's marketing culture as presidents of Quaker. The grandson, Robert D. Stuart, Jr., stressed in 1964 that "marketing was the ultimate goal, which could be accomplished only as the end effort in a complex process of production and distribution. Costs were to be controlled. Quality was to be maintained without fail. Every job was important as a step forward to that payoff in the marketplace."[1]

The Stuart family no longer manages Quaker, but the corporate commitment to the marketplace still exists. William D. Smithburg, the chief executive officer since 1983, was promoted through the ranks at Quaker. True to his corporate heritage, Smithburg acquired the Gatorade brand with the intent to grow the product through marketing.

---

[1] Arthur F. Marquette, *Brands, Trademarks, and Goodwill* (New York: McGraw-Hill, 1967), p. 258.

EXHIBIT 1.1 The Quaker Oats Company Financial Statement
(In millions except per share data)

Consolidated Statements of Income Year Ended June 30

	1988	1989	1990
Net Sales	$4,508.0	$4,879.4	$5,030.6
Cost of Goods Sold	2,397.0	2,655.3	2,685.9
Gross Profit	2,111.0	2,224.1	2,344.7
Selling, General, and Administrative Expenses	1,697.8	1,799.0	1,844.1
Interest Expense—Net of $11.0, $12.4, and $15.1 Interest Income	41.0	56.4	101.8
Other Expense—Net	57.6	149.6	16.4
Income from Continuing Operations before Income Taxes	314.6	239.1	382.4
Provision for Income Taxes	118.1	90.2	153.5
Income from Continuing Operations	196.5	148.9	228.9
Income (loss) from Discontinued Operations—Net of Tax	59.2	54.1	(59.9)
Net Income	255.7	203.0	169.0
Preferred Dividends—Net of Tax	—	—	4.5
Net Income Available for Common	$ 255.7	$ 203.0	$ 164.5
Per Common Share			
Income from Continuing Operations	$ 2.46	$ 1.88	$ 2.93
Income (Loss) from Discontinued Operations	.74	.68	(.78)
Net Income	3.20	2.56	2.15
Dividends Declared	$ 1.00	$ 1.20	$ 1.40
Average Number of Common Shares Outstanding (In thousands)	79,835	79,307	76,537

Consolidated Balance Sheets

	1988	1989	1990
Assets			
Current Assets			
Cash and Cash Equivalents	$ 47.4	$ 21.0	$ 17.7
Short-Term Investments, at Cost which Approximates Market	35.6	2.7	.6
Receivables—Net of Allowances	555.0	594.4	629.9
Inventories			
Finished Goods	281.5	326.0	324.1
Grain and Raw Materials	95.3	114.1	110.7
Packaging Materials and Supplies	37.0	39.0	39.1
Total inventories	413.8	479.1	473.9
Other Current Assets	29.8	94.2	107.0
Net Current Assets of Discontinued Operations	342.4	328.5	252.2
Total Current Assets	1,424.0	1,519.9	1,481.3
Other Receivables and Investments	20.7	26.4	63.5
Property, Plant, and Equipment	1,403.1	1,456.9	1,745.6
Less Accumulated Depreciation	480.6	497.3	591.5
Properties—Net	922.5	959.6	1,154.1
Intangible Assets, Net of Amortization	414.3	484.7	466.7
Net Noncurrent Assets of Discontinued Operations	104.6	135.3	160.5
Total Assets	$2,886.1	$3,125.9	$3,326.1

Exhibit 1.1   (Cont.)

	1988	1989	1990
Liabilities and Common Shareholders' Equity			
Current Liabilities			
Short-Term Debt	$ 310.3	$ 102.2	$ 343.2
Current Portion of Long-Term Debt	29.2	30.0	32.3
Trade Accounts Payable	262.2	333.8	354.0
Accrued Payrolls, Pensions, and Bonuses	107.3	118.1	106.3
Accrued Advertising and Merchandising	70.6	67.1	92.6
Income Taxes Payable	41.5	8.0	36.3
Other Accrued Liabilities	185.4	164.9	173.8
Total Current Liabilities	1,006.5	824.1	1,138.5
Long-Term Debt	299.1	766.8	740.3
Other Liabilities	101.0	89.5	100.3
Deferred Income Taxes	228.4	308.4	327.7
Preferred Stock, No Par Value, Authorized 1,750,000 shares; Issued 1,282,051 of $5.46 Cumulative Convertible Shares in 1989 (liquidating preference $78 per share)	—	100.0	100.0
Deferred Compensation	—	(100.0)	(98.2)
Common Shareholders' Equity			
Common Stock, $5 Par Value, Authorized 200,000,000 Shares; Issued 83,989,396 Shares	420.0	420.0	420.0
Additional Paid-in Capital	19.5	18.1	12.9
Reinvested Earnings	998.4	1,106.2	1,164.7
Cumulative Exchange Adjustment	(36.5)	(56.6)	(29.3)
Deferred Compensation	(17.4)	(165.8)	(164.1)
Treasury Common Stock, at Cost, 8,402,871 Shares; 5,221,981 Shares and 4,593,664 Shares, respectively	(132.9)	(184.8)	(386.7)
Total Common Shareholders' Equity	1,251.1	1,137.1	1,017.5
Total Liabilities and Common Shareholders' Equity	$2,886.1	$3,125.9	$3,326.1

Source: Quaker Oats, *Annual Report,* 1990.

Quaker Oats Organization.   Quaker is a decentralized company organized by product groups or categories. Quaker's grocery products divisions include breakfast foods, frozen foods, grocery specialties, pet foods, Golden Grain, and food service. Exhibit 1.2 lists the major brands included in each of Quaker's divisions. Gatorade was included in the grocery specialties division, which also contained Van Camp's Beans and Wolf Brand Chili. Gatorade constituted 65 percent of the sales of the division, and the grocery specialties division accounted for 20 percent of Quaker's total sales. Thus, Gatorade contributed approximately 13 percent to Quaker's overall sales. The president of the Grocery Specialties Division, Peter J. Vituli, was a 13-year veteran with Quaker. He had been responsible for introducing Quaker Oat Squares cereal and two products for pets, plus the relaunch of Cap'n Crunch cereal. He also spent two years marketing products in the United

EXHIBIT 1.2   Quaker Oats Divisions and Brands

North American Foods $1,583.2 million	Food Service $460.2 million

Old Fashioned Quaker Oats
Old Fashioned Quick Quaker Oats
Instant Quaker Oatmeal
Cap'n Crunch
Quaker Oat Squares
Life
Oh!s
Quaker 100% Natural
Aunt Jemima Syrup
Aunt Jemima Pancake Mix
Aunt Jemima frozen waffles, pancakes,
    French toast, etc.
Quaker Chewy Granola Bars
Dipps
Quaker Rice Cakes
Celeste Frozen Pizza
	Quaker Breakfast Products
	Grocery Specialty Products
	plus:
	    Ardmore Farms
	    Liqui-Dri Foods
	    Richardson/Snyder Foods
	    Continental Coffee
	
	Golden Grain
	$275 million
	
	Rice-A-Roni
	Noodle Roni
	Savory Classics
	Golden Grain
	Mission
	Ghirardelli (chocolate)

Pet Foods **$517.7 million** Kibbles 'n Bits 'n Bits 'n Bits Cycle Gravy Train Ken-L Ration Gaines Puss'n Boots Ken-L Ration Sausages PupPeroni Puss'n Boots Pounce	**Grocery Specialities** **$764.9 million** Gatorade Wolf Brand Chili Van Camp's Beans **International Grocery Products** **$1,420.6 million** Various Quaker brands in Europe and South America

Kingdom. The sales structure under Mr. Vituli's control began with a vice president for broker sales and included individual territory managers who provided the company's contact with food brokerage companies. The food brokers represented Quaker's direct point of distribution to the retailer.

THE MARKET

Gatorade competes in the isotonic beverage category, typically referred to as the sports drink market. These thirst quenchers are designed to replace the fluids and minerals lost during physical activity. Competition centers on rehydration performance, taste, health, and calories. According to research done for Gatorade, the effectiveness of fluid replacement beverages depends on several factors:

> *Fluid absorption*—A sports beverage should promote rapid fluid absorption; glucose/sucrose and sodium must be present in proper concentrations to help stimulate fluid absorption. Research shows that exercising people can absorb fluids containing 2 to 8 percent carbohydrate at rates similar to water. Above 10 percent carbohydrate has been shown to slow absorption rate.
>
> *Carbohydrate percentage/type*—A sports beverage should provide enough carbohydrates for use as a fuel by working muscles, yet avoid slowing fluid absorption. Research indicates formulations containing 6 to 8 percent carbohydrates are optimal for achieving a balance between energy and fluid delivery. Formulations below 6 percent provide less energy; there is no added performance advantage at levels above 6 percent. Glucose and sucrose, working in combination, deliver the most effective energy; fructose, as a sole source of carbohydrate, has been shown to be less effective.
>
> *Electrolytes*—To help the body maintain physiological homeostasis, electrolytes, particularly sodium, are needed in fluid replacement beverages for strenuous and lengthy exercise. Research indicates that 55 milligrams to 275 milligrams of sodium per serving enhance fluid absorption. (Gatorade contains less sodium than one cup of 2 percent milk.) An amount less than that found in Gatorade may not be effective in promoting optimal fluid electrolyte balance during exercise.
>
> *Taste*—Research shows that noncarbonated beverages with a mild, slightly sweet flavor are preferred by most people when they are hot and sweaty. If a sports drink tastes good, it is more likely to be consumed in the quantities necessary for proper rehydration.

Gatorade contained no vitamins, as there is no scientifically substantiated evidence to indicate that vitamins are advantageous in a rehydration product. An eight-ounce serving of Gatorade contained 50 calories (from the glucose and sucrose), which is about half the calories found in fruit drinks and nondiet soft drinks.

Each competitor in the isotonic category claims that it has the superior product for thirst quenching. With the exception of the carbonated drinks, most formulations could be argued to be adequate for fluid and mineral replacement. Therefore, flavor or taste is going to be the key competitive issue in the category.

The market is highly seasonal; the majority of sales occur during the hot summer months. Thus, it is no surprise that the majority of the sports drinks are distributed in the South, Southeast, and Southwest, where warm weather is prevalent. In Gatorade's case, 38 percent of total volume is sold in the states of Florida, Texas, and California, the very states being targeted by competition. Although most of the new brands are regional in scope, their concentration is in Gatorade's prime markets.

Competition

Gatorade management expected the sports drink category to continue to grow at a forecasted rate of about 15 percent per year during the 1990s. This meant continued growth for Gatorade, but its success had not gone unnoticed by potential competitors. Each one considered Gatorade to be its main competition, and each one was trying to capture a portion of Gatorade's 91 percent share in this $700 million sports drink market. This forced Gatorade to defend its position and placed a drain on funds previously set aside for growth. The major competing brands in the industry are summarized in Exhibit 1.3.

The international market offered the greatest growth potential. Gatorade was successfully introduced in Italy, Germany, and Brazil. Giulio Malgara, president of Quaker, Europe, predicted that Gatorade would be sold throughout the continent within five years. In Italy, Gatorade captured 93 percent of the sports drink market and induced two competing products—Isotar (4 percent share) and Acqusport (2 percent share). The next major area targeted for expansion was the Far East. In 1992, Gatorade was only marketed under license in Japan, where it competed with Coca-Cola's Aquarius drink. Quaker's international experience and expertise made global growth very appealing, plus the competition outside the United States was minimal at this time.

10-K

10-K, Gatorade's top competitor, was a subsidiary of the Japanese beverage giant, Suntory. The company had the financial strength to aggressively market its product and had achieved impressive results in key areas. Introduced in 1985, 10-K was a noncarbonated drink made from salt-free spring water that featured 100 percent of the USRDA of vitamin C, all-natural flavors and sweeteners (fructose), 60 calories per serving, and half the sodium of other thirst quenchers. 10-K contained no caffeine, Nutrasweet, or saccharin. Flavors offered were fruit punch, lemonade, orange, lemon-lime, and tea. Sizes available were 16-, 32-, 46-, and 64-ounce plastic containers. In 1991, distribution was in 28 states in the Southeast, Southwest, and Northeast. The brand captured almost 20 percent of the New Orleans market, 12 percent of the San Francisco market, and was doing 37 percent of its total volume in Florida and the Carolinas. 10-K was channeled to grocery stores and team sports' dealers. In 1989, the product market share increased from 1.9 percent to 4.5 percent of the total U.S. market and from 4.5 percent to 9 percent in 10-K's market areas. In a head-to-head taste test with Gatorade, 10-K was rated a better-tasting drink. 10-K's thirst satisfaction was rated equal to Gatorade's. Test results from respondents who used both Gatorade and 10-K over a three-month period indicated a higher repurchase rate for 10-K over Gatorade.[2]

---

[2] Tracey L. Walker, "Sports Drinks, Suddenly Everyone Wants to Play," *Beverage Industry*, February 1991, pp. 3–4.

EXHIBIT 1.3   Sports Drink Competitors

Brand and Introduction	Manufacturer	Distribution	Flavors/Sizes
Gatorade 1966	Stokely Van Camp, subsidiary of Quaker Oats Company	National	5 flavors; 3 sizes in glass bottles; 64-oz plastic bottles; 11.6-oz cans; powder pouches; aseptic packages (3-pack, 8.45-oz)
Gatorade Light April 1990	Stokely Van Camp, subsidiary of Quaker Oats Company	Southeast, Southwest, California	3 flavors; 2 sizes in glass bottles
Freestyle July 1990	Stokely Van Camp, subisidary of Quaker Oats Company	California and Arizona	3 flavors; 4-pack bottles in 2 sizes
10-K 1986	Beverage Products, division of Suntory Water Group, Atlanta; subsidiary of Suntory International	28 states in the Southeast, Southwest, and Northeast	5 flavors; 4 sizes in glass bottles
PowerBurst January 1989	PowerBurst Corporation Fresno, California	Los Angeles to New Orleans; Alaska and Hawaii; 21 states	4 flavors; 4 sizes in cans; aseptic packs; 3 sizes powdered
Workout, Workout Light, April 1989	White Rock Products Corporation, White Stone, New York	Illinois, Michigan, Ohio, North Carolina, South Carolina, New York, California, Florida	5 flavors; 16-oz
Pro-formance July 1990	Pro-formance Charlotte, NC	North Carolina, South Carolina, Tennessee, Atlanta, North Florida	4 flavors; 3 sizes
Pro Motion developed 1985 tested 1988	Sports Beverage Plano, Texas	Texas, Louisiana, Arkansas, Oklahoma, Minnesota, North Dakota, New Mexico, Colorado, Illinois, Indiana, Yuma, Arizona	4 flavors; 3 sizes in bottles, 2 sizes in cans
Mountain Dew Sport regular/diet 1990	Pepsi-Cola Company Somers, New York	Philadelphia, Minneapolis, San Diego, Eau Claire, Charlotte	12-oz cans; 2 sizes in bottles
PowerAde March 1990	Coca-Cola USA Houston, Texas	Exclusively through fountains in convenience stores, nationwide	3 flavors

Source: Pat Natschke Lenius, "New Sports Drinks Heating Up Competition," *Supermarket News,* October 1, 1990, p. 20, and promotional literature from PowerBurst Corporation and Pro-formance.

Suntory planned to spend $9 million on advertising in 1991. 10-K's promotional strategy targets men aged 18–34 and women aged 25–54. The company used television, radio, free-standing inserts (FSIs), coupons, print media, direct mail, sports marketing, local events, outdoor, and point-of-purchase merchandising to reach 90 percent of its targeted customers. The brand's advertising message focused on claims that consumers prefer 10-K because it:

- Tasted better than the leading competitor
- Was lower in sodium—no salty aftertaste
- Was enriched with Vitamin C
- Contained fructose for prolonged energy
- Was available in three popular sizes and five popular flavors

The pitch to retailers was that 10-K helped the thirst quencher category grow and that this growth meant faster turnover. The company reminded retailers that competition builds category profits and incremental sales.

PowerBurst

Introduced in December 1988 by PowerBurst Corporation and designed as an "advanced performance beverage," PowerBurst claimed nutritional superiority to existing products because it was lower in sodium and less salty in taste; had no artificial color, flavor, or preservatives; and had more sports vitamins and minerals.

Edward Debartolo, Jr., owner of the San Francisco 49ers and the Pittsburgh Penguins, had controlling interest in this privately held company that was headquartered in Fresno, California. His team ownership enabled PowerBurst to enlist quarterback Joe Montana and running back Roger Craig as endorsers. The product was promoted with full-scale television, radio, and outdoor exposure in 1990. Its goal was to capture a 15 percent share in its distribution markets. Currently, the company holds the third position in the category (nationally) at a little less than 2 percent share.

PowerBurst strayed from the traditional market of males between ages 14 and 34, claiming that its better flavor would attract younger consumers. Marketing was also directed toward sports-minded females. PowerBurst's marketing focused around its alleged superiority to Gatorade in a comparison of seven product points. Advertisements generally included a comparison scoreboard similar to the one in Exhibit 1.4.

PowerBurst sports drink was noncarbonated and offered four flavors: orange, berry punch, lemon-lime, and lemonade. Packaging provided seven different sizes ranging from 16-ounce glass bottles to 120-ounce plastic bottles and 11.5-ounce powder canisters. In 1991, distribution was in 17 states as far west as

EXHIBIT 1.4   **PowerBurst "Scoreboard"**

Points	Powerburst	Gatorade
Better tasting	1	0
Easier to Drink	1	0
Less Salty Taste	1	0
No Brominated Oils	1	0
No Artificial Color	1	0
Lower in Sodium	1	0
Essential Sports Vitamins and Minerals	1	0
Score	7	0

Montana and into the southern states of Arkansas, Louisiana, and Oklahoma. PowerBurst was available in large supermarket chains, convenience stores, and athletic and sports clubs.[3]

Mountain Dew Sport/AllSport

Pepsi-Cola Corporation introduced Mountain Dew Sport (MDS) in 1989 as its entry to the sports drink market. It was a lightly carbonated, caffeine-free beverage that came in regular and two-calorie formulas. Similar to other competitors, MDS asserted that it was better tasting than Gatorade. However, too much carbonation in this isotonic drink reduced its appeal to consumers and, as indicated earlier, Gatorade encouraged positioning on the shelf with other "soda pops." Subsequently Pepsi replaced MDS with AllSport. Unlike Mountain Dew, AllSport was offered in four flavors: orange, fruit punch, lemon-lime, and diet lemon-lime. This more lightly carbonated drink was available in 16- and 32-ounce glass containers and 12-ounce cans. Distributed in Philadelphia, Minneapolis, San Diego, Eau Claire (Wisconsin), and Charlotte, AllSport was channeled to grocery and convenience stores.[4] PepsiCo had the financial and promotional strength to provide extensive marketing support. Pepsi used its own distribution network instead of food brokers. This allowed Pepsi to move into stores quickly and to maintain optimal shelf conditions—all at a lower cost because of enormous volume. (When Pepsi test-marketed MDS in Eau Claire, 100 percent distribution was achieved in five days.) Additionally, a global distribution system was already in place in 1991, should the company decide to go international with a sports drink brand.

[3] Ibid.
[4] Ibid.

PowerAde

After a four-month test in Bakersfield, California, Coca-Cola went national with its second attempt at developing a successful thirst quencher drink. The first entry, Maxx, was a failure. PowerAde was "designed to rapidly replace body fluids lost through perspiration during physical exertion." Caffeine free and noncarbonated, PowerAde came in lemon, orange, and fruit punch flavors and was sold only at fountains. Its advertising in print and radio featured the slogan, "When you're sweating bullets . . . reach for PowerAde."

Snap-Up

Snapple Natural Beverage Company introduced Snap-Up in 1990 as a noncarbonated, mineral and fluid-replacing sports drink. Snap-Up contained maltodextrin and fructose, which reportedly enters the blood stream at a more gradual rate for a more sustained energy boost. Flavors offered were orange, lemon, lemon-lime, and fruit punch. Snap-Up was available in 16- and 32-ounce sizes and powder in 11.5-ounce cans. It was distributed on the East Coast, in the Midwest and the South, and California through health clubs, retail outlets, and convenience stores.

Pro Motion

Introduced by Sports Beverage in 1989, Pro Motion was a low-sodium, high-potassium, noncarbonated drink. It offered 100 percent recommended daily allowance for vitamin C and reportedly satisfied thirst with no salty or sweet aftertaste. Pro Motion flavors included lemon-lime, fruit punch, citrus cooler, and orange. Available in several sizes of plastic containers, Pro Motion was marketed in 20 states around the country. It was channeled through convenience stores, grocery store chains, independent stores, and institutions such as hospitals, hotels, and vending machines.

Workout

White Rock Products Corporation introduced Workout in April 1989 as an all-natural, complex carbohydrate, low-sodium, no-caffeine thirst reliever. This noncarbonated sports drink was also available in a diet formulation that contained Nutrasweet. Flavors included lemonade, lemon-lime, orange, punch, and Workout Light Iced Tea. It was packaged in a 16-ounce glass bottle and was marketed in 30 states around the country. Shelf space was sought at convenience and small independent stores.

Nautilus

Test marketed by Dr Pepper in October 1990 in Mobile, Alabama, Nautilus combined the attributes of soft drink refreshments with the benefits of a sports drink. This lightly carbonated thirst quencher offered low calories, vitamin C,

60 milligrams of sodium per 6-ounce serving, and two flavors: lemon-lime and orange. It was packaged in 2-liter plastic bottles and 12-ounce cans. It was available in grocery and convenience stores, and vending machines.

Pro-formance

Pro-formance was introduced by a Charlotte sports drink company of the same name. Joey Caldwell, North Carolina State karate champion in 1976 and 1977, developed a sports drink to help competitors "carb up" for training and competition. Pro-formance was noncarbonated and had 165 calories per 8-ounces (70 percent more than the same amount of Coca-Cola Classic and the equivalent of nine teaspoons of sugar).[5] Positioned as an energy drink, it was made from mountain water and all-natural fruit flavors and contained no sodium. Its real benefit was that it was made from a powder containing complex carbohydrates, which burn more slowly than sugar or corn syrup. It offered 12-ounce, 0.5-liter, and 1-liter servings. Pro-formance was marketed in five states and was shelved at supermarkets, convenience stores, and Wal-Mart.

GATORADE

When Quaker Oats purchased Gatorade in 1983, it was the only isotonic sports drink on the national market. Positioned as *the* sports drink, its name was almost generic. When competitors claimed their product tasted better, the Gatorade stance was that "when you're hot and sweaty Gatorade was the taste you reached for, the fluid your body craved, and ordinary taste tests were irrelevant. It was the quintessential sports drink, not a soda pop."

As the market has matured, Gatorade expanded its product line to stave off competition in various segments of the sports drink market and to reach secondary markets that would extend the franchise and build volume and profit. Although Gatorade was targeted toward "hard-core" athletes, Gatorade Light and Freestyle were introduced to compete in the low-calorie and flavor segments of the sports drink market.

Product Line Extensions

Introduced in 1990, Gatorade Light is aimed at the calorie-conscious aerobic exercisers, women, and joggers. They exercise for short or moderate lengths of time at low or moderate intensity. Gatorade Light contained 25 calories in an 8-ounce serving—about half the number of calories of regular Gatorade—and it had less sodium (80 milligrams). It was offered in three flavors and three package

---

[5] "Will Pro-formance Be a Pop Star?" *Business North Carolina*, March 1991, p. 10.

sizes. Gatorade Light sought and generally received placement on the juice aisle near regular Gatorade, thereby extending the family of products and shelf space.

Freestyle, a new, more flavorful product made with fruit juice, was aimed at people more interested in taste than the rehydration aspects of the product. Light exercisers and moderate exercisers of short to moderate duration were in the target market for this brand. Freestyle generally scored higher on taste tests than other sports drinks that did not contain fruit juice. It contained only 10 milligrams of sodium.

In 1991, Gatorade was available in six flavors. New tropical fruit flavor Gatorade was introduced to appeal to male and female teens and female adults and to broaden the product line. Each flavor had a unique appeal as indicated in Exhibit 1.5.

Packaging Options

The Gator Gallon was targeted to mothers, who purchase approximately 35 percent of Gatorade. Available in lemon-lime and orange, the plastic container was shatterproof and recyclable and had built-in handles. It was thought to be appropriate for warehouse-type (club) stores. Actually the most economical form of Gatorade was the powdered drink packaged to make four or eight quarts. Powdered Gatorade was promoted heavily at the beginning of the warm weather season and targeted to team mothers and heavy users. In 1991, eight different packages were available (Exhibit 1.6 contains the percentage of sales for each).

Newly available in convenience stores, the 23.5-ounce aluminum can was dubbed "the Slammer" and was heavily advertised in connection with Michael Jordan. Appearing in May 1991, the large can played directly on the popularity of wide-mouthed, slammable containers.[6] Also, test marketing included a 32-ounce recyclable plastic bottle and a 12-pack of 12-ounce cans. Consumers are felt to have strong preferences for their favorite flavors and packages.

In 1989, Quaker tested a fountain drink system and brought it to food service and convenience stores in 1990. The company saw this system as a source for future growth.

Distribution

In 1991, Gatorade was marketed in all states except Alaska. It was distributed primarily through food brokers who called on grocery stores and convenience stores, and institutional purchases by professional and college sports programs. Plans were under way to market Gatorade in Europe (France, Germany, Italy, and Spain) and South America (Brazil). Expansion to Europe and South America was another opportunity. Quaker viewed Gatorade as a worldwide trademark with significant opportunity for profitable growth.

---

[6] "Gatorade Bites Back with the 'Slammer,' " *Beverage Industry*, June 1991, pp. 4, 36.

EXHIBIT 1.5   Gatorade Flavors by Percent of Sales and Appeal

Flavor	Percent of Sales	Appeal
Lemon-Lime	38	Original flavor, loyal users
Orange	21	Improved taste, popular with ethnics
Fruit Punch	16	Improved taste, popular with kids
Citrus Cooler	13	Attracts new, light users
Lemonade	12	Popular summertime flavor
Tropical Fruit	new	Family appeal

Similar to other consumer packaged goods companies, Gatorade had to first sell its product to the trade. The retailers would then serve as the distribution mechanism to get the products into the hands of the ultimate consumers. In the case of retailers, demand is dependent on the profits the product generates. That profit can come in the form of increased sales volume, or in increased profit margins due to discounts or other promotional incentives.

A part of Gatorade's strategy was to point out that large shelf space and inventory were required to prevent consumers from going to another store for their purchases. Sales reps sold retail store managers on the idea that the sports beverage category should have as much shelf space on the juice aisle as the Nielsen share. For example, if a juice aisle were 64 feet long, 10 feet should be devoted to sports beverages (64-foot juice aisle $\times$ 15.3 percent sports beverage share = 10 feet). With a margin of 35 plus percent, the argument carried clout. Out-of-stocks can be costly to a given retailer. A Gatorade study found that 42 percent of consumers would not buy Gatorade if their favorite item was not available and that 18 percent would continue to shop for Gatorade at another store. Not wanting to miss a single detail in regard to visibility, the lid on Gatorade containers were changed in 1991 to heighten shelf awareness.

EXHIBIT 1.6   Gatorade Package Sizes as a Contribution to Sales

Package	Percent of Sales
64-ounce	36
32-ounce	21
46-ounce	13
Powder	11
16-ounce	9
Aseptic	8
Gallon	1
Cans	1

Gatorade distributed its products through two separate retailing industries—retail grocery stores and convenience stores. In retail sales, grocery stores represented about 55 percent of Gatorade's distribution and convenience stores accounted for the other 45 percent. Gatorade pushed for further development in convenience stores. The rationale underlying this strategy was that bottles and canned drinks were the fourth most popular item sold in convenience stores and they were a logical distribution point for Gatorade. The number of convenience stores grew 15 percent between 1988 and 1990.

The use of food brokers may prove to be a serious disadvantage for Gatorade if Pepsi or Coke develop viable products. They both offered direct store delivery (DSD), which provided greater control over shelf facings and reduced costs to retailers because DSD personnel stock the shelf, rotate product, attend to and set up displays, and monitor facings (a facing is one product width on the shelf regardless of the package's size) on a regular basis. This approach translated into fewer out-of-stocks and as a result fewer lost sales. Initial distribution was also accomplished faster through DSD. Direct sales personnel were in a store about three times a week; a food broker might be in the store only once a month and was responsible for a large number of products. Thus, interest and attention to a given product line may wane if a greater incentive is offered on another of their products. However, this problem can be circumvented by supplying enough business to the broker to make its very existence dependent on the manufacturer's business. Gatorade pursued this strategy whenever possible.

Because Gatorade had such a limited line of products and limited volume, management believed that it did not make economic sense to offer DSD. Gatorade sold approximately $600 million in product. Pepsi, on the other hand, sold syrup and licensed the name to bottlers that collectively did approximately $25 billion in business in a year. Management thought it would be difficult for Gatorade to be distributed along with other Quaker products, such as Ken-L Ration pet foods, because that would spread the Quaker personnel too thin. "They would have so many products that they would only be able to get finished with about two stores a day," commented Chris Nowokunski, Gatorade brand manager.

The shift in the balance of power from manufacturers to retailers in the food industry resulted in greater difficulty in introducing new products. "Slotting allowances" are fees charged by retailers for their shelf space. In effect, retailers are leasing shelf space to manufacturers for new products. Existing products are having to prove their value, resulting in almost continuous trade incentives (such as reduced price deals, display building contests and Gatorade cooler give-aways for store managers, and others) to maintain shelf space.

Pricing

In 1991, Gatorade pricing tended to be higher than 10-K, the only serious competitor, but with heavy in-store couponing, it was often less expensive. Gatorade's pricing strategy was in part designed to maintain a perception of quality. The use of in-store coupons promoted value because they brought Gatorade's cost below 10-K's but maintained a higher price. Although Gatorade set its price to be the quality brand, the company had no control over the price set by the retailer. Sometimes retailers set Gatorade's price low to act as a loss leader (low price on a product to induce shopping at that store). Exhibit 1.7 provides a price comparison of Gatorade and some of its competitors in various markets.

Promotion

Gatorade used a variety of promotional activities. The primary selling season was March through October; however, the heaviest promotion occurred from May to August. Advertising was designed to further strengthen Gatorade's posi-

EXHIBIT 1.7   Gatorade Price Comparisons in Selected Markets, February 1992

Brand/Package	Birmingham	Charlotte	Dallas	New Orleans	Tampa
Gatorade 32-oz	Hi $1.09 Lo .89 Avg .978	Hi $ .89 Lo .89 Avg .89	Hi $1.09 Lo .89 Avg .99	Hi $1.19 Lo .75 Avg .975	Hi $1.19 Lo .89 Avg 1.064
Gatorade 64-oz	Hi $2.25 Lo 1.89 Avg 1.99	Hi $1.89 Lo 1.89 Avg 1.89	Hi $2.35 Lo 2.09 Avg 2.22	Hi $2.49 Lo 1.79 Avg 2.055	Hi $1.98 Lo 1.75 Avg 1.87
10-K 32-oz	Hi $ .99 Lo .99 Avg .99[a]	Hi $ .99 Lo .99 Avg .99[a]	Hi $ .99 Lo .99 Avg .99[a]	Hi $ .99 Lo .72 Avg. .918	Hi $ .85 Lo .85 Avg .85[a]
10-K 64-oz	Hi $1.75 Lo 1.75 Avg 1.75[a]	Hi $1.97 Lo 1.59 Avg 1.78	n/a	Hi $2.39 Lo 1.74 Avg 1.93	Hi $1.77 Lo 1.77 Avg 1.77[a]
PowerBurst 32-oz	Hi $ .89 Lo .89 Avg .89[a]	Hi $ .95 Lo .95 Avg .95[a]	n/a[b]	n/a	Hi $1.08 Lo .69 Avg .93
Workout 16-oz	n/a	n/a	n/a	n/a	n/a
Pro-formance 1-liter	n/a	Hi $1.49 Lo 1.29 Avg 1.39	n/a	n/a	n/a
Pro Motion 32-oz	n/a	n/a	n/a	n/a	n/a
AllSport 32-oz	n/a	n/a	n/a	n/a	n/a
PowerAde 16-oz cup	n/a	n/a	n/a	n/a	n/a

Miscellaneous brands:

Enduro .5 liter	$ .75	Tampa
Daily's 1-qt	.59	Tampa, 2/$.89 Charlotte
Sports Shot 64-oz	1.50	Dallas
Quick Kick 2-liter	1.59	Dallas

[a] Only one store that was visited carried the package size and brand.

[b] The 64-oz size was available for $2.25.

n/a = not available in February 1992.

tion as the undisputed sports beverage leader. In 1989, commercials were aired during NBA games, major league baseball games, Atlantic Coast Conference (ACC) games, South Eastern Conference (SEC) games, and South West Conference (SWC) games. Prime-time television included *The Cosby Show, Wiseguy, The Wonder Years, thirtysomething*, and *Moonlighting*. Late night included David Letterman and Johnny Carson. In 1991, print ads ran in *Sports Illustrated, Inside Sports, Sporting News, Rolling Stone, GQ, Family Circle, Good Housekeeping, Better Homes & Gardens*, and *Parents* magazines. Free-standing inserts (FSIs) were often used in newspapers for coupon delivery.

Michael Jordan, basketball superstar, was featured in TV and print ads (see Exhibit 1.8). Gatorade was advertised during major collegiate and professional sporting events and on prime-time and late-night shows on network TV from April to August. During March and September, additional spots were purchased for the Sunbelt areas. Ads focused on product benefits and strong sports imagery. The TV plan reached over 95 percent of all households. Spots were primarily cast with men who were dressed in the clothing attributed to a particular sport. Models were attractive and athletic looking. The product appeared cold and refreshing—something to be gulped down, not sipped.

Print and billboards primarily reinforced these images. Because women do much of the buying, ads were placed on daytime TV and in women's magazines. The Gatorade Light campaign was targeted slightly more to female athletes than the traditional Gatorade ads. Full-season coverage targeted a growing Hispanic market and radio programming reached teens. In 1991, the advertising budget was approximately $31 million. The next closest competitor was 10-K, with $9 million in advertising.

Gatorade planned to increase its in-store presence and maintain shelf space with trade incentives and promotions in an effort to keep the competition out. Gatorade took advantage of its entrenched position and cost advantages while its competitors had to battle high costs of entry, such as slotting allowances (both 10-K and PowerBurst had to pay $1,500 in slotting allowances to each store for each item).

During the 1991 season, Gatorade was the official sports beverage of all major sports. Exhibit 1.9 summarizes the sponsorship activities.

Other promotional efforts were aimed at very aggressively maintaining outstanding retail conditions. The objective of the flurry of display activity was to increase shelf space within the juice aisle by adding a new section for Gatorade Light and reducing space devoted to competitors' beverages. Because 46 percent of Gatorade's sales were considered to be impulse purchases, displays were a critical part of the retail strategy. Regular displays were further enhanced by point-of-purchase (POP) signs, cards, and posters. Stores were encouraged to place coolers of iced units near doors or in heavily trafficked areas.

EXHIBIT 1.8   Gatorade Print Advertisement

After leading the league in scoring,

After taking the Bulls to the
Eastern Conference Championship,

And after winning the NBA title,
what is there left to reach for?

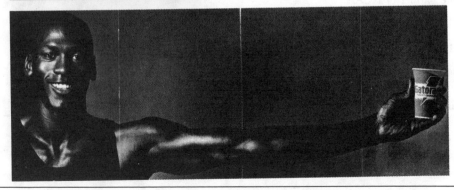

EXHIBIT 1.9   Gatorade Sponsorships in 1991

National Football League

Sideline presence at all play-off, Super Bowl, and Pro Bowl games.
Sideline presence with 27 of 28 teams.

National Basketball Association

Continued sponsorship of the Gatorade Slam Dunk Championship.
Sideline presence with all teams.

Major League Baseball

Dugout presence at League Championship Series, World Series, and All-Star games.
Sponsorship of Home Run Derby on Gatorade All Star Day Workout Day.
Dugout presence with all teams.

PGA Tour/LPGA

Golf course presence at over 100 tournament events.
Junior golf clinics with PGA tour.

NASCAR

New sponsor of Daytona 500 qualifiers—Gatorade Twin 125s.
Continued sponsorship of Gatorade 200 and Gatorade Circle of Champions.

National Hockey League

Sideline presence at Stanley Cup.
Sideline presence with all clubs.

NCAA

Corporate partner of NCAA.
Individual sponsorships with many leading colleges and universities.

National Federation of High School Associations

Title sponsor of "High School Games of the Week" on Sports Channel America.
Official sports beverage of the federation.
First participant in the "National Sponsor of High School Sports" program.

Divisional Objectives

Each division of Quaker Oats was subject to company-wide goals and objectives. As one of Quaker's high-growth products (others were ready-to-eat and hot cereals, microwave meals, food service, and international operations), Gatorade played a major role in the company's effort to reach inflation-adjusted earnings growth of 7 percent per year, and a return on equity of 25 percent or more. Gatorade's goal, however, was to continue its growth of about 28 percent annually and to maintain its 91 percent market share. President Vituli stated, "The division intends to take a very aggressive approach and try things we've never done before. . . . Specifically that means increasing the frequency with which customers use the product, improving convenience, leading segmentation of the sports beverage category and increasing distribution of Gatorade to everywhere people get hot and thirsty."[7] Plans for 1991 called for $150 million in advertising plus merchandising expenditures, with the majority being spent on sports promotions and tie-ins.

Gatorade's strategic objectives included achieving high visibility and presence in order to establish Gatorade as the undisputed sports beverage leader, dominating sports beverage merchandising, and controling the sports beverage shelf sets (position on the shelf).

THE FUTURE PRESENTS CHALLENGES AND OPPORTUNITIES

The fitness trend that has driven growth in the isotonic category is expected to continue. The category is expected to reach $2 billion by the year 2000. Demographically, however, the isotonic market faces a decline in its traditional target ages of 12 to 34. The aging of the population will force reassessment of the targeted age group in order to continue growth. Opportunities may exist if aging Americans actively pursue better health through exercise and more active lives. The aging population is expected to fuel the growth of the sunbelt region, a factor that must be considered in Gatorade's marketing strategy. In addition, growing minority groups represent a highly concentrated market that should not be ignored. Estimates are that blacks and Hispanics will constitute nearly 25 percent of the U.S. population by the year 2000.

Timothy Ramey, analyst at County NatWest Securities USA, commented, "It's going to be a David vs. Goliath-type battle for Coke and Pepsi, but it's hard to see how over time Gatorade can avoid giving away a lot of this market." Michael Bellas, president of Beverage Marketing Corporation, made a similar comment: "The market is gearing up for a substantial battle. These are some big players looking at the category in a substantial way."[8]

[7] *Quaker Quarterly*, first quarter, 1991, p. 12.
[8] Julie Liesse and Patricia Winters, "Gatorade Set to Bench New Rivals," *Advertising Age*, March 19, 1990, p. 4.

—————————— CASE 9 ————————

Wal-Mart Stores:
Strategies for Market Dominance

It was dusk in the foothills of the Ozark mountains in north central Arkansas. A battered red 1980 Ford pickup, minus two hubcaps with a hunting dog named Buck seated inside the cab, was headed down the rural road for some coffee and conversation with friends at Fred's Hickory Inn in Bentonville. Inside the truck, driving, was one of the most successful retailing entrepreneurs in modern history, who continues to be down-to-earth and old fashioned in his views of the past, the present, and the future. "I didn't sit down one day and decide that I was going to put a bunch of discount stores in small towns and set a goal to have a billion-dollar company some day," Sam Walton said. "I started out with one store and it did well, so it was a challenge to see if I could do well with a few more. We're still going and we'll keep going as long as we're successful." From these humble beginnings, Wal-Mart emerged as a modern retail success story.

This case was prepared by James W. Camerius of Northern Michigan University as a basis for class discussion rather than to illustrate either effective or ineffective handling of an administrative situation. All rights reserved to the author. Copyright © 1992 by James W. Camerius. Used with permission from James W. Camerius.

EMERGING ORGANIZATION

Wal-Mart Stores, with corporate offices in Bentonville, Arkansas, had completed its 28th consecutive year of growth in both sales and earnings in 1991. The firm operated stores under a variety of names and retail formats including Wal-Mart stores, which existed as discount department stores; Sam's Wholesale Clubs, which were wholesale/retail membership warehouses; Hypermart*USA, which were combination grocery and general merchandise stores in excess of 200,000 square feet; Wal-Mart Supercenters, scaled-down versions of hypermarkets; Dot Discount Drugstores, a super discount drug chain; and Bud's, off-price outlet stores. In sales volume, it was not only the nation's largest discount department store chain, but it had recently surpassed Sears, Roebuck, & Co. as the largest retail organization in the United States.

The Sam Walton Spirit

Much of the initial and continuing success of Wal-Mart was attributed to the entrepreneurial spirit of its founder and chairman of the board, Samuel Moore Walton. Sam Walton, or "Mr. Sam" as some referred to him, traced his down-to-earth, old-fashioned, home-spun, evangelical ways to growing up in rural Oklahoma, Missouri, and Arkansas. Although he was remarkably blasé about his roots, some suggested that it was a simple belief in hard work and ambition that had "unlocked countless doors and showered upon him, his customers, and his employees . . . the fruits of . . . years of labor in building [this] highly successful company."

"Our goal has always been in our business to be the very best," he said in an interview, "and, along with that, we believe that in order to do that, you've got to make a good situation and put the interests of your associates first. If we really do that consistently, they in turn will cause . . . our business to be successful, which is what we've talked about and espoused and practiced.

"The reasons for our success," Sam Walton said, "is our people and the way that they're treated and the way they feel about their company." Many have suggested it is this people-first philosophy that guided the company through the challenges and setbacks of its early years and allowed the company to maintain its consistent record of growth and expansion in later years.

There was little about Walton's background that reflected his amazing success. He was born in Kingfisher, Oklahoma, on March 29, 1918, to Thomas and Nancy Walton. Thomas Walton was a banker at the time and later entered the farm mortgage business and moved to Missouri. Sam Walton, growing up in rural Missouri in the depths of the Great Depression, discovered early that he "had a fair amount of ambition and enjoyed working," as he suggested in a company interview. He completed high school in Columbia, Missouri, and received a Bachelor of Arts in Economics from the University of Missouri in 1940. "I really had no idea what I would be," he said. He added as an afterthought, "At one point in time, I thought I wanted to become President of the United States."

A unique, enthusiastic, and positive individual, Sam Walton was called "just your basic home-spun billionaire" by *Business Week* magazine. One source suggested that "Mr. Sam is a life-long small-town resident who didn't change much as he got richer than his neighbors." Walton drove an old Ford pickup truck, would grab a bite to eat at Fred's Hickory Inn in Bentonville, and as a matter of practice would get his hair cut at the local barbershop. He had tremendous energy, enjoyed bird hunting with his dogs, and flew a corporate plane. When the company was much smaller, he could boast that he personally visited every Wal-Mart store at least once a year. A store visit usually included Walton leading Wal-Mart cheers that began "Give me a W, give me an A. . . ." To many employees, he had the air of a fiery Baptist preacher. Paul R. Carter, a Wal-Mart executive vice president, said: "Mr. Walton has a calling." He became the richest man in the United States, and by 1991 he had created a personal fortune for his family in excess of $21 billion.

For all that Walton's success has been widely chronicled, its magnitude is hard to comprehend. Sam Walton was selected by the investment publication *Financial World* in 1989 as the "CEO of the Decade." He had honorary degrees from the University of the Ozarks, the University of Arkansas, and the University of Missouri. He received many of the most distinguished professional awards from the industry such as "Man of the Year," "Discounter of the Year," and "Chief Executive Officer of the Year" and was the second retailer to be inducted into the Discounting Hall of Fame. He was the recipient of an Horatio Alger Award in 1984 and acknowledged by *Discount Stores News* as "Retailer of the Decade" in December of 1989. "Walton does a remarkable job of instilling near-religious fervor in his people," said analyst Robert Buchanan of A. G. Edwards. "I think that speaks to the heart of his success." In late 1989 Sam Walton was diagnosed as having multiple myeloma, or cancer of the bone marrow. Although he curtailed some activities, he planned to continue in the firm as chairman of the board.

THE MARKETING CONCEPT

Genesis of An Idea

Sam Walton started his retail career in 1940 as a management trainee with the J.C. Penney Company in Des Moines, Iowa. He was impressed with the Penney method of doing business and later modeled the Wal-Mart chain on "The Penney Idea" as reviewed in Exhibit 9.1. The Penney Company had found strength in calling employees "associates" rather than clerks. Founded in Kemerer, Wyoming, in 1902, Penney stores were located on the main streets of small towns and cities.

Following service in the U.S. Army during World War II, Sam Walton acquired a Ben Franklin variety-store franchise in Newport, Arkanas, which he operated successfully until losing the lease in 1950. He opened another store

EXHIBIT 9.1   The Penney Idea—1913

1. To serve the public, as nearly as we can, to its complete satisfaction.
2. To expect for the service we render a fair remuneration and not all the profit the traffic will bear.
3. To do all in our power to pack the customer's dollar full of value, quality, and satisfaction.
4. To continue to train ourselves and our associates so that the service we give will be more and more intelligently performed.
5. To improve constantly the human factor in our business.
6. To reward men and women in our organization through participation in what the business produces.
7. To test our every policy, method, and act in this wise: "Does it square with what is right and just?"

Source: Vance H. Trimble, *Sam Walton: The Inside Story of America's Richest Man* (New York: Dutton, 1990).

under the name of Walton's 5 and 10 in Bentonville, Arkansas, the following year. By 1962, he was operating a chain of 15 stores.

The early retail stores owned by Sam Walton in Newport and Bentonville, Arkansas, and later in other small towns in adjoining southern states, were variety-store operations. They were relatively small stores of 6,000 square feet, located on "main street," and displayed merchandise on plain wooden tables and counters. Operated under the Ben Franklin name and supplied by Butler Brothers of Chicago and St. Louis, they were characterized by a limited price line, low gross margins, high merchandise turnover, and concentration on return on investment. The firm, operating under the Walton 5 and 10 name, was the largest Ben Franklin franchise in the country in 1962. The variety stores were phased out by 1976 to allow the company to concentrate on the growth of Wal-Mart stores.

Foundation of Growth

The original Wal-Mart discount concept was not a unique idea. Sam Walton became convinced in the late 1950s that discounting would transform retailing. He traveled extensively in New England, the cradle of off-pricing. "He visited just about every discounter in the United States," suggested William F. Kenney, the retired president of the now-defunct Kings Department Stores. He tried to sell the discount store concept to Butler Brothers executives in Chicago. The first Kmart, as a "conveniently located one-stop shopping unit where customers could buy a wide variety of quality merchandise at discount prices," had opened in 1962 in Garden City, Michigan. Walton's theory was to operate a discount store in a small community where he would offer name-brand merchandise at low prices and would add friendly service. Butler Brothers executives rejected the idea. Undaunted, he opened the first Wal-Mart Discount City in late 1962 in Rogers, Arkansas.

Wal-Mart stores would sell nationally advertised, well-known brand merchandise at low prices in austere surroundings. As corporate policy, they would cheerfully give refunds, credits, and rain checks. Management conceived the firm as a "discount department store chain offering a wide variety of general merchandise to the customer." Early emphasis was placed upon opportunistic purchases of merchandise from whatever sources were available. Heavy emphasis was placed upon health and beauty aids (H&BA) in the product line and "stacking it high" in a manner of merchandise presentation. By the end of 1979, there were 276 Wal-Mart stores located in 11 states.

The firm developed an aggressive expansion strategy as it grew from its first 16,000-square-foot discount store in Rogers. New stores were located primarily in towns of 5,000 to 25,000 in population. The stores' sizes ranged from 30,000 to 60,000 square feet with 45,000 being the average. The firm also expanded by locating stores in contiguous areas, town by town, state by state. When its discount operations came to dominate a market area, it moved to an adjoining area. Although other retailers built warehouses to serve existing outlets, Wal-Mart built the distribution center first and then spotted stores all around it, pooling advertising and distribution overhead. Most stores were less than a six-hour drive from one of the company's warehouses. The first major distribution center, a 390,000-square-foot facility opened in Search, Arkansas, outside Bentonville in 1978.

National Perspectives

At the beginning of 1991, the firm had 1,573 Wal-Mart stores in 35 states with expansion planned for adjacent states. Wal-Mart became the largest retailer and the largest discount department store by continuing to follow the unique place strategy of first locating discount stores in small-town America and later in suburban markets. As a national discount department store chain, Wal-Mart Stores offered a wide variety of general merchandise to the customer. The stores were designed to offer one-stop shopping in 36 departments that included family apparel, health and beauty aids, household needs, electronics, toys, fabric and crafts, automotive supplies, lawn and patio, jewelry, and shoes. In addition, at certain store locations, a pharmacy, automotive supply and service center, garden center, or snack bar was included. The firm operated its stores with an "everyday low price" as opposed to putting heavy emphasis on special promotions, which called for multiple newspaper advertising circulars. Stores were expected to "provide the customer with a clean, pleasant, and friendly shopping experience."

Although Wal-Mart carried much the same merchandise, offered similar prices, and operated stores that looked much like the competition, there were many differences. In the typical Wal-Mart store, employees wore blue vests for easy identification, aisles were wide, apparel departments were carpeted in warm colors, a store employee followed customers to their car to pick up their shopping carts, and the customer was welcomed at the door by a "people greeter," who gave directions and struck up conversations. In some cases, merchandise was bagged in brown paper sacks rather than plastic bags because customers seemed to prefer them. A simple Wal-Mart logo in white letters on a brown background on the front of the store served to identify the firm. In consumer studies it was determined that the chain was particularly adept at striking the delicate balance needed to convince customers its prices were low without making people feel that its stores were too cheap. In many ways, competitors such as Kmart, sought to emulate Wal-Mart by introducing people greeters, by upgrading interiors, by developing new logos and signage, and by introducing new inventory response systems. In 1989, sales per square foot of retail space at Wal-Mart were $227. Kmart, in contrast, sold only $139 per square foot worth of goods annually.

A satisfaction guaranteed refund and exchange policy was introduced to inspire customer confidence in Wal-Mart's merchandise and quality. Technological advancements like scanner cash registers, hand-held computers for ordering merchandise, and computer linkages of stores with the general office and distribution centers improved communications and merchandise replenishment. Each store was encouraged to initiate programs that would make it an integral part of the community in which it operated. Associates were encouraged to "maintain the highest standards of honesty, morality, and business ethics in dealing with the public."

The External Environment

Industry analysts had labeled the 1980s as an era of economic uncertainty for retailers. Some firms faced difficulty with merger or acquisition. After acquiring U.S.-based Allied Department Stores in 1986 and Federated Department Stores in 1988, Canadian developer Robert Campeau declared bankruptcy with over $6 billion in debt. Upon reevaluation, several divisions and units of this organization were either sold or closed. Rich's flagship downtown Atlanta store, a division of Federated, was closed after completing a multi-million-dollar remodeling program. Specific merchandise programs in divisions such as Bloomingdale's were reevaluated to lower inventory and to raise cash. The notion of servicing existing debt became a significant factor in the success or failure of a retailing organization in the latter half of the decade. Selected acquisitions of U.S. retailers by foreign firms over the past decade are summarized in Exhibit 9.2

Other retailers experienced change in ownership. The British B.A.T. Industries PLC sold the Chicago-based Marshall Field department store division to the Dayton-Hudson Corporation. L. J. Hooker Corporation, the U.S. arm of Australia's Hooker Corporation, sold its Bonwit Teller and Sakowitz stores; it liquidated its B. Altman chain after fruitless sales efforts. The R.H. Macy Company saddled itself with $4.5 billion in debt as a result of acquiring Bullock's and I. Magnin specialty department stores. Chicago-based Carson, Pirie, Scott & Company was sold to the P. A. Bergner & Company, operator of the Milwaukee Boston Store and Bergner Department Stores. Bergner declared Chapter 11 bankruptcy in 1991.

EXHIBIT 9.2   Selected Acquisitions of U.S. Retailers by Foreign Firms, 1980–1990

U.S. Retailer	Foreign Acquirer	Country of Acquirer
Allied Stores (General Merchandise)	Campeau	Canada
Alterman Foods (Supermarkets)	Delhaie-Le Leon	Belgium
Bonwit Teller (General Merchandise)	Hooker Corp.	Australia
Brooks Brothers (Apparel)	Marks & Spencer	Great Britain
Federated Department Stores (Diversified)	Campeau	Canada
Great Atlantic & Pacific (Supermarkets)	Tengelmann	West Germany
Herman's (Sporting Goods)	Dee Corp.	Great Britain
International House of Pancakes (Restaurants)	Wienerwald	Switzerland
Talbots (Apparel)	Jusco	Japan
Zale (Jewelry)	PS Associates	Netherlands

Source: Barry Berman and Joel R. Evans, *Retail Management: A Strategic Approach,* 4th ed. (New York: Macmillan, 1989).

Many retail enterprises confronted heavy competitive pressure by lowering prices or changing merchandise strategies. Sears, Roebuck & Company, in an effort to reverse sagging sales and less than defensible earnings, unsuccessfully introduced a new policy of "everyday low pricing" in 1989. It later introduced name-brand items alongside its traditional private-label merchandise and introduced the store-within-a-store concept to feature the name-brand goods. For example, Whirlpool appliances were sold next to Kenmore (Sears brand) appliances. Montgomery Ward, and to a lesser extent Kmart and Ames Department Stores, followed similar strategies. The J.C. Penney Company, despite repositioning as a more upscale retailer, felt that an impending recession plus concerns about the Persian Gulf War had combined to erode consumer confidence. "As a result," the company noted in its 1990 annual report, "sales and profits within the industry were more negatively impacted than at any time since the last major recession of 1980 to 1982."

The discount department store industry by the early 1990s had changed in a number of ways and was thought to have reached maturity by many analysts. Several formerly successful firms like E.J. Korvette, W.T. Grant, Atlantic Mills, Arlans, Federals, Zayre, Heck's, and Ames had declared bankruptcy and as a result either liquidated or reorganized. Regional firms like Target Stores and Shopko Stores began carrying more fashionable merchandise in more attractive facilities and shifted their emphasis to more national markets. Specialty retailers such as Toys 'R' Us, Pier 1 Imports, and Oshmans were making big inroads in toys, home furnishings, and sporting goods. The superstores of drug and food chains were rapidly discounting increasing amounts of general merchandise. Other firms such as May Department Stores Company (Caldor and Venture) and the F.W. Woolworth Co. (Woolco) had withdrawn from the field by either selling their discount divisions or closing them down entirely.

Several new retail formats had emerged in the market place to challenge the traditional discount department store format. The superstore, a 100,000- to

300,000-square-foot operation, combined a large supermarket with a discount general-merchandise store. Originally a European retailing concept, these outlets were known as "malls without walls." Super Kmart and American Fare owned by Kmart and Supercenter stores and Hypermart*USA owned by Wal-Mart were examples of this trend toward large operations. Warehouse retailing, which involved some combination of warehouses and showroom facilities, used warehouse principles to reduce operating expenses and thereby offer discount prices as a primary customer appeal. Home Depot combined the traditional hardware store and lumber yard with a self-service home improvement center to become the largest home center operation in the nation.

Some retailers responded to changes in the marketplace by selling goods at price levels 20 to 60 percent below regular retail prices. These off-price operations appeared as two general types: (1) factory outlet stores like Burlington Coat Factory Warehouse, Bass Shoes, and Manhattan's Brand Name Fashion Outlet, and (2) independents like Loehmann's, T.J. Maxx, Marshall's, and Clothesline, which bought seconds, overages, closeouts, or leftover goods from manufacturers and other retailers. Others chose to dominate a product classification. Some superspecialists such as Sock Appeal, Little Piggie, and Sock Market, offered a single narrowly defined classification of merchandise with an extensive assortment of brands, colors, and sizes. Others, as niche specialists, such as Kids Mart, a division of F.W. Woolworth, and McKids, a division of Sears, targeted an identified market with carefully selected merchandise and appropriately designed stores. Some retailers such as Silk Greenhouse (silk plants and flowers), Office Club (office supplies and equipment), and Toys 'R' Us (toys) were called "category killers" because they had achieved merchandise dominance in their respective product categories. Firms such as The Limited, Victoria's Secret, and the Banana Republic became mini-department specialists by showcasing new lines and accessories alongside traditional merchandise.

Wal-Mart became the nation's largest retail and discount department store chain in sales volume in 1991. Kmart Corporation, now the industry's second largest retailer and discount department store chain, with over 2,300 stores and $32,070,000 in sales in 1990, was perceived by many industry analysts and consumers in several independent studies as a laggard, even though it had been the industry sales leader for a number of years. In the same studies, Wal-Mart was perceived as the industry leader even though according to the *Wall Street Journal*: "They carry much the same merchandise, offer prices that are pennies apart, and operate stores that look almost exactly alike." "Even their names are similar," noted the newspaper. The original Kmart concept of a "conveniently located, one stop shopping unit where customers could buy a wide variety of quality merchandise at discount prices," had lost its competitive edge in a changing market. As one analyst noted in an industry newsletter: "They had done so well for the past 20 years without paying attention to market changes. Now they have to." Wal-Mart and Kmart sales growth over the past 10 years is reviewed in Exhibit 9.3. A competitive analysis is shown of four major retail firms in Exhibit 9.4.

EXHIBIT 9.3   Competitive Sales and Store Comparison

	Kmart		Wal-Mart[a]	
Year	Sales (In thousands)	Number of Stores	Sales (In thousands)	Number of Stores
1990	$32,070,000	2,350	$32,601,594	1,573
1989	29,533,000	2,361	25,810,656	1,402
1988	27,301,000	2,307	20,649,001	1,259
1987	25,627,000	2,273	15,959,255	1,114
1986	23,035,000	2,342	11,909,076	980
1985	22,035,000	2,332	8,451,489	859
1984	20,762,000	2,173	6,400,861	745
1983	18,597,000	2,160	4,666,909	642
1982	16,772,166	2,117	3,376,252	551
1981	16,527,012	2,055	2,444,997	491
1980	14,204,381	1,772	1,643,199	330

[a] Wal-Mart fiscal year ends January 31. Figures are assigned to previous year.

Some retailers like Kmart had initially focused on appealing to professional, middle-class consumers who lived in suburban areas and were likely to be price sensitive. Other firms like Target, which had adopted the discount concept early, generally attempted to go after an upscale consumer who had an annual household income of $25,000 to $44,000. Fleet Farm and Menard's served the rural consumer, and some firms such as Chicago's Goldblatt's Department Stores returned to their immigrant heritage to serve blacks and Hispanics in the inner city.

In rural communities Wal-Mart success often came at the expense of established local merchants and units of regional discount store chains. Hardware stores, family department stores, building supply outlets, and stores featuring fabrics, sporting goods, and shoes were among the first to either close or relocate elsewhere. Regional discount retailers in the Sunbelt states, including Roses, Howard's, T.G.& Y, and Duckwall-ALCO, that once enjoyed solid sales and earnings, were forced to reposition by renovating stores, opening bigger and more modern units, remerchandising assortments, and offering lower prices. In many cases, stores such as Coast-to-Coast, Pamida, and Ben Franklin closed upon a Wal-Mart announcement to build in a specific community. "Just the word that Wal-Mart was coming made some stores close up," indicated a local newspaper editor.

Corporate Strategies

The corporate and marketing strategies that emerged at Wal-Mart to challenge a turbulent and volatile external environment were based upon a set of two main objectives that had guided the firm through its growth years in the 1980s. In the first objective the customer was featured: "Customers would be provided

EXHIBIT 9.4 An Industry Competitive Analysis, 1991

	Wal-Mart	Sears, Roebuck	Kmart	J.C. Penney
Sales (Thousands)	$32,601,584	$55,972,000	$32,070,000	$17,410,000
Net Income (Thousands)	1,291,024	902,000	756,000	577,000
Net Income per Share	1.14	2.63	3.78	4.33
Dividends per Share	.14	2.00	1.72	2.64
Number of Stores (see Note)	1,724	1,765	4,180	3,889
Percent Sales Change	26.0%	1.2%	.6%	2.1%

Note: Wal-Mart and Subsidiaries (Number of Outlets)
      Wal-Mart Stores—1,573
      Sam's Wholesale Club—148
      Hypermart*USA—3

   Sears, Roebuck & Company
   Sears Merchandise Group (Number of Outlets)
      Department Stores—863
      Paint and Hardware Stores—98
      Catalog Outlet Stores—101
      Western Auto—504
      Eye Care Centers of America—94
      Business Systems Centers—65
      Pinstripes Petites—40

   Allstate Insurance Group
   Dean Witter Financial Services Group
   Coldwell Banker Real Estate Group

   Kmart Corporation (Number of Outlets)
   General Merchandise—2,350
   Specialty Retail Stores—1,830
      PACE Membership Warehouse
      Builders Square
      Payless Drug Stores
      Waldenbooks
      The Sports Authority

   J.C. Penney Company (Number of Outlets)
   Stores—1,312
      Metropolitan Market Stores—697
      Geographic Market Stores—615
   Catalog Units—2,090
      J.C. Penney Stores—1,312
      Free-Standing Sales Centers—626
      Drug Stores—136
      Other, Principally Outlet Stores—16
   Drug Stores (Thrift Drug or Treasury Drug)—487

what they want, when they want it, all at a value." In the second objective the team spirit was emphasized: "Treating each other as we would hope to be treated, acknowledging our total dependency on our Associate-partners to sustain our success." The approach included aggressive plans for new store openings; expansion to additional states; upgrading, relocation, refurbishing, and remodeling of existing stores; and opening new distribution centers. The plan was to avoid having a single operating unit that had not been updated in the past seven years. In the 1991 annual report to stockholders, the 1990s were described as "A new era for Wal-Mart; an era in which we plan to grow to a truly nationwide retailer, and should we continue to perform, our sales and earnings will also grow beyond where most could have envisioned at the dawn of the 80s." Appendix 9.A contains a 10-year financial summary for Wal-Mart.

In the 1980s, Wal-Mart developed a number of new retail formats. The first Sam's Wholesale Club opened in Oklahoma City in 1983. The wholesale club was an idea that had been developed earlier by other firms but that found its greatest success and growth in acceptability at Wal-Mart. Sam's Wholesale Club featured a vast array of product categories with limited selection of brand and model, cash-and-carry business with limited hours, large (100,000-square-foot) bare-bones facilities, rock-bottom wholesale prices, and minimal promotion. The limited membership plan permitted wholesale members who bought a membership and others who usually paid a percentage above the ticket price of the merchandise. At the beginning of 1991, there were 148 Sam's Wholesale Clubs open in 28 states. Effective February 2, 1991, Sam's Clubs merged the 28 units of the Wholesale Club of Indianapolis, Indiana, into the organization.

The first Hypermart*USA was a 222,000-square-foot superstore that combined a discount store with a large grocery store and contained a food court of restaurants and a variety of other service businesses such as banks or videotape rental stores. It opened in 1988 in the Dallas suburb of Garland. A scaled-down version of Hypermart*USA was called the Wal-Mart SuperCenter. It had similar merchandise offerings, but with about half the square footage of hypermarkets. These expanded store concepts also included convenience stores and gasoline distribution outlets to "enhance shopping convenience." The company proceeded slowly with these plans and later suspended its plans for building any more hypermarkets in favor of the supercenter concept.

The McLane Company, a provider of retail and grocery distribution services for retail stores, was acquired in 1991. In October 1991, management announced that it was starting a chain of stores called Bud's, which would sell damaged, outdated, and overstocked goods at discounts even deeper than regular Wal-Mart stores.

Several programs were launched to "highlight" popular social causes. The "Buy American" theme was a Wal-Mart retail program initiated in 1985. Additionally, "Bring It Home to the USA" was selected to communicate the company's support for U.S. manufacturing. In the program, Wal-Mart encouraged manufacturers to produce goods in the United States rather than import them from other countries. Vendors were attracted into the program by encouraging manufacturers to initiate the process of contracting the company directly with proposals to sell goods that were made in the United States. Buyers also targeted specific import items in their assortments on a state-by-state basis to encourage domestic manufacturing. According to Haim Dabah, president of Gitano Group, a maker of fashion discount clothing that at one time imported 95 percent of its clothing and now makes about 20 percent of its products in the United States, "Wal-Mart let it be known loud and clear that if you're going to grow with them, you sure better have some products made in the U.S.A." Farris Fashion (flannel shirts); Roadmaster Corporation (exercise bicycles); Flanders Industries (lawn chairs); and Magic Chef (microwave ovens) were examples of vendors that chose to participate in the program.

From the Wal-Mart perspective, the "Buy American" program centered on value—producing and selling quality merchandise at a competitive price. The promotion included television advertisements featuring factory workers, a soaring American eagle, and the slogan "We buy American whenever we can, so you can, too." Prominent in-store signage and store circulars were also included. One store poster read "Success Stories—These items formerly imported, are now being purchased by Wal-Mart in the U.S.A."

Wal-Mart was one of the first retailers to embrace the concept of "green" marketing. The program offered shoppers the option of purchasing products that were better for the environment in three respects: manufacturing, use, and disposal. Introduced through full-page advertisements in the *Wall Street Journal* and *USA Today,* in-store signage identified the environmentally safe products. As Wal-Mart executives saw it, "Customers are concerned about the quality of land, air, and water, and would like the opportunity to do something positive." To initiate the program, 7,000 vendors were notified that Wal-Mart had a corporate concern for the environment and to ask for their support in a variety of ways. Wal-Mart television advertising showed children on swings, fields of grain blowing in the wind, and roses. Green and white store signs printed on recycled paper marketed products or packaging that had been developed or redesigned to be more environmentally sound.

Wal-Mart was the channel commander in the distribution of many brand name items. As the nation's largest retailer and in many geographic areas the dominant distributor, it exerted considerable influence in negotiations for the best price, delivery terms, promotion allowances, and continuity of supply. Many of these benefits could be passed on to consumers in the form of quality name-brand items available at lower-than-competitive prices. As a matter of corporate policy, management often insisted on doing business only with a producer's top sales executives rather than going through a manufacturer's representative. Wal-Mart had been accused of threatening to buy from other producers if firms refused to sell directly to it. In the ensuing power struggle, Wal-Mart executives refused to talk about the controversial policy or admit that it existed. As suggested by a representative of an industry association, "In the Southwest, Wal-Mart's the only show in town." Added an industry analyst, "They're extremely aggressive. Their approach has always been to give the customer the benefit of any corporate savings. That builds customer loyalty and market share."

Another key factor in the mix was an inventory control system that was recognized as the most sophisticated in retailing. A high-speed computer system linked virtually all the stores to headquarters and the company's distribution centers. It electronically logged every item sold at the checkout counter, automatically kept the warehouses informed of merchandise to be ordered, and directed the flow of goods to the stores and even to the proper shelves. Most important for management, it helped detect sales trends quickly and speeded up market reaction time substantially.

Decision Making in a Market-Oriented Firm

One factor that distinguished Wal-Mart from other companies was the unusual depth of employee involvement in company affairs. Corporate strategies put emphasis on human resources management. Employees of Wal-Mart became "associates," a name borrowed from Sam Walton's early association with the J.C. Penney Company. Input was encouraged at meetings at the store and corporate level. The firm hired employees locally, provided training programs, encouraged employees to ask questions through a "Letter to the President" program, and made words like "we," "us," and "our" a part of the corporate language. A number of special award programs recognized individual, department, and division achievement. Stock ownership and profit-sharing programs were introduced as part of a "partnership concept."

The corporate culture was acknowledged by the editors of the trade publication *Mass Market Retailers* when it recognized all 275,000 associates collectively as the 1989 "Mass Market Retailers of the Year." The editors noted, "In this decade that term [Wal-Mart associate] has come to symbolize all that is right with the American worker, particularly in the retailing environment and most particularly at Wal-Mart." The store-within-a-store concept, as a Wal-Mart corporate policy, trained individuals to be merchants by being responsible for the performance of their own departments as if they were running their own businesses. Seminars and training programs afforded them opportunities to grow within the company. "People development, not just a good 'program' for any growing company but a must to secure our future," was how Suzanne Allford, vice president of the Wal-Mart People Division, explained the firm's decentralized approach to retail management development.

"The Wal-Mart Way" was a phrase that was used by management to summarize the firm's unconventional approach to business and the development of the corporate culture. Referring to a recent development program, the 1991 annual report noted, "We stepped outside our retailing world to examine the best managed companies in the United States in an effort to determine the fundamentals of their success and to 'benchmark' our own performances." The term "total quality management" (TQM) was used to identify this "vehicle for proliferating the very best things we do while incorporating the new ideas our people have that will assure our future."

The Growth Challenge

David Glass, 53 years old, had assumed the role of president and chief executive officer at Wal-Mart, the position previously held by Sam Walton, founder of the company. Known for his hard-driving managerial style, Glass gained his experience in retailing at a small supermarket chain in Springfield, Missouri. He joined Wal-Mart as executive vice president for finance in 1976. He was named president and chief operating officer in 1984.

And what of Wal-Mart without Mr. Sam? "There's no transition to make," said Glass, "because the principles and the basic values he used in founding this company were so sound and so universally accepted." "As for the future," he suggested, spinning around in his chair at his desk in his relatively spartan office at corporate headquarters in Bentonville, "there's more opportunity ahead of us than behind us. We're good students of retailing and we've studied the mistakes that others have made. We'll make our own mistakes, but we don't repeat theirs. The only thing constant at Wal-Mart is change. We'll be fine as long as we never lose our responsiveness to the customer."

For over 25 years Wal-Mart Stores experienced tremendous growth and as one analyst suggested was "consistently on the cutting edge of low-markup mass merchandising." Much of the forward momentum came from the entrepreneurial spirit of Samuel Moore Walton. Mr. Sam remained chairman of the board of directors and corporate representative for the immediate future. A new management team was in place. As the largest retailer in the country, the firm had positioned itself to meet the challenges of the next decade as an industry leader. The question now was: Could the firm maintain its blistering growth pace—outmaneuvering the competition with the innovative retailing concepts that it has continued to develop better than anyone else?

REFERENCES

"A Supercenter Comes to Town," *Chain Store Age Executive,* December 1989, pp. 23–30+.

ABEND, JULES, "Wal-Mart's Hypermart: Impetus for U.S. Chains?" *Stores,* March 1988, pp. 59–61.

The Almanac of American Employers (Chicago: Contemporary Books, 1985), p. 280.

"Another Record Year at Wal-Mart," *Chain Store Age,* General Merchandise Edition, June 1987, p. 70.

BARD, RAY, and SUSAN K. ELLIOGG, *The National Director of Corporate Training Programs* (New York: Doubleday, 1988), pp. 351–352.

BARRIER, MICHAEL, "Walton's Mountain," *Nation's Business,* April 1988, pp. 18–20+.

BEAMER, WAYNE, "Discount King Invades Marketer Territory," *National Petroleum,* April 1988, pp. 15–16.

BERGMAN, JOAN, "Saga of Sam Walton," *Stores,* January 1988, pp. 129–130+.

BLUMENTHAL, KAREN, "Marketing with Emotion: Wal-Mart Shows the Way," *Wall Street Journal,* November 20, 1989, p. B3.

BRADFORD, MICHAEL, "Receiver Sues to Recoup Com Payments," *Business Insurance,* September 11, 1989, p. 68.

BRAGG, ARTHUR, "Wal-Mart's War on Reps," *Sales & Marketing Management,* March 1987, pp. 41–43.

BRAUER, MOLLY, "Sam's: Setting a Fast Pace," *Chain Store Age Executive,* August 1983, pp. 20–21.

BROOKMAN, FAYE, "Will Patriotic Purchasing Pay Off?" *Chain Store Age,* General Merchandise Edition, June 1985, p. 95.

CAMINITI, SUSAN, "What Ails Retailing," *Fortune,* January 30, 1989, pp. 63–64.

COCHRAN, THOMAS N., "Chain Reaction," *Barron's,* October 16, 1989, p. 46.

CORWIN, PAT, JAY L. JOHNSON, and RENEE M. ROULAND, "Made in U.S.A.," *Discount Merchandiser,* November 1989, pp. 48–52.

"David Glass's Biggest Job Is Filling Sam's Shoes," *Business Month,* December 1988, p. 42.

"Discounters Commit to Bar-code Scanning," *Chain Store Age Executive,* September 1985, pp. 49–50.

"The Early Days: Walton Kept Adding 'a Few More' Stores," *Discount Store News,* December 9, 1985, p. 61.

EDGERTON, JERRY, and JORDAN E. GOODMAN, "Wal-Mart for Hypergrowth," *Money,* March 1988, p. 12.

ENDICOTT, R. CRAIG, " '86 Ad Spending Soars," *Advertising Age,* November 23, 1987, pp. S-2+.

ENDICOTT, R. CRAIG, "Leading National Advertisers (Companies Ranked 101–200)," *Advertising Age,* November 21, 1988, pp. S-1+.

"Explosive Decade," *Financial World,* April 4–17, 1984, p. 92.

"Facts about Wal-Mart Stores, Inc.," Press Release, Corporate and Public Affairs, Wal-Mart Stores.

FISHER, CHRISTY, and JUDITH GRAHAM, "Wal-Mart Throws 'Green' Gauntlet," *Advertising Age,* August 21, 1989, pp. 1+.

FISHER, CHRISTY, and PATRICIA STRAND, "Wal-Mart Pulls Back on Hypermart Plans," *Advertising Age,* February 19, 1990, p. 49.

"The Five Best-Managed Companies," *Dun's Business Month,* December 1982, p. 47.

GILLIAM, MARGARET A., "Wal-Mart and the Investment Community," *Discount Merchandiser,* November 1989, pp. 64+.

"Glass Is CEO at Wal-Mart," *Discount Merchandiser,* March 1988, pp. 6+.

"Great News: A Recession," *Forbes,* January 8, 1990, p. 194.

GRUBER, CHRISTINA, "Will Competition Wilt Rose's," *Chain Store Age,* General Merchandise Edition, May 1984, p. 40.

HARTNETT, MICHAEL, "Resurgence in the Sunbelt," *Chain Store Age,* General Merchandise Edition, October 1985, pp. 13–15.

HELLIKER, KEVIN, "Wal-Mart's Store of the Future Blends Discount Prices, Department-Store Feel," *Wall Street Journal,* May 17, 1991, pp. B1, B8.

HIGGINS, KEVIN T., "Wal-Mart: A Pillar in a Thousand Communities," *Building Supply Home Centers,* February 1988, pp. 100–102.

HUEY, JOHN, "America's Most Successful Merchant," *Fortune,* September 23, 1991, pp. 46–48+.

HUEY, JOHN, "Wal-Mart, Will It Take over the World?" *Fortune,* January 30, 1989, pp. 52–56+.

"Hypermart*USA Makes a Few Adjustments," *Chain Store Age Executive,* May 1988, p. 278.

"In Retail, Bigger Can Be Better," *Business Week,* March 27, 1989, p. 90.

"Jack Shewmaker, Vice Chairman, Wal-Mart Stores, Inc.," *Discount Merchandiser,* November 1987, pp. 26+.

JACOBER, STEVE, "Wal-Mart: A Boon to U.S. Vendors," *Discount Merchandiser,* November 1989, pp. 41–46.

JACOBER, STEVE, "Wal- Mart: A Retailing Catalyst," *Discount Merchandiser,* November 1989, pp. 54–58.

JOHNSON, JAY L., "Are We Ready for Big Changes?" *Discount Merchandiser,* August 1989, pp. 48, 53–54.

JOHNSON, JAY L., "The Future of Retailing," *Discount Merchandiser,* January 1990, pp. 70+.

JOHNSON, JAY L., "Hypermart*USA Does a Repeat Performance," *Discount Merchandiser,* March 1988, pp. 52+.

JOHNSON, JAY L., "Hypermarkets and Supercenters—Where Are They Heading?" *Discount Merchandiser,* November 1989, pp. 60+.

JOHNSON, JAY L., "Internal Communication: A Key to Wal-Mart's Success," *Discount Merchandiser,* November 1989, pp. 68+.

JOHNSON, JAY L., "The Supercenter Challenge," *Discount Merchandiser,* August 1989, pp. 70+.

JOHNSON, JAY L., "Supercenters: Wal-Mart's Future?" Discount Merchandiser, May 1988, pp. 26+.

JOHNSON, JAY L., "Walton Honored by Harvard Business School Club," *Discount Merchandiser,* June 1990, pp. 30, 34.

KEITH, BILL, "Wal-Mart Places Special Emphasis on Pharmacy," *Drug Topics,* July 17, 1989, pp. 16–17.

KELLY, KEVIN, "Sam Walton Chooses a Chip off the Old CEO," *Business Week,* February 15, 1988, p. 29.

KELLY, KEVIN, "Wal-Mart Gets Lost in the Vegetable Isle," *Business Week,* May 28, 1990, p. 48.

KERR, DICK, "Wal-Mart Steps up 'Buy American,'" *Housewares,* March 7–13, 1986, pp. 1+.

KLAPPER, MARVIN, "Wal-Mart Chairman Says His Buy American Program Working," *Women's Wear Daily,* December 3, 1985, p. 8.

"Leader in New Construction," *Chain Store Age Executive,* November 1985, p. 46.

LLOYD, BRUCE A., "Wal-Mart to Build Major Distribution Center in Loveland, Colorado," *Site Selection,* June 1989, pp. 634–635.

"Management Style: Sam Moore Walton," *Business Month,* May 1989, p. 38.

MARSCH, BARBARA, "The Challenge: Merchants Mobilize to Battle Wal-Mart in a Small Community," *Wall Street Journal,* June 5, 1991, pp. A1, A4.

MASON, TODD, "Sam Walton of Wal-Mart: Just Your Basic Homespun Billionaire," *Business Insurance,* October 14, 1985, pp. 142–143+.

MCLEOD, DOUGLAS, "Micro Exceeded Authority on Wal-Mart Cover: Judge," *Business Insurance,* July 20, 1987, p. 28.

"$90 Million Expansion Bill at Wal-Mart," *Chain Store Age Executive,* November 1982, p. 73.

"Number of Units Set to Climb by 62%," *Chain Store Age Executive,* November 1983, p. 34.

"Our People Make the Difference: The History of Wal-Mart," Video Cassette (Bentonville, Arkansas: Wal-Mart Video Productions, 1991).

PADGETT, TIM, "Just Saying No to Wal-Mart," *Newsweek,* November 13, 1989, p. 65.

"Perspectives on Discount Retailing," *Discount Merchandiser,* April 1987, pp. 44+.

RAWN, CYNTHIA DUNN, "Wal-Mart vs. Main Street," *American Demographics,* June 1990, pp. 58–59.

REED, SUSAN, "Talk About a Local Boy Making Good: Sam Walton, the King of Wal-Mart, Is America's Second-Richest Man," *People,* December 19, 1983, pp. 133+.

REIER, SHARON, "CEO of the Decade: Sam M. Walton," *Financial World,* April 4, 1989, pp. 56–57.

"Rex Chase—Pure Wal-Mart Lore," *Chain Store Age,* General Merchandise Edition, March 1983, p. 35.

RUDNITSKY, HOWARD, "How Sam Walton Does It," *Forbes,* August 16, 1982, pp. 42–44.

RUDNITSKY, HOWARD, "Play It Again Sam," *Forbes,* August 10, 1987, p. 48.

"Sam Moore Walton," *Business Month,* May 1989, p. 38.

"Sam Walton, the Retail Giant: Where Does He Go from Here?" *Drug Topics,* July 17, 1989, p. 6.

"Sam's Wholesale Club Racks up $1.6 Billion in Sales in 1986," *Discount Merchandiser,* February 1987, p. 26.

SAPORITO, BILL, "The Mad Rush to Join the Warehouse Club," *Fortune,* January 6, 1986, pp. 59+.

SCHACHNER, MICHAEL, "Wal-Mart Chief Fined $11.5 Million for Court Absence," *Business Insurance,* January 9, 1989, pp. 1+.

SCHWADEL, FRANCINE, "Little Touches Spur Wal-Mart's Rise," *Wall Street Journal,* September 22, 1989, p. B1.

SHEETS, KENNETH R., "How Wal-Mart Hits Main Street," *U.S. News & World Report,* March 13, 1989, pp. 53–55.

"Small Stores Showcase Big Ideas," *Chain Store Age,* General Merchandise Edition, September 1985, pp. 19–20.

"Small Town Hit," *Time,* May 23, 1983, p. 43.

SMITH, SARAH, "America's Most Admired Corporations," *Fortune,* January 29, 1990, pp. 56+.

SPROUT, ALISON L., "America's Most Admired Corporations," *Fortune,* February 11, 1991, pp. 52+.

TAUB, STEPHEN, "Gold Winner: Sam M. Walton of Wal-Mart Stores Takes the Top Prize," *Financial World,* April 15, 1986, pp. 28+.

TAYLOR, MARIANNE, "Wal-Mart Prices Itself in the Market," *Chicago Tribune,* April 28, 1991, Section 7, pp. 1+.

"Tending Wal-Mart's Green Policy," *Advertising Age,* January 29, 1991, pp. 20+.

THURMOND, SHANNON, "Sam Speaks Volumes about New Formats," *Advertising Age,* May 9, 1988, p. S-26.

TRIMBLE, VANCE H., *Sam Walton: The Inside Story of America's Richest Man* (New York: Dutton, 1990).

"Wal-Mart Associates Generate over $5.5 Million for United Way," January 2, 1990, Corporate and Public Affairs, Wal-Mart Stores.

"Wal-Mart Beats the Devil," *Chain Store Age*, August 1986, p. 9.

"Wal-Mart Expands: Tests New 'Wholesale' Concept," *Chain Store Age*, General Merchandise Edition, June 1983, p. 98.

"Wal-Mart Has No Quarrel with 1984," *Chain Store Age*, General Merchandise Edition, June 1985, p. 36.

"Wal-Mart on the Move," *Progressive Grocer*, August 1987, p. 9.

"Wal-Mart Policy Asks for Supplier Commitment," *Textile World*, May 1985, pp. 27–28.

"Wal-Mart Raises over $3 Million for Children's Hospital," Press Release, June 1989, Corporate and Public Affairs, Wal-Mart Stores.

"Wal-Mart Rolls out Its Supercenters," *Chain Store Age Executive*, December 1988, pp. 18–19.

"Wal-Mart Stores Penny Wise," *Business Month*, December 1988, p. 42.

"Wal-Mart: The Model Discounter," *Dun's Business Month*, December 1982, pp. 60–61.

"Wal-Mart to Acquire McLane, Distributor to Retail Industry," *Wall Street Journal*, October 2, 1990, p. A8.

"Wal-Mart's Glass to Reps: 'That's a Bunch of Baloney!'" *Discount Merchandiser*, September 1987, p. 12.

"Wal-Mart's Goals," *Discount Merchandiser*, January 1988, pp. 48–50.

"Wal-Mart Goes on Its Own," *Progressive Grocer*, June 1987, p. 9.

"Wal-Mart's 'Green' Campaign to Emphasize Recycling Next," *Adweek's Marketing Week*, February 12, 1990, pp. 60–61.

"Wal-Mart's 1990 Look," *Discount Merchandiser*, July 1989, p. 12.

WEINER, STEVE, "Golf Balls, Motor Oil, and Tomatoes," *Forbes*, October 30, 1989, pp. 130–131+.

WEINER, STEVE, "Pssst! Wanna buy a Watch? A Suit? How about a Whole Department Store?" *Forbes*, January 8, 1990, pp. 192+.

"Wholesale Clubs," *Discount Merchandiser*, November 1987, pp. 26+.

"Why Wal-Mart Is Recession Proof," *Business Week*, February 22, 1988, p. 146.

"Work, Ambition—Sam Walton," Press Release, June 1990, Corporate and Public Affairs, Wal-Mart Stores.

ZWEIG, JASON, "Expand It Again, Sam," *Forbes*, July 9, 1990, p. 106.

APPENDIX 9.A   Wal-Mart Stores, Inc.—Financial Performance (In thousands except per share data)[a]

10-Year Financial Summary	1982	1983	1984	1985	1986	1987	1988	1989	1990	1991
Earnings										
Net Sales	$2,444,997	$3,376,252	$4,666,909	$6,400,861	$8,451,489	$11,900,076	$15,959,255	$20,649,001	$25,810,656	$32,601,594
Licensed Department Rentals and Other Income—Net	17,650	22,435	36,031	52,167	55,127	84,623	104,783	136,867	174,644	261,814
Cost of Sales	1,787,496	2,458,235	3,418,025	4,722,440	6,361,271	9,053,219	12,281,744	16,056,856	20,070,034	25,499,834
Operating, Selling, and General and Administrative Expenses	495,010	677,020	892,887	1,181,455	1,485,210	2,007,645	2,599,367	3,267,864	4,069,695	5,152,178
Interest Costs										
Debt	16,053	20,297	4,935	5,207	1,903	10,422	25,262	36,286	20,346	42,716
Capital Leases	15,351	18,570	29,946	42,506	54,640	76,367	88,995	99,395	117,725	125,920
Taxes on Income	65,943	100,416	160,903	230,653	276,119	395,940	441,027	488,246	631,600	751,736
Net Income	$ 82,794	$ 124,140	$ 196,244	$ 270,767	$ 327,473	$ 450,086	$ 627,743	$ 837,221	$ 1,075,900	$ 1,291,024
Financial Position										
Current Assets	589,161	720,537	1,005,567	1,303,254	1,784,275	2,353,271	2,905,145	3,630,987	4,712,616	6,414,775
Net Property, Plant, Equipment, and Capital Leases	333,026	457,509	628,151	870,309	1,303,450	1,676,282	2,144,852	2,661,954	3,430,059	4,712,039
Total Assets	937,513	1,187,448	1,652,254	2,205,229	3,103,645	4,049,092	5,131,809	6,359,668	8,198,484	11,388,915
Current Liabilities	339,961	347,318	502,763	688,968	992,683	1,340,291	1,743,763	2,065,909	2,845,315	3,990,414
Long-Term Debt	104,581	106,465	40,866	41,237	180,682	179,234	185,672	184,439	185,152	740,254
Long-Term Obligations under Capital Leases	154,196	222,610	339,930	449,886	595,205	764,128	866,972	1,009,046	1,087,403	1,158,621
Preferred Stock with Mandatory Redemption Provisions	7,438	6,861	6,411	5,874	4,902					
Shareholders' Equity	$ 323,942	$ 488,109	$ 737,503	$ 984,672	$1,277,659	$1,690,493	$ 2,257,267	$ 3,007,909	$ 3,965,561	$ 5,365,524
Stores in Operation at the End of this Period										
Wal-Mart Stores	491	551	642	745	859	980	1,114	1,259	1,402	1,573
Sam's Wholesale Clubs	—	—	3	11	23	49	84	105	123	148

Source: Wal-Mart Annual Report, January 31, 1991

[a] On beginning year balance.

_____ CASE 21 _____

Verbatim Challenges 3M for Market Leadership

A satisfied smile appeared on Bob Falco's face as he was reading the January 19, 1992, issue of *PcWeek*. As manager of branded marketing at Verbatim, he was pleased with the figures he saw in the computer publication. According to figures released by the Santa Clara Consulting Group, 3M had a 15.5 percent share of the floppy disk market, and Verbatim was right behind the market leader with a 15.2 percent share. "We *are* going to be the leader in this market," he though to himself. "But we're more than just a floppy disk manufacturer. With our excellent tape storage products and optical disk technology, we're going to be the leader in the overall computer media market."

COMPANY HISTORY

In 1969, Information Terminals Corporation was formed in Sunnyvale, California, to manufacture computer screens (terminals). In the early days, there was virtually no competition and profits for the company and its distributors were substantial. However, as personal computer use in business expanded rapidly, competitors entered the market and the high costs of producing screens persuaded the company managers to look to more profitable emerging markets and products. Recognizing that the sales potential for magnetic recording materials for personal computers was much larger than that of computer screens, the company began manufacturing 8″ floppy disks and changed its name to Verbatim. Research and development concentrated on digital data cassettes and floppy disks. Having the new technology for data storage available during rapid market growth, management was in a position to choose a few key distributors; they refused other potential distributors in order to enhance the profit potential for both Verbatim and its selected distributors.

Attracted by the projected $4 billion market, a number of competitors entered the floppy disk field in the late 1970s and early 1980s and threatened

This case was prepared by Linda E. Swayne, Peter M. Ginter, and Chris M. Tucker as a basis for class discussion rather than to illustrate either effective or ineffective handling of an administrative situation. The authors wish to thank Bob Falco and Carol Hull, Verbatim Corporation, for their assistance. Used with permission from Linda E. Swayne.

Verbatim's dominant position.[1] Competitors such as 3M, Maxwell, Fuji, and Sony all looked for ways to differentiate their products. In the early 1980s, Verbatim was slow to adapt to the increasingly competitive market. "For a number of years Verbatim was making a lot of money and increasing its business—and that hid a lot of sins," said Bob Falco, Verbatim's manager of North American branded marketing. Several distributors began to carry the products of Verbatim's new competitors. These distributors were the very ones that Verbatim had previously refused to supply. When the marketplace continued expanding, many of these distributors in turn refused to deal with Verbatim.

Because of substantial reductions in profits, Verbatim cut 127 U.S. staff positions in November 1984 to reduce costs.[2] At the same time, the company invested more than $40 million in the development of 3.5″ diskettes for personal computers under the DataLife label.[3] Leading the demand for higher disk capacities was the rapid expansion in user data bases. Software programs required more storage capacity. Generally, the easier new software programs were to use, the more sophisticated the set of instructions had to be between the software and the computer and the greater the disk capacity. Software programs were becoming available to the general consumer during this time and the popular IBM-PC required higher capacity disks.

The Kodak Era

In 1985, Eastman Kodak acquired Verbatim for $175 million and changed the company's marketing focus, manufacturing methods, and channels of distribution.[4] Kodak had been buying 8″, 5.25″, and 3.5″ disks from Xidex (a competitor of Verbatim) for over a year before the purchase, and Kodak marketed a line of accessories including computer paper, printer stands, and surge suppressors. A new philosophy came to Verbatim with the transfer of ownership to Kodak: Product development was the key to increasing success. Both Kodak- and Verbatim-brand diskettes were available from Verbatim. Although Kodak-brand diskettes were a late entrant to the disk market, the high brand recognition for the Kodak name enabled the company to be a major competitor in the branded market. Mass merchandisers such as discount stores, warehouse clubs, and other retailers were particularly accepting of the Kodak name because of its recognition by consumers.

Sweeping changes occurred in 1987 with the hiring of Mark Welland as Verbatim vice president of North American marketing and sales. Welland, the former national sales and marketing manager for Maxell, recognized that prices for floppy disks were plummeting and concentrated on repositioning the majority of Verbatim's sales from low-priced, nonlabeled disks for the original equipment

---

[1] "Malcolm Northrup Needs a Flip-flop," *Industry Week,* January 7, 1985, p. 58.
[2] Ibid.
[3] Ibid.
[4] Sue Kapp, "Mechanic for Mending," *Business Marketing,* June 1988, p. 8.

manufacturer (OEM) market to a premium-priced floppy disk manufacturer for the branded market. Ironically, the fact that Verbatim already was a low-cost producer had allowed it to remain in business during the shake-out years in the mid-1980s. Welland wanted not only to be successful in the market, but to be first in the market with new products. Under Welland's direction, all efforts were put into branded items, especially the disks differentiated by a patented Teflon coating. The DataLifePlus brand name was superscripted by "Verbatim—A Kodak Company." The diskette line was extended with the addition of the Bonus brand for the price-sensitive market.

Mitsubishi Takes Over

Announced in March 1990 and completed in May 1990, Kodak sold Verbatim to Mitsubishi Kasei, the chemical division of the $9 billion Japanese conglomerate. Industry experts believed the undisclosed price to be $240 million, $65 million more than Eastman Kodak paid for Verbatim in 1985.[5]

A year before acquiring Verbatim, Mitsubishi had started manufacturing 3.5" disks under its own brand as well as other OEM diskettes in its Chesapeake, Virginia, facility. As a late entrant in the industry, Mitsubishi found it difficult to build brand awareness against 3M, Verbatim, Sony, and other well-established competitors. Therefore, Mitsubishi purchased Verbatim for its established brand name, distribution channels, and market share. Kodak agreed to allow Mitsubishi to continue using the Kodak name until May 1992, which provided Welland and Falco, who both continued with Verbatim after the sale, some time to formulate new marketing and promotional strategies.

The purchase of Verbatim by Mitsubishi offered a much-needed capital infusion that was limited under Kodak's ownership. Mitsubishi management subscribed to the belief inherent in many Japanese companies: Invest heavily in the present with an eye on long-term profitability. Mitsubishi provided more capital for Welland's ongoing advertising campaign. In contrast, Kodak had been lean in advertising dollars allotted directly to Verbatim and the DataLife brand. Instead, Kodak depended on increased sales through corporate advertising of its name, which capitalized on the fact that Kodak was the second most recognized name in the world (behind Coca-Cola).

THE INDUSTRY

The deluge of technology in the computer industry changed the way America did business. The introduction of the personal computer gave individual workers the power to write and edit documents, produce electronic spreadsheets, and compile large databases. Not only could businesspeople hook up to a company's mainframe, they could do it away from the office. The lap-top computer

[5] Clifford Glickman, "After Floppies, What?" *Charlotte Observer*, January 7, 1991, p. 7D.

meant that professionals could sit in a customer's office and work as easily as if they were sitting in their own office. Computer purchasers appeared to be interested in greater use of color and graphics, the ability to store more information on a single disk, and higher-quality printers.

In 1991, most Americans were concerned with the continuing weak economy. As a result of low consumer confidence and rising unemployment, Americans became extremely conscious of their spending behavior especially for big-ticket items such as personal computers. PCs at the office were considered a necessity. Although office managers were cutting operating costs, computer disks were not something that could be eliminated. In part because of the economy, more people were working at home. According to Falco, "The home office is driving the business now." Sales of diskettes to this market were up substantially. On the other hand, personal computers purchased for recreational use at home were considered to be a luxury, and disk expenditures by the recreational user were expected to decrease. The costs of manufacturing data storage products, such as rewritable optical disks and 8-mm and 4-mm tape products, were expected to rise as new technologies were researched and implemented. As a result, a highly competitive industry would have to be even more concerned with differentiating its products on something other than price.

The computer media market boasted $1.8 billion in total sales during 1990 as compared to $1.2 billion in 1989. Twenty-seven percent of the sales were attributed to 5.25" disks, while 3.5" disks made up over 30 percent of sales. Exhibit 21.1 outlines the market share for the various computer media. The overall growth of the 5.25" and the 3.5" segment of the media market averaged about 25 percent in the first three quarters of 1989. Sales of 5.25" diskettes did not decline as much as was forecasted but did decline about 3 percent because of the weakening demand for low-end machines for the home market. Sales of high-density (HD) 3.5" disks increased slightly, although they represented less than 20 percent of the total 3.5" units sold.[6]

EXHIBIT 21.1   Computer Media Market Shares

Medium	Percent Share
1/2" Reel-to-Reel Tape	16
1/2" Tape Cartridges	2
8" Disks	11
5.25" Disks	27
3.5" Disks	30
Data Cartridges	14

Source: "Floppy Disks," *Purchasing*, February 22, 1990, p. 76.

[6] "Say Good-bye to 3.5" Disk Shortage," *Purchasing*, February 20, 1990, p. 76.

EXHIBIT 21.2   **Sales of Disks Worldwide, All Formats**

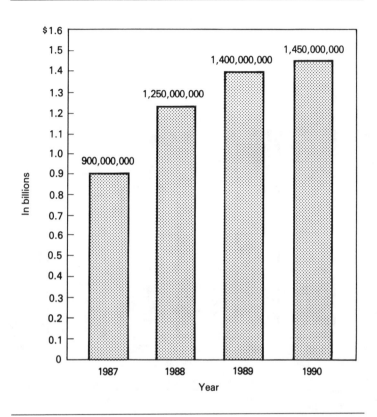

Source: Santa Clara Consulting Group.

According to the Santa Clara Consulting Group, worldwide sales of floppy disks in 1990 increased slightly above 1989 sales (Exhibit 21.2). Computer Industry Forecasts, published by the Data Analysis Group, projected 1991 sales of floppy disks to be $2.7 billion.[7]

Magnetic floppy disks were viewed as commodities, and price competition was fierce. Welland stated, "We've experienced a price erosion of about 23 percent in 1990 and about the same the year before. It was probably the purest form of open market competition—but brutal competition." Exhibit 21.3 provides the average price of 5.25″ floppy disks from 1985 to 1990. Although the price of branded double-density (DD) 5.25″ disks and generic brands fell drastically (to as low as 17 cents each), the introduction of HD 5.25″ disks kept the average higher.

[7] Computer Industry Forecast, Data Analysis Group, Georgetown, California, first quarter report, 1991.

EXHIBIT 21.3   Average Price for All 5.25" Floppy Disks, 1985–1990

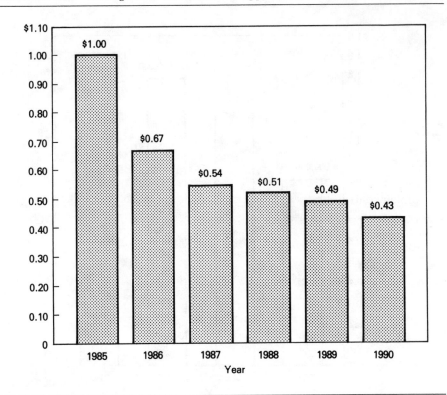

Source: Santa Clara Consulting Group.

Interestingly, worldwide sales of computers were expected to grow by only 6.5 percent in 1991, compared to the 8.4 percent growth in 1990. Personal computer sales were forecasted to drop from 13 percent of the market to 8 percent.[8] Slow sales growth could be partially attributed to fears of recession, office budget cutting, and a slowdown in the switching from large computer systems to less expensive desktop systems in business.[9] Price competition was expected to limit lap-top and microcomputer revenues in 1991.

COMPETITION

Verbatim was faced with a number of key competitors in a highly competitive industry. Several of the competitors such as 3M, Maxell, Sony, and

[8] John W. Verity, "Computers Will See Lots of Downtime," *Business Week*, January 14, 1991, p. 101.
[9] David P. Brousell, "Industry Outlook—1991," *Datamation*, January 1, 1991, p. 38.

BASF had highly recognized brand names that were used on a variety of products with synergistic effects.

"The market for data storage products contains three segments: premium, price, and economy," according to Falco. The premium market segment included 3M, Verbatim, Sony, and Maxell brands. Fuji, BASF, and Memorex competed in the price segment, which was typically 15 percent lower in price than the premium brands. The economy segment featured value through lower prices achieved by lower manufacturing costs and included the Bonus, TDK, and Highland (3M) brands. The premium category accounted for approximately 60 percent of the market. The remaining 40 percent of the market was divided between the price segment and the economy segment.

Verbatim operated primarily in the premium market. Although the majority of its products were targeted to the upper end of the mass market, Verbatim maintained its Bonus brand diskette at the lower end of the market. "This product is offered for people who want a quality brand name and are value conscious. They don't want the cheapest thing they can find, but a brand name they recognize and trust at a moderate price point," Falco stated.

Figures from a 1990 Magnetic Media Industry report for 1989 activity placed Verbatim as third in market share with 8.59 percent of the industry (Exhibit 21.4). The category leader, 3M, had 12.14 percent market share. Maxell (Hitachi) held the second position with 10.96 percent share. Falco commented that the January 1992 figures placed Verbatim second to 3M in market share worldwide. He felt that the market was so fiercely competitive that each quarter could register a different market share leader from among the top three. Companies have literally

EXHIBIT 21.4   Revenue and Unit Market Share Data for Floppy Disks

Company	Revenues (In millions)	Percent Total Industry Revenues	Percent Total Industry Units
3M	$205	12.14	12.13
Hitachi/Maxell	185	10.96	9.37
Verbatim	145	8.59	8.46
Sony	117	6.93	6.22
Xidex	99	5.86	9.62
BASF	93	5.51	5.59
Kao	92	5.45	3.87
Fuji	78	4.62	4.06
TDK	67	3.97	3.92
Nashua	35	2.07	2.66
Totals	$1,116	66.10	65.90

Source: Magnetic Media Information Services Floppy Disk Industry Report, February 15, 1990.

come and gone in the 1980s. Xidex, Elephant, and Syncom have all left the industry, although newcomers, primarily from Japan and Mexico, appeared occasionally.

A major factor affecting competition in the data storage industry was that the products (primarily diskettes) were relatively undifferentiated. The market was characterized by increasing technological advances by manufacturers that kept attempting to differentiate the products. Rumors were always circulating that some brands with low market share would be pulling out of the diskette market as competition heated up.

3M

Although the market share leader, 3M had only established disk production in the early 1980s and it represented only a small part of the multi-billion-dollar company. 3M was a strong global competitor in all areas of marketing, manufacturing, and distribution with worldwide visibility. In 1992, it was the only large U.S. manufacturer of diskettes that offered a complete line of media as well as many other well-known office products (Scotch tape, Post-It Notes, and so forth). The company had a strong reputation as a creative innovator of quality products. Considered the technology leader, 3M committed significant resources to R&D.

Maxell

Hitachi-Maxell was one division of Hitachi, Limited, Japan's largest electrical and electronics manufacturer. Maxell began disk production in the late 1970s; diskettes accounted for approximately 20 percent of the company's total business. The company has a reputation for high quality, especially in audio-visual products. Although it did not manufacture a full line of computer media, the company did produce diskettes and 4-mm and 8-mm tape, and purchased data cartridges with its brand name on them.

Sony

Sony Corporation was a leading manufacturer of electronic and entertainment products. In the United States, Sony's business activities shifted from electronics to entertainment with the purchase of CBS Records in 1988 and Columbia in 1989. Sony and the Japanese electronics conglomerate, Matsushita, developed a 2″ disk in 1988 and claimed that these would eventually be the industry standard. As of early 1992, this had not occurred.

Sony produced a full product line of computer media except for cassettes, 1/2″ reel-to-reel tape, and 1/2″ tape cartridges. Sony supplied many OEM customers with nonlabeled 3.5″ disks and both optical drives and optical disks.

Other Competitors

Fuji and BASF entered into a joint venture to produce 3.5″ disks in the late 1980s. Fuji had strength in the film market, and BASF had a strong brand image in the audio-visual market. Both competed in the lower-priced-value market for computer media. KAO manufactured for the OEM market and private-label customers. The company pursued bulk and bid business based on low prices. Through 1991, KAO had little success in the branded market.

Share of Mind

All of Verbatim's top competitors were manufacturers of a broad range of products that enhanced their ability to generate high levels of awareness through corporate advertising. In 1990 and 1991, 3M and BASF both used mass-media corporate advertising for all their products, which led to high levels of awareness. In 1991, BASF began an advertising campaign that emphasized its role in technological innovation and claimed, "We don't make many of the products you buy—we make them better." In 1989, 3M spent almost three times the level of Verbatim (Exhibit 21.5). Such a large budget enhanced 3M's already high name recognition. 3M, in particular, received the fringe benefit of positive brand perceptions from its many other, quality products.

As indicated in Exhibit 21.6, there seemed to be a lack of consistency among competitors' advertising themes. Campaigns had no central focus or else they held the focus for a short period of time. Exhibit 21.6 summarizes the advertising campaigns of Verbatim's major competitors.

A top-of-mind awareness survey completed in 1991 by Verbatim found 3M leading, followed by Maxell, and then Verbatim (Exhibit 21.7). This corresponded to market-share sales figures (in Exhibit 21.5).

EXHIBIT 21.5   Competitive Advertising Expenditures, 1989

Company	1989 Total Diskette Advertising Budget	Percent of Total
3M	$2,705,716	40
Maxell	1,214,368	18
BASF	1,113,618	16
Verbatim	976,481	14
Sony	542,930	8
Mitsubishi	283,853	4
Totals	$6,836,966	100

Source: Kodak in-house study, 1989.

EXHIBIT 21.6   Advertising Campaigns of Major Competitors

3M

1988–89 Theme:	"Supporting the Dream."
Ad Message:	Teamwork that provides you with technological breakthroughs, superior quality and selection.
1990 Theme:	No consistent tag line, emphasis on reliability.
Ad Message:	"Wanted for breaking Murphy's Law" (3M diskettes); exclusive formulation and "Mark Q" manufacturing process. Secondary emphasis on convenience (preformatted diskettes).
Promotions:	11th disk free.

Maxell

1988–89 Theme:	"The Gold Standard."
Ad Message:	Maximum safety and reliability: "Ten times more reliable than conventional floppy disks, twice the durability, twice the resistance to dirt and dust."
1990 Theme:	"The Gold Standard."

BASF

1988–89 Theme:	"The Spirit of Innovation."
Ad Message:	100% error free, compatibility, data protection.
1990 Theme:	"Try it. Depend on it."
Promotions:	Cash sweepstakes.

Sony

1988–89 Theme:	"Sony. The One and Only" (corporatewide).
Ad Message:	World leader in high-densisty magnetic media.
1990 Theme:	No consistent tag line.
Ad Message:	Reliability.

EXHIBIT 21.7   Top-of-Mind Awareness for the Major Floppy Disk Competitors

Company	Percent Unaided Awareness*
3M	45
Maxell	24
Verbatim	23
Sony	16
BASF	7
Fuji	3

* Multiple responses

Source: Verbatim floppy disk tracking study, 1991.

VERBATIM CORPORATION MISSION

The mission of Verbatim was to be the recognized leader of the magnetic and optical media-data storage industry by being a profitable, worldwide quality manufacturer and marketer.

Verbatim Corporate Vision

Verbatim, on a worldwide basis, will:

- Be obsessed with customer satisfaction.
- Be known for product quality.
- Be dedicated to continuous quality improvement.
- Be a technology leader, positioned to provide new products to our customers when needed.
- Give people the information and resources necessary to continuously improve quality to their customers.
- Be #1 in revenue market share.
- Nurture partnerships with our suppliers to meet or exceed our quality goals.

Having purchased Verbatim, Mitsubishi planned to become the leader in diskette revenue market share with a continued emphasis on the most effective use of dollars for advertising, promotions, and new product introductions. CEO Nicky Hartery recently reminded employees of the importance of being ''number one'' in revenue market share as opposed to unit market share by saying, ''You can't deposit units in the bank.'' Verbatim directed its advertising and promotions to attain market share equal to or greater than 3M, the industry leader.

PRODUCT STRATEGY

Product Line

Verbatim manufactured and marketed a wide variety of data storage media including magnetic storage media (floppy disks) and advanced mass storage devices (back-up tapes and optical disks). Exhibit 21.8 shows the Verbatim product line. Floppy disks were produced in 3.5", 5.25", and 8" sizes with varying features and were backed by Verbatim's lifetime guarantee. A new product for this market was the DataLife 3.5" extra-high-density (ED) microdisk that provided 4 MB of storage compared to 1 MB for DD and 2 MB for HD disks.

One segment of mass storage devices included 4-mm and 8-mm computer grade data cartridges, 1/4" data cartridges, high-density streamer cassettes, digital data cassettes, and 1/2" reel tape. These products were used for back-up and restoration of computer files, and archival purposes. As hard drives expanded in size, back-up media increased in importance, as it would take numerous floppy disks to back up a hard drive.

EXHIBIT 21.8   Verbatim's Product Line

OfferThe Best Storage Space InTown.

Offer your customers superior quality Verbatim disks. In addition to our regular line of data storage products, we now offer exciting value-added products like DataLifePlus disks with Teflon® coating, vivid DataLife Colors disks and DataLife factory formatted disks. Plus data cartridges, data cassettes and reel tapes. Which means now your customers can get any kind of data storage they need all from one **Verbatim**

The other segment of mass storage and the newest area for Verbatim was optical disk manufacturing. Within the industry, optical disks came in three formats: ROM (read-only memory), WORM (write once, read many), and rewritable disks. "We are on the threshold of optical being a very big product," Falco stated in 1991. Verbatim was one of the first companies to offer 5.25" rewritable optical disks and the first with the 3.5" rewritable optical disks.

Branded Products

Verbatim continued marketing the DataLife brand after being purchased by Kodak. Kodak wanted to use its name on disks that would be sold in mass merchant outlets because of the high recognition of the brand name. Verbatim and DataLife were better-recognized brand names in computer stores.

In the agreement with Mitsubishi, Kodak allowed Verbatim to use the Kodak name until May of 1992. The transition from Kodak to Verbatim brands progressed smoothly. The Kodak brand was sold primarily by the mass merchants such as Kmart and Target, where Verbatim did not have much brand recognition. While owned by Kodak, the box showed Verbatim in large letters with smaller letters underneath that stated, "A Kodak Company." Throughout 1991, as packages were redesigned, the Kodak brand was deleted. There was some resistance from the mass merchants to the conversion. The Verbatim product did not sell as well as the Kodak brand in the mass market, so at first, Verbatim sales reps had to convince the mass merchants to continue carrying the DataLife product, while advertising and promotion dollars were spent to reach the end user with information about Verbatim's brands. Sales of DataLife increased; most former purchasers of Kodak switched to Verbatim's DataLife.

During the time Kodak was being deleted from packages, there was a great deal of discussion concerning branding. Should Verbatim be the highlighted brand name with DataLife superscripted or subscripted, or should DataLife be highlighted with Verbatim superscripted or subscripted? Or should there be only one brand? If only one brand name was to be selected, should it be Verbatim or DataLife? Although "Verbatim" perfectly expressed the performance wanted from disks, it was difficult for many non-English speaking people to pronounce. As the company supplied media storage worldwide, careful study was required to make the decision.

Product Differentiation

Magnetic Floppy Disks. In 1986, Verbatim introduced an antistatic lining for diskettes called DataHold. It discharged static electricity, protecting disks from data loss. Every disk sold by Verbatim contained this protection.

Verbatim secured a patent on its Teflon coating process introduced in October 1987. DataLifePlus disks were protected from spills, fingerprints, and other office mishaps that might cause data loss. Many computer users were afraid of "mysterious data loss." The Teflon coating allowed the liner to wipe the disk clean inside the jacket as it was being used in the drive. Falco commented, "DataLifePlus is about 20 percent of our business. A lot of people don't worry about data loss until they have lost data." An agreement prohibited DuPont from selling Teflon to other disk manufacturers through 1991 and gave Verbatim a guaranteed, but short-lived competitive advantage in the marketplace. Although competitors could purchase Teflon from Dupont after 1991, they had to develop a process that did not infringe on the Verbatim coating patent. Apparently the competition did not judge the market to be of sufficient size to spend the R&D funds—especially when floppy disks became essentially a commodity product. As of the beginning of 1992, none of the competitors had challenged Verbatim for this segment.

Although Verbatim was the first in October 1987 to offer preformatted diskettes, 3M and others soon followed with this slightly more expensive, but more convenient product. Buyers could purchase diskettes preformatted for any number of machines from IBM and related machines, to Apple Macintosh.

In 1988, Verbatim introduced colored disk jackets for easier office organization. The new jackets tended to be more appealing to the consumer's eye. Branded under the DataLife Colors label, the colored diskettes encouraged brand loyalty by providing continuity to existing color filing systems. Other manufacturers developed their own versions of color disks since Verbatim's introduction.

In late 1990, Verbatim announced an additional enhancement for its 3.5″ disks. Diskettes contained a metal shutter that is worn down by a computer's disk drive over time and could deposit potentially damaging shavings into the disk drive. Verbatim pioneered a flexible, nonmetallic DataSeal shutter that did not wear down and deposit shavings into the computer. Verbatim began shipping the product in March 1991; competitors quickly developed similar protection devices.

Magnetic Tape.   In the spring of 1989, Kodak began to manufacture 1/2″ reel-to-reel computer tape (with finish processing at Verbatim) under the DataLife brand name. However, other competitors, such as 3M, BASF, and Memorex were already established in this mature market. The tape was a late entrant to a mature market; data processing managers were not very interested in any new brands.

Expansion into highest density tape products occurred in 1991. DataLife high capacity tape in 8-mm and 4-mm widths competed against Sony, Maxell, and 3M.

Optical Disks.   Although the technology had been available since 1985, it was not until August 1989 that 3M announced its entrance into the erasable (rewritable) optical disk market. Similar to popular compact disks, this product could be used repeatedly for media storage. One month after 3M, Verbatim announced that it would manufacture optical disks. This new product had required huge cash investments to develop a drastically different manufacturing process. Both Verbatim and 3M hoped that the cost of manufacturing and change in format to optical disks would prevent some competitors from entering the new market.

Unfortunately, purchases of the optical disk drives have not met expectations, thus the demand for optical disks has been disappointing as well. In early 1992, optical disk drives were too slow and expensive to replace magnetic media for most uses. Verbatim was still hoping to capitalize on the erasable optical disks. Unlike regular floppy disks, erasable optical disks were not yet considered commodities; therefore, there was little price erosion. In actuality, optical disks were not positioned to replace floppy disks. Optical disks had a huge storage capacity— 128 megabytes of storage on a 3.5" disk compared to 1 or 2 megabytes for most 3.5" floppies. The 5¼" optical disks store up to 650 MB. The conversion to optical disk drives has been slow because of the high cost of the hardware, but optical drive prices have started to come down. In addition, the optical disks have declined in price. There has been a problem within the industry concerning standardization and compatibility.

The legality of supplying evidence on optical disks was another issue of critical importance. When WORM technology was the only form of optical disk available, legal concerns were not a problem. However, with the development of multifunction disk drives that can use WORM *and* rewritable disks, the courts were not certain how they could be sure that evidence had not been changed. Another unknown, because the product was so new, was the "life" of an optical disk. This was particularly important for hospitals, which required a guarantee that data would "stay" on a disk for a minimum of 25 years.

International Data Corporation expected customers to buy about $100 million worth of erasable optical disks in 1991.[10] Purchasers of optical disks tend to be involved with huge data storage needs such as libraries, government agencies, and large corporations. Some industry analysts expected optical disks to develop into an economical and popular product. Others felt that optical disks would never achieve more than a limited share of the market, and still others predicted that the 3.5" optical disk would eventually replace the floppy disk. IBM introduced new personal computers that could use 3.5" optical disks in June 1991.

Sony was expected to announce a 2.5" optical disk drive in late 1992. It would combine video, audio, and data into a process called optical imaging. The new drive would require further miniaturization of optical disks.

THE FLOPPY DISK CUSTOMER

Verbatim's products were directed at two broad categories of users, the original equipment manufacturer market and the branded market. Exhibit 21.9 contains a summary of the computer media market. In the OEM market, manufacturers produced nonlabeled diskettes for companies that developed software packages or manufactured hardware that included operating system software. Lotus and Microsoft were two of Verbatim's OEM customers. Labels were added

---

[10] "Say Good-bye," p. 76.

EXHIBIT 21.9   Verbatim Market Opportunities

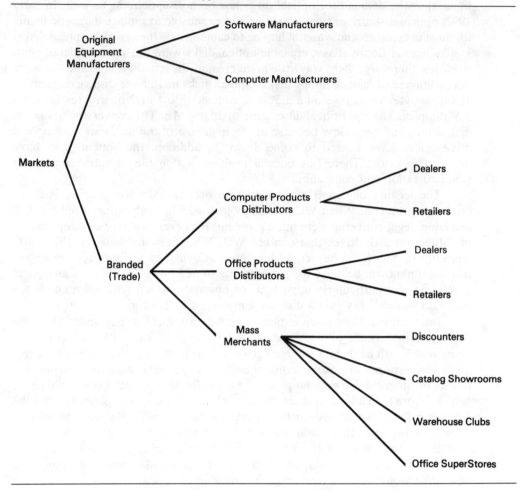

carrying the name of the purchaser rather than Verbatim's name. The branded market consisted of buyers who purchased Verbatim brands of unformatted or preformatted diskettes for personal or business use.

The OEM Market

Verbatim enjoyed a strong position in the OEM market. In fact, Verbatim was the largest nonlabeled supplier in the United States to OEMs and software publishers. The price competition in the OEM market forced Verbatim to search for economies in production and for product differentiation through quality and service. To speed delivery, Verbatim established East and West Coast distribution facilities. Although price remained an important factor, Verbatim differentiated its product through quality, durability, and meeting customers' specifications; these factors carried more weight with hardware and software producers when purchasing diskettes that would/bear their company's name. Quality was an extremely important factor in the OEM market, and Verbatim's reputation for quality products anchored its strong position in this area.

The Branded Market

The branded market was very price competitive at all levels. According to Falco, "Salespeople frequently come to me and say, 'I can sell 20,000 more diskettes to this account if we lower the price by 10 cents a diskette,' and I tell them that's not the type of business we're after. We could have made $40 million more in 1990 if we could have maintained the same price levels that existed in 1989." Despite the price decline, Verbatim continued to give attention to research and development of new products in addition to its enhancement of existing products. Falco characterized the market as a "pennies industry" alluding to the fact that margins are constantly squeezed by price competition on one side and R&D, production, and new technology costs on the other.

The branded market can be divided into home users or business users, buying from Verbatim's trade customers. Bob Falco commented, "Media Market Research profiled the end user, whether he or she is a home or office user, to be 35 years old; well educated; high income; married with children; a reader who is interested in new products, electronics, self-improvement and investments; and an active participant in individual sports activities."

Home Users. In 1992, more than 26 million Americans performed job-related work at home. By 1993, that number was predicted to reach nearly 35 million. According to LINK Resources, a research and consulting firm, there were several different categories of homeworkers. These included salaried corporate employees, self-employed workers, contract workers, and freelancers. LINK profiled the average homeworker as 39 years old, part of a dual-career family with a family income of $42,000. This was and will be an important market for Verbatim as the numbers continue to grow. The phenomenal growth of homeworkers was credited for much of the growth in sales for office equipment, including copiers, fax units, calculators, and computers. The annual investment in home-office equipment including computers, copiers, fax units, calculators, and cellular phones in 1989 was $5.3 billion, and experts predicted 1993 sales to top $8.4 billion.[11]

Business Users. The profile of users in a large business was similar to other end users, although their purchasing patterns were different. Large companies tended to have longer sales cycles, to buy in larger quantities, to buy in a highly organized

---

[11] "Working at Home: Growth Is Phenomenal," *The Office*, March 1991, p. 58.

fashion, and to look for value-added services. Seventy percent of large businesses purchased diskettes through a central purchasing agent primarily for efficiency and lower costs. Instead of multiple departments within a company each placing a single order, purchasing needs were pooled and one large order for one brand was placed, generally earning significant quantity discounts.

According to a 1987 in-house study by Kodak, business users had slightly larger diskette libraries than home users. Whether business or home user, the largest acquisition of disks occurred during the first year of computer usage. Hard disk drive owners purchased more disks in the first year, but that dropped off more in the second year than that of the nonowner of a hard disk drive. Both business and home users generally owned two brands of disks.

Trade Customers. Verbatim sold branded products to various channel members (the trade) to resell to a variety of end users. The trade audience included computer distributors, computer dealers/retailers, software dealers/retailers, national/regional wholesalers, and office megastores such as Staples, Office Depot, and OW (Office Warehouse). Mass merchants could be divided into discount chains, catalog showrooms, warehouse clubs, hypermarkets, and drugstore chains.

A shift was under way in the branded market as sales of diskettes at computer specialty stores were leveling off but increasing in superstores such as Sam's Wholesale, Pace, Office Depot, and Office America. This was attributed to growing computer literacy among end users who once felt that a specialist was needed to aid in the selection of diskettes. Verbatim shifted much of its advertising and promotional attention to end users to correspond with this trend.

ADVERTISING AND OTHER PROMOTIONAL STRATEGIES AT VERBATIM

In 1991, Verbatim used its promotional budget to shift away from "push" advertising to the trade toward a focus on "pull" advertising to end users. Verbatim's advertising and promotion had become more dedicated to this facet of the business. Verbatim's branded advertising objectives included:

- Increasing brand name and advertising awareness levels of Verbatim above 3M,
- Establishing a preference for Verbatim,
- Establishing a specific position for Verbatim and its brands,
- Creating advertising that supports the chosen position and,
- Supporting the advertising program with sales promotions and public relations.

Verbatim used both vertical and horizontal trade publications. Full-page ads in the typical computer publications such as *Byte* and *PcWeek* were used to reach a variety of users. The vertical publications included magazines that specialized in the hospital, accounting, and legal professions. These publications targeted the corporate user and were a relatively inexpensive method of advertising. Ads would continue to be placed in trade journals. Verbatim hoped to increase advertising expenditures to match the spending of competitors resulting in increased visibility and name recognition.

Direct mail had been used occasionally to reach some specialized markets that would have a particular interest in a new product. It was used to introduce the Verbatim tape products to data processing managers in the New York City area and to introduce the worry-free DataLifePlus disks to CEOs.

Promotions

Promotions focused on each member in the channel of distribution. Rebates in the form of a credit on future Verbatim purchases to trade customers were based on volume and growth relative to history. Occasionally "spiffs" were offered to trade customers for each unit of Verbatim sold in a selected category. (Spiffs were cash payments by trade customers to their sales reps that were reimbursed by Verbatim.) End-user promotions included on-pack or in-pack (free 11th disk, rebates, coupons, free storage box, or cleaning kit).

Public Relations

Greater emphasis was sought in the public relations arena with attempts to place stories about Verbatim in various print media that would offer a form of "free" advertising. Case histories about the usage of Verbatim products were the best way to get placement in a publication.

Sales Force

The United States/Canada branded sales division consisted of five regional managers that each supervised up to eight sales representatives. The OEM sales group consisted of nine Verbatim sales representatives. Overall sales objectives for 1991 included increasing sales revenue by 19 percent and taking market share away from Verbatim's primary competitors. Verbatim had approximately 200 trade customers of which 35 contributed the majority of sales.

BACK TO THE BUSINESS OF CHALLENGING THE LEADER

As Bob Falco developed his plan to become the market share leader, he thought about the current situation in the industry. "In other recessions in the 1970s and 1980s floppy disks were not really affected. But the 1991–92 recession is a white collar recession and there has been a definite slowdown in the media business—particularly in the New England area. Fortunately, sales to the home office market are doing well. That market is really carrying the business right now. We're ready for the breakthrough in optical disks, but the way the life cycle for any new technology is compressed, that will probably become a commodity market, too, and in a very short period of time."

_____ CASE 34 _____

American Greetings
Faces New Challenges in the 1990s

_____

As CEO Morry Weiss looked at the corporate rose logo of the world's largest publicly owned manufacturer of greeting cards and related social-expression merchandise, American Greetings (AG), he reflected upon the decade of the 1980s. In 1981, he had announced the formulation of a corporate growth objective to achieve $1 billion in annual sales by 1985, which would represent a 60 percent increase over 1982 sales of $623.6 million.

It was 1986 before AG reached that goal with sales of $1.035 billion. The profit margin, however, was 5.75 percent, the lowest in five years and down from its high of 8.09 percent in 1984. In its fiscal year ending February 28, 1990, AG reported sales of $1.286 billion with a profit margin of 5.51 percent. Weiss looked at the 10-year sales, net income and selling, distribution, and marketing costs summary prepared by his corporate staff (Exhibit 34.1). He realized that AG's increase in sales had come at a high cost with an escalated and intensified battle

This case was prepared by Daniel C. Kopp and Lois Shufeldt as a basis for class discussion rather than to illustrate either effective or ineffective handling of an administrative situation. The authors would like to acknowledge the cooperation and assistance of American Greetings. Used with permission from Daniel C. Kopp. ˝

EXHIBIT 34.1   Consolidated Statements of Financial Position, 1981–1990

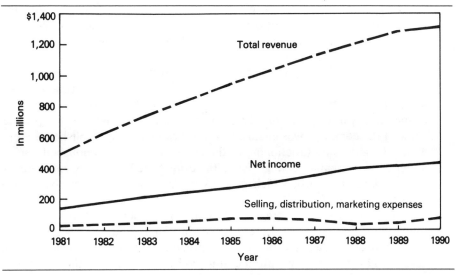

for market share dominance among the three industry leaders, Hallmark, Gibson, and AG. In the final analysis, market shares had not really changed that much among the big three. Each was determined to defend its respective market share, and the nature of the greeting card industry changed dramatically. Previously, the two leading firms, Hallmark and AG, peacefully coexisted by having mutually exclusive niches. Hallmark offered higher-priced, quality cards in department stores and card shops, and AG offered inexpensive cards in mass-merchandise outlets. However, AG's growth strategy to attack the industry leader and its niche, followed by Gibson's growth strategy and Hallmark's defensive moves, changed the industry. AG was now engaged in defending its competitive position.

HISTORY OF AMERICAN GREETINGS

The story of American Greetings is one of an American dream of a Polish immigrant who came to the land of promise and opportunity to seek his fortune. Jacob Sapirstein was born in 1884 in Wasosz, Poland, and because of the Russian-Japanese war of 1904, was sent by his widowed mother, along with his seven brothers and one sister, to live in America.

Jacob, also known as J. S., began his one-man business buying postcards made in Germany from wholesalers and selling them to candy, novelty, and drug stores in Cleveland in 1906. From a horse-drawn card wagon, the small venture steadily flourished.

J. S. and his wife Jennie, also a Polish immigrant, had three sons and a daughter; all three sons became active in their father's business. At the age of nine, Irving, the oldest, kept the family business afloat while J. S. was recovering from the flu during the epidemic of 1918. The business had outgrown the family living room and was moved to a garage at this time.

J. S. had a basic philosophy of service to the retailer and a quality product for the consumer. He developed the first wire rack as well as a rotating floor stand to make more attractive, convenient displays. In the 1930s the Sapirstein Card Company began to print its own cards to ensure the quality of its product. The name of the company was changed to American Greeting Publishers to reflect the national stature and functioning of the company. Its first published line of cards under the American Greetings name, the Forget Me Not line, went on sale in 1939 for a nickel. One card, which remains the company's all-time best seller, was designed by Irving.

The company saw great expansion throughout the 1940s, as loved ones found the need to communicate with World War II soldiers. The most significant effect of this was the widespread use of greeting cards by the soldiers. In the past, cards had been primarily a product utilized by women; thus, the expansion to the male market was a significant breakthrough for the card industry.

The 1950s marked the first public offering of stock, and the name change to American Greetings Corporation. Ground was broken for a new world headquarters, which led the way for expansion to world markets. The company made connections with several foreign markets and acquired a Canadian plant.

In 1960, J. S. stepped down at the age of 76. His son Irving succeeded him as president. Under Irving's leadership and with the assistance of his brothers, Morris and Harry Stone (all three brothers had changed their names from Sapirstein, meaning sapphire, to Stone in 1940 for business reasons), the company continued to expand into gift wrapping, party goods, calendars, stationery, candles, ceramics, and perhaps, most importantly, the creation of licensed characters.

Expansion into these related items somewhat diminished AG's recession-proof profits. Greeting card sales typically increase during recessions as people refrain from gift buying and instead remember others with a less expensive card. The supplemental items now constituted one-third of the company's sales, not enough to seriously jeopardize AG during down economies, yet greatly augmented the company's sales during good economic times.

AG's world expansion became a major pursuit throughout the 1960s and 1970s. Morry Weiss, a grandson-in-law of J. S., became the new president of AG in 1978; Irving continued as chairman of the board of directors.

THE GREETING CARD INDUSTRY

According to GM News, in 1988 Americans exchanged more than 7.1 billion cards—around 29 per person, which was down from the highest per capita card consumption of 30 per person in 1985.[1] And with the average retail price per card of $1.10, that made "social expression" nearly an $8 billion business. According to the Greeting Card Association, card buyers sent the following:

Holiday	Units Sold (In millions)	Percent
Christmas	2,200	30.99
Valentine's Day	850	11.97
Easter	180	2.54
Mother's Day	140	1.97
Father's Day	85	1.20
Graduation	80	1.13
Thanksgiving	40	0.56
Halloween	25	0.35
St. Patick's Day	16	—
Grandparent's Day	10	—
Chanukah	9	—
Other Seasons	5	—

Half of the total greeting cards purchased in 1988 were seasonal cards. The remainder were in the category of everyday cards. People living in the northeast and the northcentral parts of the country bought more cards than average, and southerners 30 percent fewer. People who bought the majority of them tended to be between 35 and 54 years of age, came from large families, lived in their own homes in the suburbs, and had an average household income of $30,000.

Women purchased over 90 percent of all greeting cards. Many women enjoyed browsing and shopping for cards, and tended to purchase a card only if it was appropriate—when the card's verse and design combined to convey the sentiment she wished to express. However, because an increasing number of women were working, they were shopping less frequently and buying less impulse merchandise.

Everyday cards, especially nonoccasion cards or alternative cards, were on the increase. According to *Forbes* and *American Demographics,* the alternative card market was the fastest-growing segment at 25 percent a year, and the card industry as a whole grew 5 percent a year.[2] Alternative cards were not geared to any holiday, but could be inspirational, satirical, or ethnic in nature. This segment was directed toward the estimated 76 million baby boomers. Changes in society—demographic and social—were fueling the growth of alternative cards. These changes included increases in the numbers of blended families, single-parent households, working women, divorcees and remarriages, and population seg-

[1] "Greeting Cards Departments . . . Mass Retail Outlets," *GM News,* October 1989, p. 10.
[2] "Flounder," *Forbes,* April 25, 1988, p. 352; "Funny Valentines," *American Demographics,* February 1989, p. 7.

ments that traditionally included the heaviest greeting card users—35- to 65-year-olds. Formerly, it was the focus strategy of the many small card makers who had 70 percent of the alternative card market. However, the big three captured 87 percent of this segment.

Most industry analysts considered the greeting card industry to be in or near the maturity stage. According to Prudential-Bache, the industry unit growth rate was 2 to 4 percent from 1946 to 1985. The greeting card industry was comprised of from 500 to 900 firms, which ranged from three major corporations to many small family organizations. The industry was dominated by the big three: Hallmark, American Greetings, and Gibson. The estimated market shares were:

Company	1977	1985	1989
Hallmark	50%	42%	40–42%
AG	24	33	32–33
Gibson	5	9	8–10

(Estimates vary according to the source.)

During the 1980s the big three engaged in market share battles through intense price, product, promotion, and place competition. The primary price competition (through discounts to retailers) was during the period 1985–1987, although it continued at a lesser rate. According to Value Line, the end result was the reduction of profits with little change in market shares.

Generally, there was a soft retailing environment. Overall slowdown in retail traffic resulted in reduced sales. The retailing industry was overstored and promotion oriented, which could result in retailers asking greeting card suppliers for lower prices to assist them in keeping their margins from shrinking. Retailers were losing their loyalty to manufacturers that supplied a full line of products—cards, gift wrap, and other items, and were looking instead for the lowest-cost supplier of each, according to Kidder, Peabody & Company.[3] Retailer concessions made to gain accounts were difficult to remove; retailers were reluctant to give them up. Competition in the industry was expected to intensify, especially in the areas of price, sales promotion, distribution, and selling.

Market niches were also attacked. According to the *Insider's Chronicle,* the biggest battlefields were the gift and specially card shops, which once were the exclusive domain of Hallmark and alternative cards.[4] A 1989 comparison of the three firms reveals the following:

---

[3] E. Gray Glass III, Research Reports on American Greetings and Greeting Card Industry, Kidder, Peabody & Company, May 16, 1986; May 20, 1986; December 11, 1986; January 20, 1987.
[4] "American Greetings," *Insider's Chronicle,* February 8, 1988, p. 3.

Firm	Sales (In billions)	Net Income (In millions)	Number of Employees	Number of Products	Number of Outlets
Hallmark	$2.0	n/a	28,000	20,300	37,000
AG	$1.3	$44.2	29,000	20,000	90,000
Gibson	$0.4	$35.0	7,900	n/a	50,000

n/a = not available.

OBJECTIVES

When asked about AG's 1989 performance, Morry Weiss replied, "Our goal was to improve competitiveness and enhance future earnings prospects in order to maximize shareholder value. AG refocused its world wide business operating strategies. While we have not reached the upper levels of that goal, substantial progress was made in 1989. We are reducing seasonal product returns, accounts receivable, and inventories. These are indicators of how well a business is being operated, and the results show that our people have made substantial progress. We are committed to making even further improvement in these areas."[5]

Weiss further explained, "Sales in 1989 increased despite the loss of revenue caused by the divestiture during the year of the company's AmToy and Plymouth divisions and several foreign subsidiaries . . . net income was affected by restructuring costs which included the cost of relocating Carlton Cards/US to Cleveland, Ohio; consolidating certain manufacturing operations; and selling, consolidating or downsizing several unprofitable businesses." His assessment of AG's 1990 performance was: "It was the kind of year you have to feel good about. Our performance demonstrated our ability to produce outstanding earnings, even in a year when the revenue gain was modest. To accomplish this required enormous effort in every department. It required a diligent watch over expenses while increasing productivity."[6]

Morry Weiss also commented about AG's growth: "We are building a more synergistic relationship between our core business and our subsidiary operations in order to increase our value to our retailers. Our goal is to be a full-service provider to our retailer accounts. The more we represent a single source for a variety of consumer products, the more important a resource we become."[7]

To reach this aim of providing retailers not only greeting cards, but complementary products, AG made the following acquisitions:

[5] American Greetings *Annual Report*, 1989, p. 3.
[6] *Annual Report*, 1990. p. 2.
[7] *Annual Report*, 1989, p. 3.

Company	Products
Acme Frame Products	Picture Frames
Wilhold Hair Care Products	Hair Care Products
Plus Mark	Promotional Christmas Products
A.G. Industries	Greeting Card Cabinets/Displays

MARKETING STRATEGIES

Product

AG produced a wide product line, including greeting cards, gift wrap, party goods, toys, and gift items. Greeting cards accounted for 65 percent of the company's 1990 fiscal sales. The breakdown of sales by major product categories follows:

Category	1980	1984	1986	1990
Everyday Greeting Cards	34%	36%	37%	41%
Holiday Greeting Cards	27	27	29	24
Gift Wrap and Party Goods	21	21	18	17
Consumer Products (Toys, etc.)	9	7	7	9
Stationery	9	9	9	9

Source: AG's Annual Reports.

The essence of AG's product strategy was identifying consumer needs, creating responses that sold, and pretesting to determine the winners. AG believed in identifying consumer needs and responding to them with creative products. Research was a key ingredient. Over 12,000 North American households were surveyed annually to obtain information about every greeting card purchased and received. AG utilized focus group sessions, simulated shopping surveys, and shopping mall interviews. Especially important was ongoing lifestyle research to identify changing tastes and consumer needs for product development.

Research efforts resulted in new products. Couples, an everyday card line that answered the trend back to more sincere romantic relationships, and Kid Zone, which responded to the need for more effective communication with children, were introduced during fiscal 1990. Holly Hobbie designs, popular in the 1960s, were reintroduced when research indicated a trend toward more traditional values.

Morry Weiss commented on the Couples line: "We've proven our ability to meet the challenge of the marketplace. Couples takes its place alongside a pantheon of our major greeting card innovations."[8]

AG had one of the largest creative staffs in the world with over 550 artists, stylists, writers, designers, photographers, and planners who were guided by the latest research data available from computer analysis, consumer testing, and information from AG's sales and merchandising departments. Careful monitoring of societal changes, fashion and color trends, and consumer preferences provided further guidance to product development. They created more than 20,000 new greeting card designs each year. AG adhered to uncompromising quality—in papers, inks, and printing procedures.

AG also engaged in retail pretesting to determine which product ideas had the greatest chance of sales. This was extremely important because of the competitiveness of the market and retailers' needs for fast turnover. A network of retail test stores was used. New cards were rated based upon actual sales performance, and those with the best sales ratings were distributed worldwide.

AG was trying to take advantage of the alternative card segment. In 1992, alternative cards commanded 20 percent of the everyday greeting card market, and the double-digit annual growth rate was expected to continue. Carlton Cards was AG's speciality card subsidiary and recently moved from Dallas to AG's Cleveland headquarters. Carlton was to concentrate on "swiftly developing products unique to the more avant-garde tastes of the specialty store consumer."

AG pioneered licensing and was an industry leader in character licensing. Their strategy was to maximize the potential of their creative and marketing expertise. The following identifies some of AG's character licenses:

Character	Year
Holly Hobbie	1968/1989
Ziggy	1971
Strawberry Shortcake	1980
Care Bears	1983
Herself the Elf	1983
Popples	1983

Strawberry Shortcake was one of the most popular licensed characters. According to *Forbes,* however, all of AG licensed characters have not been successful.[9] One flop, Herself the Elf, was perceived by retailers as being too much like Strawberry Shortcake; it also missed the Christmas season because of

---

[8] "Flounder," p. 352.
[9] American Greetings *Form 10-K,* 1989, 1.

production problems. Another failure was Get Along Gang, which tried to appeal to both little girls and boys. Another licensing creation, Popples, added a new dimension to a field crowded with look-alikes. Poppies literally "popped out" from a plush ball to a lovable, furry, playmate. A plush toy that folded into its own pouch, Popples enabled children to make its arms, legs, and fluffy tail appear and disappear at will. AG's licensing income is shown below:

Year	Income (In millions)
1984	$17.5
1985	$20.9
1986	$17.6
1987	$17.0
1988	$16.5
1989	$13.3
1990	$11.8

Source: AG's Annual Reports.

Distribution

AG distributed its products in 90,000 retail outlets in 50 countries throughout the world and in 12 languages. AG's major channels of distribution, in order of importance, included drug stores, mass merchandisers, supermarkets, stationery, and gift shops, combo stores (stores combining food, general merchandise, and drug items), variety stores, military post exchanges, and department stores.[10]

AG's primary channels of distribution (which included supermarkets, chain drug stores, and mass retail merchandisers) experienced growth due to demographic and lifestyle changes. The increase of working women changed the location for many card purchases. In 1992, 55 percent of all everyday greeting cards were purchased in convenient locations.

AG's five largest customers accounted for about 17.4 percent of net sales. These customers included mass merchandisers, major drug stores, and military exchanges.

AG had 26 regional and 58 district sales offices in the United States, Canada, United Kingdom, France, and Mexico.

Promotion

Service was a key value to AG's marketing effort as reflected in the following statement by Morry Weiss: "One of our cornerstone values is service to the customer. Although we are a leader in marketing innovation, we earned our reputation for superior customer service by clinging to old-fashioned ideas. We

---

[10] *Annual Report*, 1990, p. 2.

get to know our customers—and their customers—and learn how their businesses operate."[11]

The services that AG provided its retailers were based upon three key ingredients: knowledgeable sales force, in-store service personnel, and quick response to needs. AG offered the following:

- Largest full-time sales force in the industry, which was composed of highly trained experts.
- National sales force of 12,000 part-time in-store merchandising representatives who visited mass retail stores to restock goods, realign products, set up new displays and point-of-purchase materials, generate reorders, and process returns.
- A computerized network that allowed AG to more quickly and consistently ship complete and accurate orders to retailers[12].

According to Weiss, "AG is focusing on building a strong partnership with retailers and consumers. We will expand distribution of our products in the global marketplace. We will 'partner' with retail accounts by making greeting card departments more profitable. And we will improve our response to consumers' needs for appropriate products and attractive, easy to shop departments."[13]

AG tried to achieve more sales and profits by making the space allocated by retailers more productive. This was accomplished by sophisticated merchandising that made greeting card displays more "consumer friendly." Since women purchased approximately 90 percent of all greeting cards, AG redesigned greeting card cabinets to respond to the fact that women spent less time in stores than previously. Redesigned greeting card cabinets displayed 40 percent more cards in the same amount of space. Point-of-purchase signs and new caption locators ("Mother," "Stepdaughter," and so forth) helped customers in a hurry find the right card.

Themes were becoming more important in merchandising. These were used for particular seasons or occasions that project a strong message to consumers and evoke an immediate awareness of the occasion. Related to this was a new concept called "occasion merchandising," which grouped various products for everyday occasions such as cards, gift wrap, candles, invitations, party goods, and so on.

AG tried to design its marketing programs to increase customer traffic and profitability of the greeting card department. Realizing the need for retailers to differentiate themselves and their products, AG attempted to work on an individual basis to customize the greeting card department for each retailer. This was accomplished via market research and technology. This was especially important to large chains that had to contend with regional differences. Greeting card

[11] Ibid.
[12] Ibid.
[13] Ibid., p. 5.

departments could be customized to reflect a specific area's demographics. If, for example, the demographic profile was comprised of a large number of elderly or "Yuppies," specific products would be featured to target that segment.

In 1982, AG became recognized nationwide, first through television commercials and then through a new corporate identity program. The updated corporate rose logo was featured prominently at retail outlets; the logo became a standard and highly recognizable feature on all product packaging, store signage, point-of-purchase displays, and even the truck fleet. The year-round advertising campaign in 1982 included the promotion of the major card-sending holidays and nonseasonal occasions during daytime and prime-time programming.

The aim of AG's national consumer advertising and public relations programs was to remind people to send cards, in that one of AG's chief competitors was consumer forgetfulness. AG was the only company in the industry to sponsor national consumer retail promotions. These consumer-directed programs served to establish brand identity and generate retail store traffic.

A summary of AG's selling, distribution, and marketing expenses as a percentage of sales is displayed below:

Year	Percent
1981	28.2
1982	28.7
1983	29.2
1984	29.3
1985	29.0
1986	29.9
1987	31.6
1988	33.4
1989	32.6
1990	32.9

PRODUCTION STRATEGIES

AG had 34 plants and facilities in the United States, Canada, the United Kingdom, France, and Mexico. This was down from the 49 plants and facilities in 1986. The company owned approximately 4.8 million square feet and leased 11.3 million square feet of plant, warehouse, store, and office space. It met its space needs in the United States through long-term leases of properties constructed and financed by community development corporations and municipalities.

AG had taken steps in 1987 to 1990 to decrease production costs. It tried to improve its production efficiency by cutting costs and reducing work-in-process inventories. AG also invested heavily in automated production equipment to cut labor costs in 1988. AG benefited from lower costs for raw materials and fewer product returns because of better inventory control. AG's material, labor, and other production costs are as follows:

Year	Percent of Sales
1981	44.7
1982	44.3
1983	41.3
1984	40.5
1985	39.9
1986	40.2
1987	42.3
1988	45.1
1989	42.8
1990	41.5

PERSONNEL STRATEGIES

In 1989, American Greetings employed over 15,000 full-time and 14,000 part-time people in the United States, Canada, Mexico, and Europe. This equated to approximately 20,500 full-time employees.

When asked about AG employees, Morry Weiss commented: "But perhaps our greatest strength is the men and women who create, manufacture, distribute, sell, and support our products. They are committed to knowing our customers, meeting their needs with quality products and providing service before and after the sale."[14]

AG had a noncontributing profit-sharing plan for most of its U.S. employees, as well as a retirement income guarantee plan. It also had several pension plans covering certain employees in foreign countries.

FINANCE STRATEGIES

Exhibits 34.2, 34.3, and 34.4 contain relevant financial information for American Greetings. The financial condition of AG has fluctuated over the years. In the early to mid-1980s, AG profit margins increased from 5.42 percent in 1981 to its high of 8.09 percent in 1984. However, AG's financial performance in the mid- to late 1980s was disappointing, with the profit margin falling to 2.84 percent in 1988 and a return on investment of 2.90 percent. In 1990, AG's profit margin had risen to 5.51 percent with a return on investment of 6.33.

[14] Ibid., p. 1.

EXHIBIT 34.2 Consolidated Statements of Financial Position (In thousands)

	1986	1987	1988	1989	1990
Assets					
Current Assets					
Cash and Equivalents	$ 26,853	$ 17,225	$ 36,534	$ 94,292	$ 122,669
Trade Accounts Receivable, Less Allowances for Sales Returns and Doubtful Accounts	240,471	284,135	278,559	242,582	254,285
Inventories					
Raw Material	59,343	56,057	56,122	48,478	51,075
Work in Process	60,179	69,668	61,406	51,625	42,139
Finished Products	181,237	202,412	245,801	197,618	208,918
	300,759	328,137	363,329	297,721	302,132
Less LIFO Reserve	76,552	75,392	77,274	83,017	85,226
	224,207	252,745	286,055	214,704	216,906
Display Material and Factory Supplies	26,826	29,770	30,299	25,192	25,408
Total Inventories	251,033	282,515	316,354	239,896	242,314
Deferred Income Taxes	36,669	26,593	39,935	49,542	51,315
Prepaid Expenses and Other	6,228	9,679	8,672	11,020	10,362
Total Current Assets	561,254	620,147	680,054	637,332	680,945
Other Assets	47,085	89,488	95,752	92,285	107,788
Property, Plant and Equipment					
Land	7,523	7,956	7,548	6,471	6,229
Buildings	165,241	183,481	223,491	216,545	215,458
Equipment and Fixtures	222,718	269,644	319,353	340,233	354,979
	395,482	461,081	550,392	563,249	576,666
Less Accumulated Depreciation and Amortization	130,519	148,097	175,917	205,246	224,383
Property, Plant, and Equipment—Net	264,963	312,984	374,475	358,003	352,283
Total Assets	$873,302	$1,022,619	$1,150,281	$1,087,620	$1,141,016

Liabilities and Shareholders' Equity

Current Liabilities					
Notes Payable to Banks	$ 15,921	$ 25,092	$ 13,956	$ 17,201	$ 36,524
Accounts Payable	66,685	69,175	98,270	79,591	75,146
Payrolls and Payroll Taxes	28,675	31,230	33,759	38,839	10,878
Retirement Plans	11,697	10,966	4,148	8,573	10,878
State and Local Taxes	2,763	3,056	—	—	—
Dividends Payable	5,317	5,343	5,338	5,311	5,281
Income Taxes	18,988	—	13,782	6,693	6,430
Sales Returns	23,889	29,964	28,273	24,543	21,182
Current Maturities of Long-Term Debt	4,786	10,894	54,150	3,740	—
Total Current Liabilities	178,721	185,720	251,676	184,491	200,756
Long-Term Debt	147,592	235,005	273,492	246,732	235,497
Deferred Income Taxes	64,025	77,451	86,426	91,409	100,159
Shareholders' Equity					
Common Shares—Par Value $1:					
Class A	29,203	29,552	29,628	29,692	29,946
Class B	2,982	2,588	2,528	2,497	2,063
Capital in Excess of Par Value	94,744	102,718	104,209	105,245	110,234
Shares Held in Treasury	(1,689)	(15,409)	(14,199)	(14,767)	(26,692)
Cumulative Translation Adjustment	(16,801)	(11,604)	(7,564)	(4,790)	(8,186)
Retained Earnings	374,525	416,598	424,085	447,111	497,239
Total Shareholders' Equity	482,964	524,443	538,687	564,988	604,604
Total Liabilities and Shareholders' Equity	$873,302	$1,022,619	$1,150,281	$1,087,620	$1,141,016

Source: American Greetings.

EXHIBIT 34.3 Consolidated Statements of Income, Years Ending February 28 or 29 (In thousands except per share data)

	1986	1987	1988	1989	1990
Net Sales	$1,012,451	$1,102,532	$1,174,817	$1,252,793	$1,286,853
Other Income	23,200	23,463	24,155	22,566	22,131
Total Revenue	1,035,651	1,125,995	1,198,972	1,275,359	1,308,984
Cost and Expenses					
Material, Labor and Other Production Costs	416,322	476,725	540,143	546,214	543,602
Selling, Distribution, and Marketing	308,745	355,363	400,033	415,597	431,254
Administration and General	131,928	125,407	135,224	148,095	149,771
Depreciation and Amortization	23,471	29,059	34,191	39,527	40,251
Interest	19,125	24,875	32,787	33,479	27,691
Restructuring Charge	—	12,371	—	23,591	—
	899,591	1,023,800	1,142,378	1,206,503	1,192,569
Income before Income Taxes	136,060	102,195	56,594	68,856	116,415
Income Taxes	61,635	38,834	23,203	24,582	44,238
Net Income	$ 74,425	$ 63,361	$ 33,391	$ 44,274	$ 72,177
Net Income per Share	$2.32	$1.97	$1.04	$1.38	$2.25

Source: American Greetings.

EXHIBIT 34.4 **Selected Financial Data, Years Ending February 28 or 29 (In thousands except per share data)**

	1986	1987	1988	1989	1990
Summary of Operations					
Total Revenue	$1,035,651	$1,125,995	$1,198,972	$1,275,359	$1,308,984
Materials, Labor, and Other Products	420,747	476,725	540,143	546,214	543,602
Depreciation and Amortization	23,471	20,059	34,191	39,527	40,251
Interest Expense	19,125	24,875	32,787	33,479	27,691
Net Income	$ 74,425	$ 63,361	$ 33,391	$ 44,274	$ 72,177
Net Income per Share	$2.32	$1.97	$1.04	$1.38	$2.25
Cash Dividends per Share	.62	.66	.66	.66	.66
Fiscal Year End Market Price per Share	$35.62	$28.75	$17.63	$21.25	$31.25
Average Number Shares Outstanding	32,059,851	32,212,556	32,068,752	32,146,971	32,029,533
Financial Position					
Accounts Receivable	$ 240,471	$ 284,135	$ 278,559	$ 242,582	$ 254,285
Inventories	251,033	282,515	316,354	239,896	243,314
Working Capital	382,533	434,427	428,378	452,841	480,189
Total Assets	873,302	1,022,619	1,150,281	1,087,620	1,141,016
Capital Additions	61,799	68,740	96,682	41,938	42,869
Long-Term Debt	147,592	235,005	273,492	246,732	235,497
Shareholders' Equity	482,964	524,443	538,687	564,988	604,604
Shareholders' Equity per Share	$15.01	$16.32	$16.75	$17.55	$18.89
Net Return Average Shareholders' Equity	16.5%	12.7%	6.3%	8.0%	12.3%
Pretax Return on Total Revenue	13.1%	9.1%	4.7%	5.4%	8.9%
Summary of Operations					
Total Revenue	$ 498,272	$ 623,604	$ 742,683	$ 839,914	$ 945,658
Materials, Labor and Other Products	225,356	278,866	313,769	344,313	382,205
Depreciation and Amortization	10,863	12,752	13,890	15,507	18,799
Interest Expense	13,548	21,647	24,086	16,135	15,556
Net Income	$ 26,515	$ 32,843	$ 44,582	$ 59,658	$ 74,365
Net Income per Share	$.97	$1.20	$1.54	$1.91	$2.35
Cash Dividends per Share	.26	.27	.31	.40	.54
Fiscal Year End Market Price per Share	$5.50	$9.63	$18.69	$23.69	$33.06
Average Number Shares Outstanding	27,314,594	27,352,342	28,967,092	31,240,455	31,629,418
Financial Position					
Accounts Receivable	$ 114,051	$ 131,996	$ 148,018	$ 146,896	$ 173,637
Inventories	133,836	159,623	177,459	180,019	214,449
Working Capital	167,772	215,412	241,724	275,685	330,409
Total Assets	433,204	491,854	580,675	685,894	747,897
Capital Additions	22,768	26,720	33,967	46,418	43,575
Long-Term Debt	113,486	148,895	111,066	119,941	112,876
Shareholders' Equity	205,550	227,784	316,368	365,496	425,748
Shareholder Equity per Share	$7.52	$8.31	$10.18	$11.62	$13.35
Net Return Average Shareholders' Equity	13.7%	15.4%	17.1%	17.8%	19.2%
Pretax Return on Total Revenue	9.9%	9.2%	11.0%	13.0%	14.4%

Irving Stone commented about AG's 1990 performance: "Fiscal 1990 revenues were a record $1.31 billion. This marks the 84th consecutive year that revenues have increased since the Company's founding in 1906. And . . . revenue was driven by higher sales of everyday greeting cards, our low-cost high margin core products. Fourth quarter sales were particularly strong. We expect to continue reporting good sales results." He continued, "The market value of our common stock rose 47 percent, from $21.25 on February 28, 1989 to $31.25 at the fiscal year close on February 28, 1990. This compares favorably to 27 percent increases for both the Dow Jones Industrial Average and the Standard and Poor's 500 Stock Index. Total returns to stockholders—share price appreciation plus dividends—was 50 percent in fiscal 1990."[15]

AG's stock price ranged from a low of 9-1/2 in 1981 to a high of 37-1/8 in 1990.

MANAGEMENT

AG was organized via a divisional profit center basis. Each division had its own budget committee, although an executive management committee, comprised of five senior executives, approved the strategic plans for all the divisions. Strategic plans were established in 1-, 3-, 10-, and 20-year time frames. Corporate AG maintained strict budgetary and accounting controls.

The basic domestic greeting card business was placed under the U.S. Greeting Card Division. Domestic and international subsidiary operations, including the licensing division, were a second unit, with corporate management a third. AG decentralized its structure in 1983.

U.S. Greeting Card Division.   This division emcompassed the core business of greeting cards and related products, including manufacturing, sales, merchandising, research, and administrative services. It produced and distributed greeting cards and related products domestically. The same products were distributed throughout the world by international subsidiaries and licensees.

Domestic and International Subsidiaries.   AG's domestic and international subsidiary operations included the following:

Domestic

Acme Frame Products
A.G. Industries
Plus Mark
Summit Corporation/Summit Collection

[15] Ibid.

Those Characters from Cleveland
Wilhold Hair Care Products

International

Carlton Cards—Canada
Carlton Cards—England
Carlton Cards—France
Felicitaciones Nacionales S.A. de C.V.—Mexico
Rust Craft Canada

The number of domestic operations in 1990 included six versus seven in 1986. Firms divested included Amtoy, Drawing Board Greeting Cards, and Tower Products. The number of international operations in 1990 was 5 versus 13 in 1986. Among the international operations consolidated included one in Canada, four in Continental Europe, one in Monaco, and four in the United Kingdom.

AG's domestic and international sales are summarized below:

Sales Recap

Year	Domestic	Gross Profit Margin	Foreign	Gross Profit Margin	U.S. Percent	International Percent
1990	$1,088,438	11.86	$220,546	6.79	83.15	16.85
1989	1,039,464	7.75	235,895	9.22	81.50	18.50
1988	996,628	7.79	202,344	5.80	83.12	16.88
1987	940,565	13.28	185,430	1.19	83.53	16.47
1986	874,255	15.38	161,396	12.82	84.42	15.58
1985	799,805	16.51	145,853	13.18	84.58	15.42
1984	717,057	15.18	122,857	13.61	85.37	15.63
1983	631,143	14.29	111,549	13.94	85.00	15.00
1982	523,467	12.54	100,137	13.61	85.40	14.60
1981	440,516	12.27	57,756	14.87	88.41	11.59

Source: AG annual reports.

FUTURE OF AG

When asked about the future of AG, Morry Weiss responded, "We are poised for perhaps the most successful period in our history. We are prepared to strengthen our core business and improve our position in the greeting card industry; to provide a greater return to our shareholders; and to afford our employees even greater opportunities for growth and career advancement. The strategies we will employ to achieve our goals for the new year and beyond are clear. We have well defined corporate strengths which we will target to build even stronger partnerships with retailers and consumers.[16]

[16] *Annual Report*, 1989, p. 3.

Irving Stone's view of the future included the following: "We are optimistic about the future. We are confident that we can achieve even more exciting results . . . in the future. We face the future confident that our commitment to help people build and maintain relationships will produce even more innovative products like Couples."[17]

U.S. *Industrial Outlook* expected industry sales to grow between 3 to 4 percent annually through 1992. Moderate growth was predicted due to forecasted moderate growth in the gross national product, real disposable personal income, and personal consumption expenditures. For continued growth and profitability, U.S. *Industrial Outlook* recommended diversification into related product lines, institution of more cost-cutting strategies, monitoring of demand for current lines, divesting of unprofitable lines, and better matching of demand with supply to avoid after-holiday returns.[18]

The unit growth rate for the greeting card industry between 1987 and 2015 was estimated to be between 1 and 3 percent. Exhibit 34.5 provides the forecast according to Prudential-Bache Securities. The slowing of unit growth was primarily due to the postwar baby boomers who had already entered their high card-consumption years. With the declining birthrate of the 1970s and 1980s, consumption of cards was expected to decline.[19]

EXHIBIT 34.5   The Greeting Card Industry—Consumption Forecast

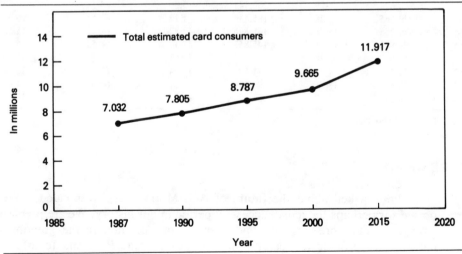

[17] U.S. *Industrial Outlook,* Department of Commerce, 1988, pp. 29–16, 29–17.
[18] "Greeting Cards Industry Update," Prudential-Bache Securities, December 30, 1988; August 9, 1989, September 27, 1989.
[19] Ibid.

However, greeting card officials optimistically projected that the rate of consumption would increase moderately from the current per-capita rate of 29 cards to 44 cards per-capita by 2015. Greeting card sources also reported that consumers were upgrading their purchases to higher priced cards, thus generating more profits per sale. The aging population, those over 55, also tended to send more cards than did younger persons.

Prudential-Bache's expectations for the future of the greeting card industry included the following:

> Price competition would remain a concern because of the maturity of the industry and the limited number of large players.
>
> At least 5 to 10 percent of the industry's current sales were to retail outlets that the industry leaders would never serve due to the small size of these outlets, which made it too expensive to reach.
>
> The greeting card industry was an area ripe for potential acquisition.
>
> AG was and would continue to experience increased competition in its promotional gift-wrap area.
>
> The big three could be challenged by any small, well-run company.
>
> It would be unlikely that the big three with combined market shares of 80 to 85 percent would continue to expand to "own the market." The dynamic competitive nature of the industry would prohibit this.
>
> There was not much room for the big three to grow by capturing more of the remaining market they were not reaching.[20]

As CEO Morry Weiss thought about the future, he wondered what changes AG should make in its competitive strategies.

[20] Ibid.

_____ CASE 22 _____

Anheuser-Busch Dominates in the 1990s

On March 28, 1990, Patrick K. Stokes was appointed president of Anheuser-Busch, the beer subsidiary of Anheuser-Busch Companies (the holding company). He succeeded August A. Busch III, who had served as president of the subsidiary for the past three years. Mr. Busch, who maintained his position as chairman of the board, president, and chief executive officer of Anheuser-Busch Companies, said that "he will continue to participate in the management of the beer subsidiary, but will devote more time to corporate duties and working with other subsidiaries."[1] One analyst expressed his belief that Mr. Stokes' main challenge would be to reach the 50 percent market-share objective by or before the mid-1990s. The analyst went on to say, "Stokes will be under extra pressure since the achievement of this [50 percent market share] objective is a top priority of Mr. Busch."

Mr. Stokes had served as chairman and CEO of Campbell-Taggart and as chairman and president of Eagle Snacks, both food subsidiaries of Anheuser-Busch Companies. Also promoted was Michael J. Roarty, director of marketing for Anheuser-Busch, the beer subsidiary, to vice president of corporate marketing and communications for the company and chairman of Busch media group. During Roarty's 13-year tenure in the beer subsidiary, sales and market share had more than doubled—to 80.7 million barrels and 42.1 percent market share. Rather than appoint a new director of marketing, three veteran Anheuser-Busch managers shared the challenge of achieving 50 percent market share with Mr. Stokes.

COMPANY HISTORY—AN ENTREPRENEURIAL SPIRIT

In 1852, George Schneider founded the Bavarian Brewery in St. Louis, Missouri. Five years later, on the brink of bankruptcy, the brewery was sold to a competitor who renamed it Hammer and Urban. By 1860, the new company

This case was prepared by Thomas L. Wheelen, David B. Croll, and Moustafa H. Abdelsamad. Research assistance was performed by Paul Parker. The case is intended as a basis for class discussion rather than to illustrate either effective or ineffective handling of an administrative situation. Copyright © 1990 by Thomas L. Wheelen. Used with permission from Thomas L. Wheelen.

[1] "August Busch III Names Beer Successor," _Beverage World_, May 1990, p. 10.

defaulted on a loan to Eberhard Anheuser. Anheuser, a successful soap manufacturer, assumed control of Hammer and Urban and four years later asked his son-in-law, Adolphus Busch, to join the brewery as a salesman. Busch, who became the driving force behind the new venture, became a partner in 1873, and then president between 1880 and 1913. In 1879, the name of the brewery was changed to Anheuser-Busch Brewing Company.

Adolphus Busch was a pioneer in the development of a new pasteurization process for beer and became the first American brewer to pasteurize beer. In 1894, he and Carl Conrad developed a new beer that was lighter in color and body. This new beer, Budweiser, gave Busch a national beer, for which he developed many marketing techniques to increase sales. By 1901, the annual sales of Anheuser-Busch had surpassed the million-barrel mark.

In 1913, August A. Busch succeeded his father as president of the company, serving as president during the prohibition era between 1920 and 1933. He led the company in many new diversification endeavors such as truck bodies, baker's yeast, ice cream, corn products, commercial refrigeration units, and nonalcoholic beverages. With the passage of the 21st Amendment, which repealed Prohibition, Anheuser-Busch returned to the manufacturing and distribution of beer on a national basis, and in 1934 the company went public. August A. Busch's son, Adolphus Busch III, was president of the company from 1934 until his death in 1946.

August A. (Gussie) Busch, Jr., succeeded Adolphus Busch III as president and CEO in 1946. He was elected chairman of the board in 1956. During his tenure, eight new breweries were constructed and sales increased 11-fold, from 3 million barrels in 1946 to 34 million barrels in 1974. He guided the company as it continued its conglomerate diversification strategies into real estate, family entertainment parks, transportation, the St. Louis Cardinals baseball team, and can manufacturing. Busch was serving as honorary chairman of the board of Anheuser-Busch Companies, and chairman and president of the St. Louis National Baseball Club at his death on September 29, 1989. He was 90. Before his death, Mr. Busch had commented, "I've had a wonderful, competitive life filled with challenges and reward." He continued, "And I'm thankful for it all. Most of all, I'm thankful for my heritage, for my family, and for my children. I'm thankful for my life with my company, Anheuser-Busch." His death marked the last of the legendary "beer barons," and the end of an era.[2]

August A. Busch III, born on June 16, 1937, was the fifth generation of the Busch brewing dynasty. He started his career hauling beechwood chips out of 31,000-gallon aging tanks. In his youth "Little Augie" was a hell-raiser, but he changed to a conservative "workaholic" after attending the University of Arizona and the Siebel Institute of Technology, a Chicago school for brewers. He was elected president in 1974, and CEO in 1975. During his tenure, sales increased by more than two and a half times, or 264 percent, from 34 million barrels in 1974 to

[2] Anheuser-Busch Companies, *Annual Report 1989*, p. 1.

89.7 million barrels in 1989. The company maintained 12 breweries having a capacity of 85.1 million barrels, and Anheuser-Busch continued its successful conglomerate diversification efforts (Exhibit 22.1).

During his 15 years of managing the company, Busch transformed it from a large, loosely run company into a tightly run organization with an emphasis on the bottom line. Busch was known for his tough-mindedness and intensity, his highly competitive nature, and his attention to detail. As Mr. Dennis Long, former president of the company's brewing subsidiary, said, "There is little that goes on that he doesn't know something about." Busch, a brewmaster, was known for making unscheduled visits to the breweries at all hours of the day and night.

Mr. Busch would start his day at 5:30 A.M., then pilot his helicopter from his 1,000-acre farm in Saint Peters, Missouri, to the company's headquarters on the South Side of St. Louis—a 30-mile flight. He would hold his first meeting over breakfast, which would take place at 7:00 A.M., and would rarely leave the office before 6:00 P.M. One of his final rituals before retiring at 8:30 P.M. would be to taste-test daily samples of beer that are flown in from the company's breweries. Few batches of Budweiser, or any Anheuser-Busch beer, were shipped without his personal approval. Busch was described "as a man who absolutely never wastes time." "When you have a meeting with him, it is boom, boom, boom," stated Jerry Steinman, publisher of *Beer Marketer's Insights*, an industry newsletter. Professor Amand C. Stalnaker, on the board of directors of the company, put it another way. "He's not the guy who sits back, puts his feet up on the desk and says, 'Let's chat about this for an hour or two.' But I would call it intensity rather

---

EXHIBIT 22.1   Anheuser-Busch Subsidiaries

Anheuser-Busch
Anheuser-Busch Investment Capital Corporation
Anheuser-Busch International
Busch Agricultural Resources
Busch Creative Service Corporation
Busch Entertainment Corporation
Busch Media Group
Busch Properties
Campbell Taggart
Civic Center Corporation
Container Recovery Corporation
Eagle Snacks
International Label Company[a]
Manufacturers Railroad Company
Metal Container Corporation
Promotional Products Group
St. Louis National Baseball Club
St. Louis Refrigerator Car Company

---

[a] This is a joint venture company.
Source: Anheuser-Busch Companies, Inc., *Fact Book—1989/90*, pp. 6–26.

than abruptness."[3] Mr. Long added, "Let there be no doubt. He's at the helm and he sets the tone. For him, planning and management are one and the same, once a plan is drawn up, he tracks the follow-through to make sure that it is carried out."[4]

Encouraging openness and participation from his executives, Busch provided them with plenty of responsibility and freedom, and promoted group decision making. Henry King, former president of the United States Brewing Association, stated, ". . . the reason Anheuser-Busch leads the field is because it's got dynamic leadership. August Busch picks very talented people; he gives them enormous responsibilities, but he gives them the authority to execute those responsibilities and he holds people accountable."[5]

His policy committee was a 12-member forum in which each member must present an opinion on the current topic or issue and substantiate his position. Mr. Busch felt that "executives do not learn from success, they learn from their failures." What is his philosophy on success? As he stated, "The more successful that we become . . . the more humble we must be . . . because that breeds future success."[6]

Robert S. Weinberg, a brewing industry analyst and former consultant to the company, felt, "The thing that is extraordinary about A-B is their depth of management talent. . . . This is a very extraordinary team. They're not competing with each other; they're all working together for the common goal." However, a former employee warned, "The biggest mistake as an Anheuser executive is to wake up one morning and think you're a Busch," even though Mr. Busch speaks in endearing, almost emotional terms about the A-B family of employees.[7]

Mr. Busch's 26-year-old son, August A. Busch IV, has been learning the business over the past five years. He was the brand manager for Bud Dry. Commenting on the success of his four children, Mr. Busch said, "If they have the competency to do so, they'll be given the opportunity. You learn from the ground up. Those of us who are in this company started out scrubbing the tanks."[8] "The fact that he [August IV] is August III's son does not mean a free lunch," stated a friend of the immediate family. "It couldn't hurt, however."[9]

THE ORGANIZATION

On October 1, 1979, Anheuser-Busch Companies was formed as a new holding company. The company's new name and organization structure more

---

3 Christy Marshall, "The Czar of Beers," *Business Month*, June 1988, p. 26.
4 "How Anheuser Brews Its Winners," *New York Times*, August 4, 1985.
5 Larry Jabbonsky, "What Keeps A-B Hot?" *Beverage World*, September 1988, p. 22.
6 "How Anheuser Brews Its Winners," p. 28.
7 Jabbonsky, "What Keeps A-B Hot?" p. 22.
8 "How Anheuser Brews Its Winners," p. 18.
9 Jabbonsky, "What Keeps A-B Hot?" p. 22.

clearly reflected Anheuser-Busch's mission and diversification endeavors of the past decades.

Reorganization of the Business Segments

As a result of the acquisition of Sea World in September 1989, Anheuser-Busch reorganized and redefined its principal business segments from prior years. For strategic planning purposes the company's three business segments became (1) beer and beer-related operations, which produced and sold the company's beer products; (2) food products, which consisted of the company's food and food-related operations (Campbell-Taggart and Eagle Snacks); and (3) entertainment, which consisted of the company's theme parks (Sea World, Cypress Gardens, Busch Gardens, Adventure Island, and Sesame Place), baseball team (St. Louis Cardinals), stadium (Busch Stadium and Civic Center), and real estate development and operations. Exhibit 22.2 is an outline of each of the 17 companies that comprise the three business segments.

Prior to the reorganization, the three principal business segments had been (1) beer and beer-related, (2) food products, and (3) diversified operations. The diversified operations segment included entertainment, real estate, transportation, and communications operations. In 1989, transportation and communications became part of the beer and beer-related segment.

In 1989, the beer and beer-related business segment contributed 78.1 percent of the corporation's net sales and 93.7 percent of the operating income. Financial information for each of these business segments is shown in Exhibit 22.3. Beer will remain the top priority according to Mr. Busch.

Because of the company's vertical integration strategy, knowledge concerning the economics of the various industries in which Anheuser-Busch competes increased, the quantity and quality of supply was better assured, and both packaging and raw materials were more strongly controlled. In cultivating internally developed businesses such as Eagle Snacks, Anheuser-Busch continued its philosophy of maintaining premium-quality and quantity of supply and control of both packaging and raw materials through self-manufacture. In 1985, Eagle Snacks added plant capacity through the acquisition of Cape Cod Chip Company and through plant expansion.

Company Philosophy

Anheuser-Busch's stated philosophy was "Anheuser-Busch's vision of greatness is today a reality. But the company isn't about to rest on its history of achievement. There are many new challenges to be met, and, as always, Anheuser-Busch will lead the way, because we believe that excellence is not just the act of achievement, but the process of constantly striving to achieve even more. We also believe that while a single achievement may signify luck, a history

EXHIBIT 22.2   Anheuser-Busch Companies—Business Segments

Beer and Beer-Related Companies

Company	Year Founded	Activities
Anheuser-Busch	1852	It ranked as the world's largest brewer, selling 80.7 million barrels of beer in 1989, and has been the industry leader since 1957. It distributed 14 naturally brewed products through 950 independent beer wholesalers and 10 company-owned wholesalers. Barrels sold have increased by 60.8 percent since 1980.
Busch Agricultural Resources	1962	It processed barley into malt. In 1989, it supplied 28 percent of the company's malt requirements. It grew and processed rice, and had the capacity to meet 50 percent of the company's rice needs.
Container Recovery Corporation	1979	It recycled more than 350 million pounds of aluminum, or more than 9 billion cans, and 29 million pounds of glass, or 58 million bottles, in 1989.
Metal Container Corporation	1974	It operated 10 can and lid manufacturing plants. In 1989, it produced nearly 10 billion cans and 12 billion lids. This represented 40 percent of the company's container requirements. This subsidiary was rapidly expanding into the soft drink container market.
Anheuser-Busch International	1981	It was the company's international licensing and marketing subsidiary. The world beer market was 3.5 times as large as the domestic market. Sales were up 20 percent in 1989. The company exported to 40 countries and license-brewed in six countries.
Busch Media Group	1985	It was the company's in-house agency to purchase national broadcast media time and to develop and place local advertising schedules.
Anheuser-Busch Investment Capital Corp	1984	It shared equity positions with qualified partners in A-B: distributorships. It had invested in 16 wholesale dealerships.
Promotional Products Group	n/a	It was responsible for licensing, development, sales, and warehousing of the company's promotional merchandise. In 1989, more than 1,500 new promotional items were created and approximately 5,000 different items were available at any one time.
Busch Creative Services	1980	It was a full-service business and marketing communications company, selling its services to Anheuser-Busch and other Fortune 500 companies. In 1986, it acquired Innervision Productions, which produced video programming and industrial films. In 1986, it acquired Optimus, which was a post-production facility.
St. Louis Refrigerator Car Company	1878	It was one of the company's transportation subsidiaries with three facilities. It provided commercial repair, rebuilding, maintenance, and inspection of railroad cars. The rail car division had record profits in 1989.

(Cont.)

EXHIBIT 22.2   (Cont.)

Beer and Beer-Related Companies

Company	Year Founded	Activities
Manufacturers Railway Company	1878	This was the other transportation subsidiary. It operated 42 miles of track in the St. Louis area, 247 insulated railroad cars used to ship beer, 48 hopper cars, and 77 boxcars. It included a fleet of 240 specially designed trailers. It also ran the warehousing for eight brewery locations.

Food Products Companies

Company	Year Founded	Activities
Campbell Taggart	1982	It had 75 plants and approximately 20,000 employees in the U.S., Spain, and France. It was a highly diversified food products company with operations in about 35 percent of this country. It consisted of the following divisions: bakery operations, refrigerated products, frozen food products (Eagle Crest Foods, Inc.), and international subsidiaries—Spain and France, and other interests—makes folding cartons.
Eagle Snacks	1978	It produced and distributed a premium line of snack foods and nuts. In 1984, it began self-manufacturing virtually all of its snack products, and in 1985 it purchased Cod Potato Chip Company. It continued to move toward its goal of gaining significant market share in the snack food industry (estimated sales in excess of $10 billion).

Entertainment

Company	Year Founded	Activities
Busch Entertainment	1959	It was the company's family entertainment subsidiary. It consisted of the Dark Continent (FL), The Old Country (VA), Adventure Island (FL), and Sesame Place (PA). These parks attracted 6.2 million people. In 1989, it acquired Sea World, Cypress Gardens, and Boardwalk and Baseball. The 1989 attendance at these parks was 14 million people.
Busch Properties	1970	It was the company's real estate development subsidiary with commercial properties in Virginia, Ohio, and California. It continued to develop a planned community, Kingsmill, in Williamsburg, VA.
St. Louis National Baseball Club	1953	St. Louis Cardinals.
Civic Center Corporation	1981	It owned Busch Stadium, the Civic Center, and two and three-fourths downtown city blocks currently used for parking.

n/a = not applicable.

of many achievements signifies great endeavor and the promise of more to come. Anheuser-Busch has lived that philosophy. And the result speaks for itself."[10]

Diversification Activities

The company acquired Sea World for $1.1 billion from Harcourt Brace Jovanovich in 1989. The acquisition consisted of three theme parks in central Florida: Boardwalk and Baseball (closed in January 1990 because it had never been profitable), Cypress Gardens (Winter Haven), and Sea World (Orlando). Harcourt Brace Jovanovich sold the parks because it had $2.9 billion of debt that occurred as it fought a 1987 hostile takeover bid from British publisher Robert Maxwell.

In 1989, Anheuser-Busch announced its plans to build a $300 million resort and theme park in Spain near Barcelona. The park would feature five theme villages—four of these would be China, Mexico, Polynesia, and old Western United States—to be opened in 1993. The resort would be modeled after the company's Kingsmill resort near Williamsburg, Virginia, and would feature a world-class hotel and conference center, 18-hole golf course, and swimming and tennis facilities.[11]

Because they did not meet objectives, a number of subsidiaries were sold in 1988 and 1989. Master Cellars Wines, Saratoga Spring Company, and Sante Mineral Water Company of the A-B Beverage Group were sold to Evian Waters of France. Busch Industrial Products Corporation (producer of yeast products) was sold to Gist-Brocades N.V. of the Netherlands. The majority interest in Exploration Cruise Lines was sold in 1988.

In 1985, the company became an investor in its first venture capital fund, Innoven, an established fund that has been very successful over the years. Anheuser-Busch gained exposure to new business areas being developed by the small start-up companies in which Innoven invested capital.

The company extended its research and development program with Interferon Sciences, which has been developing and clinically testing both material and recombinant forms of interferon, an antiviral agent found in the human body.

"Along with quality, Anheuser-Busch is committed to growth and innovation. That commitment has seen the company through rough times—two World Wars, prohibition, and the great depression. Although hundreds of breweries succumbed to difficult times like these and closed their doors, Anheuser-Busch survived and grew. During these trying periods, the company devised innovative ways to use its resources, its people, and its expertise. But in good times as well as bad, the company has always realized that while you have to do the best you can in the present, you must always keep your eyes turned toward the future."[12]

---

[10] Anheuser-Busch Companies, Inc., *Fact Book, 1989/90*, p. 3.
[11] "Busch Plans Theme Park in Spain," *Tampa Tribune*, May 25, 1989, pp. 1D, 8D; Anheuser-Busch, *Annual Report 1990*, p. 31.
[12] *Fact Book 1989/90*, p. 3.

EXHIBIT 22.3 **Financial Information for Business Segments (In millions)**

1989	Beer and Beer-Related[a]		Food Products		Entertainment[b]	
Net Sales	$7,405.7	78.1%	$1,803.0	19.0%	$ 286.3	3.0%
Operating Income	1,244.7	93.7	56.9	4.3	27.1	2.0
Depreciation and						
Amortization Expense	298.7	72.8	87.2	21.3	24.4	5.9
Capital Expenditures	846.6	78.6	120.2	11.2	109.9	10.2
Identifiable Assets	5,902.9	68.0	1,295.6	14.9	1,493.4	17.1
Corporate Assets						
Total Assets						
1988						
Net Sales	$6,902.0	77.3%	$1,680.9	18.8%		
Operating Income	1,168.2	92.4	55.0	4.4		
Depreciation and						
Amortization Expense	252.9	70.4	70.7	19.7		
Capital Expenditures	785.4	82.6	100.9	10.6		
Identifiable Assets	5,102.4	76.5	1,229.7	18.4		
Corporate Assets						
Total Assets						
1987						
Net Sales	$6,375.8	76.4%	$1,627.2	19.5%		
Operating Income	1,090.2	94.9	54.4	4.8		
Depreciation and						
Amortization Expense	215.4	67.3	70.4	22.0		
Capital Expenditures	630.4	74.9	149.1	17.7		
Identifiable Assets	4,580.5	74.7	1,230.1	20.0		
Corporate Assets						
Total Assets						
1986						
Net Sales	$5,892.0	76.0%	$1,552.7	20.0%		
Operating Income	945.2	92.9	56.6	5.6		
Depreciation and						
Amortization Expense	192.3	68.4	60.5	21.5		
Capital Expenditures	544.8	68.5	100.9	20.6		
Identifiable Assets	4,083.2	74.2	1,114.1	20.2		
Corporate Assets						
Total Assets						
1985						
Net Sales	$5,412.6	77.3%	$1,416.4	20.2%		
Operating Income	797.0	95.8	28.5	3.4		
Depreciation and						
Amortization Expense	161.7	68.5	53.2	22.5		
Capital Expenditures		76.7	103.7	17.3		
Identifiable Assets				20.2		
Corporate Assets						
Total Assets						

[a] In 1989, Communication and Transportation are included in this segment. It was part of Diversified Operations in previous years.

[b] In 1989, Entertainment became a principal business segment. It was part of diversified operations in previous years.

[c] Before 1989, Diversified Operations was a business segment. Notes a and b show how it was eliminated.

Source: Anheuser-Busch *Annual Report 1989, 1988, and 1985*, pp. 58–59; p. 46; and p. 50.

	Diversified Operations[c]		Eliminations		Consolidated
			(13.7)	(0.1)%	$9,481.3
				0.0	1,328.7
				0.0	410.3
				0.0	1,076.7
				0.0	8,691.9
					343.8
					$9,025.7
	$361.8	4.18%	($20.6)	(0.2)%	$8,924.1
	40.9	3.2		0.9	1,264.1
	35.4	9.9		0.0	359.0
	64.2	6.8		0.0	950.5
	340.0	5.1		0.0	6,673.0
					436.8
					$7,109.8
	$366.1	4.3%	($19.4)	(0.2)%	$8,349.7
	4.0	0.3		0.0	1,148.6
	34.3	10.7		0.0	320.1
	62.3	7.4		0.0	841.8
	325.0	5.3		0.0	6,135.6
					412.3
					$6,547.9
	$ 32.4	4.2%	($21.0)	(0.2)%	$7,754.3
	15.6	1.5		0.0	1,018.0
	28.4	10.1		0.0	281.2
	87.1	10.9		0.0	796.2
	307.0	5.6		0.0	5,504.9
					393.2
					$5,898.1
	$189.6	2.7%	($13.9)	(0.2)%	$7,000.3
	6.8	0.8		0.0	823.3
	21.2	9.0		0.0	236.1
	36.1	6.0		0.0	601.0
	174.6	3.8		0.0	4,626.1
					495.3
					$5,121.4

In planning for the future, Anheuser-Busch would continue its long-term commitment to diversification. These efforts were to be maintained as long as they were consistent with meeting the company's objectives.

THE PRODUCT

Beer uniquely fits contemporary lifestyles. The five hallmarks of beer as a consumer beverage are convenience, moderation, health, value, and thirst-quenching properties. Each member of the Anheuser-Busch family of 14 beers was positioned to take advantage of this lifestyle. Exhibit 22.4 shows the target market for each of the company's beers.

Domestic consumption of alcoholic beverages continued to decline by about 2 percent annually.[13] Exhibit 22.5 provides information on the consumption of beer by segments (popular, premium, superpremium, light, low-alcohol, imported, malt liquor, and ale), and growth rates by segments and per capita consumption of beer, wine, distilled spirits, and coolers. The only projected growth segments for beer appeared to be light beer and imported beers; all other beer segments had a projected negative growth factor. Some of the reasons for the decline in alcohol consumption were the rising health consciousness among consumers and the focused attention on the dangers of drinking and driving. Also, the Census Bureau indicated a drop in the 20- to 39-year-old age group (see Exhibit 22.6).

EXHIBIT 22.4   Anheuser-Busch Beers

Beer	Class	Target Market
Budweiser	Premium	Any demographic or ethnic group and any region of the country
Bud Light	Light	Young to middle-age males
Bud Dry	Premium dry	New taste
Michelob	Superpremium	Contemporary adults
Michelob Light	Light	Young, active, upscale drinker with high-quality lifestyle
Michelob Dry	Dry	Yuppies
Busch	Popular	Consumers who prefer lighter-tasting beer at a value
Busch Light	Light	Popular-priced light beer
Natural Light	Light	Beverage to go with good food
LA	Low alcohol	Health-conscious consumers (ceased production May, 1990)
O'Doul's	Nonalcoholic	Great tasting beer without alcohol
King Cobra	Malt liquor	Contemporary male adults, aged 21–24
Carlsberg	Lager	Import market
Elephant Malt Liquor	Malt liquor	Consumers who enjoy imported beer

[13] "Beverage Industry," *Value Line*, November 23, 1990, p. 1533.

EXHIBIT 22.5   Apparent Beer Consumption by Segment (Barrels in millions)

| | 1970 | | 1975 | | 1980 | | 1985 | | 1990 | | 1995 | | 2000 | |
	Barrels	Share	Barrels	Share	Barrels	Share	Barrels	Share	Barrels	Share	Barrels	Share	Barrels	Share
Popular	71.6	58.3%	65.4	43.5%	30.0	16.9%	33.3	18.2%	30.5	16.5%	28.0	15.4%	26.0	14.4%
Premium	46.1	37.5	71.6	47.6	102.3	57.5	86.1	47.1	81.5	44.0	75.7	41.6	72.5	40.2
Super-premium	1.1	0.9	5.0	3.3	11.5	6.5	8.8	4.8	7.0	3.8	6.9	3.8	6.8	3.8
Light	—	—	2.8	1.9	22.1	12.4	39.4	21.6	49.0	26.4	52.0	28.6	54.0	30.0
Low Alcohol	—	—	—	—	—	—	0.4	0.2	0.1	0.1	0.1	0.1	0.1	0.1
Imported	0.9	0.7	1.7	1.1	4.6	2.6	7.9	4.3	11.0	5.9	13.5	7.4	16.0	8.9
Malt Liquor	3.1	2.5	3.8	2.5	5.5	3.1	5.5	3.0	5.2	2.8	4.7	2.6	4.2	2.3
Ale	—	—	—	—	1.9	1.1	1.3	0.7	1.0	0.5	0.9	0.5	0.7	0.4
Total	122.8	100.0	150.3	100.0	177.9	100.0	182.7	100.0	185.3	100.0	181.8	100.0	180.3	100.0

Source: *Impact Data Bank,* 1988 ed. Table 4–E, p. 30; Table 4–6, p. 31; Table 8–A, p. 75.

EXHIBIT 22.5   (cont.)

| | *Average Annual Compound Growth Rate* | | | | | |
Segment	1970–75	1975–80	1980–85	1985–90	1990–95	1995–2000
Popular	−1.8%	−14.4%	2.1%	−1.7%	−1.7%	−1.5%
Premium	9.2	7.4	−3.4	−1.1	−1.5	−0.9
Superpremium	35.4	18.1	−5.2	−4.5	−0.3	−0.3
Light	—	51.2	12.3	4.5	1.2	0.8
Low Alcohol	—	—	+	−24.2	—	—
Imported	13.5	22.2	11.6	6.8	4.2	3.5
Malt Liquor	4.2	7.7	—	−1.1	−2.0	−2.2
Ale	n/a	n/a	−7.3	−5.1	−2.1	−4.9
Total	4.1%	3.4%	0.5%	0.3%	−0.4%	−0.2%

Source: *Impact DataBank,* 1988 Ed., Table 8B, p. 76.

EXHIBIT 22.5   (cont.)

Per Capita Consumption
(Gallons per Adult)

| | Year | |
Category	1989E	2000E
Wine	2.54	2.12
Distilled Spirits	2.15	1.63
Beers	33.79	29.37
Coolers	0.62	0.37
Total Alcoholic Beverages	39.10	33.48

Source: *Market Watch,* April 1990, p. 24.

EXHIBIT 22.6 U.S. Population Projections[a]

	1990	1995	2000	2005	2010	2015	2020	2025
All Ages[a]	250,410,000	260,138,000	268,266,000	275,604,000	282,575,000	288,997,000	294,364,000	298,252,000
Under 5 years	18,408,000	17,799,000	16,898,000	16,611,000	16,899,000	17,213,000	17,095,000	16,664,000
5 to 9 years	18,378,000	18,759,000	18,126,000	17,228,000	16,940,000	17,225,000	17,542,000	17,428,000
10 to 14 years	17,284,000	18,847,000	19,208,000	18,575,000	17,670,000	17,380,000	17,674,000	18,000,000
15 to 19 years	17,418,000	17,567,000	19,112,000	19,477,000	18,839,000	17,930,000	17,642,000	17,940,000
20 to 24 years	18,698,000	17,482,000	17,600,000	19,109,000	19,453,000	18,818,000	17,931,000	17,657,000
25 to 29 years	21,511,000	18,966,000	17,736,000	17,822,000	19,310,000	19,642,000	19,020,000	18,144,000
30 to 34 years	22,414,000	21,996,000	19,413,000	18,175,000	18,262,000	19,750,000	20,080,000	19,457,000
35 to 39 years	20,220,000	22,244,000	21,820,000	19,274,000	18,041,000	18,115,000	19,576,000	19,906,000
40 to 44 years	17,677,000	20,092,000	22,091,000	21,678,000	19,161,000	17,931,000	18,015,000	19,463,000
45 to 49 years	13,947,000	17,489,000	19,885,000	21,892,000	21,482,000	18,980,000	17,769,000	17,855,000
50 to 54 years	11,540,000	13,808,000	17,338,000	19,736,000	21,725,000	21,328,000	18,866,000	17,679,000
55 to 59 years	10,623,000	11,229,000	13,459,000	16,917,000	19,259,000	21,195,000	20,811,000	18,422,000
60 to 64 years	10,741,000	10,096,000	10,699,000	12,846,000	16,171,000	18,420,000	20,276,000	19,925,000
65 to 69 years	10,251,000	10,056,000	9,491,000	10,106,000	12,163,000	15,319,000	17,467,000	19,257,000
70 to 74 years	8,122,000	8,874,000	8,752,000	8,304,000	8,876,000	10,705,000	13,506,000	15,420,000
75 to 79 years	6,105,000	6,607,000	7,282,000	7,246,000	6,913,000	7,419,000	8,981,000	11,378,000
80 to 84 years	3,828,000	4,315,000	4,735,000	5,287,000	5,295,000	5,068,000	5,462,000	6,647,000
85 to 89 years	2,065,000	2,433,000	2,803,000	3,141,000	3,554,000	3,587,000	3,459,000	3,769,000
90 to 94 years	873,000	1,074,000	1,302,000	1,539,000	1,759,000	2,017,000	2,061,000	2,014,000
95 to 99 years	260,000	330,000	417,000	520,000	631,000	738,000	864,000	903,000
100 years and over	56,000	76,000	100,000	131,000	171,000	217,000	266,000	325,000
Median age in years	33.0	34.7	36.4	37.8	39.0	39.5	40.2	41.0
Mean age in years	35.4	36.2	37.1	38.1	39.1	39.9	40.7	41.5

[a] Includes armed forces overseas.

Source: U.S. Department of Commerce, Bureau of the Census, Population Series, p. 14.

The perennial beer drinkers' preferences can and do change. Dry beer and nonalcoholic beer appeared to be successful in the test markets, but their true staying power remains unknown. For example, LA beer was dropped from the Anheuser-Busch line in 1990 because it lost its positioning when the company introduced O'Doul's brand of nonalcoholic beer.

Anheuser-Busch had 13 breweries located in 10 states, with an annual capacity of 85.1 million barrels of beer (see Exhibit 22.7). The 13th brewery at Centerville, Georgia, became operational in 1992 at a cost of approximately $300 million; its annual capacity was 6 million barrels. The expansion by Anheuser-Busch was the opposite of other brewers, which have been consolidating capacity. Mr. Busch sees ". . . expansion as necessary for 'market penetration and growth,' never blinking from Anheuser-Busch's projected 50-share by the mid-1990s."[14]

In order to meet the increasing demand for its beer, Anheuser-Busch developed an extensive expansion and modernization program. A 3.6-million barrel expansion at the Newark brewery was completed in 1990, and the capacity at the Tampa brewery was to be expanded by 800,000 barrels to 2.7 million. Mini-expansions were occurring at six other plants, and when completed would add approximately 2.5 million barrels of capacity.

Mr. Busch, talking about the cost of the ingredients (barley, rice, corn, hops, and others) to make beers, said, "We pay premium to the market because we demand the highest quality ingredients that money can buy. We have the highest cost of ingredients of anybody in the brewing industry. I can prove it to you. We

EXHIBIT 22.7   U.S. Production Facilities

Brewery	Year Opened	Capacity (In millions of barrels)
St. Louis	1880	12.6
Newark	1951	5.8
Los Angeles	1954	12.1
Tampa	1959	1.9
Houston	1966	9.7
Columbus	1968	6.4
Jacksonville	1969	6.7
Merrimack	1970	3.1
Williamsburg	1972	9.0
Fairfield	1976	3.7
Baldwinsville	1982	8.2
Fort Collins	1988	5.9
Total in 1990		85.1
Centerville	1992	6.0
Total in 1992		91.0

[14] Jabbonsky, "What Keeps A-B Hot?" p. 28.

must make sure that we are the lowest cost producer."[15] Mr. Busch went on to say, "Quality comes first." Mr. Busch's statements tied directly into the primary reason the company gives for Anheuser-Busch's outstanding record of achievement: "Quality—First and most importantly, Anheuser-Busch believes in quality. Quality is never sacrificed for economic reasons—or for any other reason. The company is firmly convinced that its belief in and strict adherence to quality is the fundamental, irreplaceable ingredient in its successful performance for more than 100 years. That quality is there for everybody to see, to taste, to experience, and to enjoy. 'Somebody still cares about quality' is more than a corporate slogan at Anheuser-Busch. It's a way of life."[16]

PROMOTION

Anheuser-Busch, probably the largest sponsor of sporting events, racing vehicles, and broadcasts, had its beers affiliated with sports for years (see Exhibit 22.8). In 1989, the company spent $32 million on advertising during the Olympic games.

The alcoholic beverage industry spent a total of $1,318,900,000 on advertising in 1988. The advertising mix by medium and by alcoholic beverage industry segment (beer, distilled spirts, wine, and coolers) is shown in Exhibit 22.9. The brewers spent nearly $900 million on advertising, or 68.3 percent of the total industry expenditures. The number one advertising medium for brewers continued to be television; magazines remained as the primary advertising medium for distilled spirits marketers.

Total media spending by the brewers for 1988 was over double the level for 1980. The per-case expenditure for beer has more than doubled during the same period, from 18 cents to 37 cents. Anheuser-Busch's advertising expenditures increased by 8 percent to $385 million, or 61.6 percent of the company's total for promotion. The company's total for 1988 increased 3.2 percent over 1987. Anheuser-Busch's advertising expenditures were 42.8 percent of total brewers' expenditures. Adolph Coors increased its advertising outlays by 30.7 percent to 126 million. Miller Brewing cut its media expenditures by $12.8 million, or 6.3 percent, from $202 million to $189 million or 21.0 percent of the total industry expenditures. G. Heileman Brewing (Bond Corporation) increased its expenditures by 41 percent to $42 million. Sam Frank, vice president of marketing for Heileman, said, "The way you try to build a regional brand is with regional affiliations to prevent more share erosion by national brands. You have to play on the big boy's turf, so to speak, if you want to prove to consumers that you're as good as national brands. You've got to advertise heavily."[17] G. Heileman sales declined by 10.4 percent despite the substantial increase in the marketing budget.

[15] Ibid.
[16] *Fact Book 1989/90*, p. 3.
[17] "Total Media Spending Drops 3.9% in '88 as Brewers Increase Outlays to $900 Million," *Impact*, Vol. 19, Nos. 16, 17, August 15 and September 1, 1989, p. 4.

EXHIBIT 22.8 Anheuser-Busch Companies, Sports Affiliation and Sponsorships

Budweiser		Bud Light	
Horse Racing	Irish Derby Breeders' Cup Budweiser International	Powerboat Racing	Powerboat Racing Team ABC Masters
Hydroplane Racing	Miss Budweiser	Bowling	
CART/Indy Car	Truesports Indy Car	Triathlons	Ironman World Championship U.S. Triathlon Series
Drag Racing	King Funny Car		
NASCAR	Junior Johnson Ford	**Busch**	
CART/NASCAR	Budweiser International Race of Champions	NASCAR	Official Beer of NASCAR Busch Pole Award Busch Clash
Olympics	Corporate Sponsor	Pool	British Pool League
PGA Golf	Anheuser-Busch Golf Classic		
Boxing	Golden Gloves	**Michelob**	
PBA Bowling	Budweiser Hall of Fame	Skiing	Team Michelob
Soccer	Major Indoor Soccer League U.S. Soccer Federation World Cup U.S. National Team	Golf	Golf Advisory Staff
Shooting	Shooting Exhibitions by Willis Corbett		
Surfing	Pro Surfing Tour		

Source: Anheuser-Busch Companies, Inc., *Fact Book—1989/90*, p. 61

EXHIBIT 22.9   Alcoholic Beverage Advertising Expenditures by Medium[a] (In millions)

Medium	Beer	Distilled Spirits	Wine	Coolers	Total
Television	$679.7	$0.5	$64.2	$75.3	$819.7
Radio	144.8	1.0	11.6	3.9	161.3
Total Broadcast	824.5	1.5	75.8	79.2	981.0
Magazines	18.0	179.6	13.2	0.9	211.7
Outdoor	22.5	34.1	0.6	0.9	58.1
Newspapers	33.5	17.9	4.7	1.7	57.8
Newspaper Supplements	0.8	7.4	1.7	0.2	10.1
Total Print and Outdoor	74.8	239.0	20.3	3.7	337.8
	$899.3	$240.5	$96.2	$82.9	$1,318.9

[a] Columns may not add up because of rounding.
Source: *Impact DataBank,* Vol. 19, August 15 and September 15, 1989, p. 4.

Charles Fruit, vice president of corporate media for Anheuser-Busch said, "Our competitors continue to focus the majority of their television advertising in sports sponsorships and I would think that would continue to be a competitive area." In 1988, Anheuser-Busch allocated $11 million to introduce Michelob Dry on a national basis, while decreasing Michelob Light's expenditures from $33 million to $18 million. Mr. Fruit commented, "With the emergence of Michelob Dry, the whole Michelob family is registering positive trends again. Our regular Michelob brand had experienced the same softness. Dry invigorated the entire family."[18]

Anheuser-Busch Promotional Products Group had approximately 10,000 different items available at any one time. This included such items as caps, glassware, mugs, clothing, and key chains, all bearing the A & B eagle, Clydesdale, or beer-brand logos. Each year more than 1,500 new promotional items were created and authorized.

Anheuser-Busch acted as the Rolling Stones' primary U.S. sponsor for their 1989 27-city tour. A 30-second TV spot, "Honky Tonk Woman" featured the concert with a Bud bottle showing up every now and then.

In 1990, Anheuser-Busch announced its "market-share strategy," that was to pull millions of advertising dollars out of radio and television to spend more on "grass-roots" events and point-of-purchase promotions. This new strategy was announced to combat the price discounting in the industry (see Exhibit 22.10). According to Robert Weinberg, beer analyst, "Relative to competition, Anheuser-Busch was probably over advertising.[19]

[18] Ibid., pp. 3–4.
[19] Richard Gibson, "Bud Puts Stress on Promotions, Trims TV Ads," *Wall Street Journal,* February 21, 1990, p. B- 5.

EXHIBIT 22.10   Anheuser-Busch Advertising Expenditures, 1989 and 1990

Media	1989	1990
Network Television	$181,467	$129,009
Spot Television	94,835	91,646
Syndicated Television	10,753	13,703
Cable Television	26,300	26,788
Network Radio	7,707	983
Spot Radio	42,073	21,147
Magazines	8,834	7,767
Newspapers	9,537	3,989
Newspaper Magazines	399	243
Outdoor	6,148	6,058
Total Measured Media	388,055	301,331
Total Unmeasured	203,400	157,900
Total	$591,455	$459,231

Source: *Advertising Age,* September 25, 1991, p. 4.

PRICING

The brewers were in the midst of a prolonged beer price war. During 1989, both Coors, the nation's fourth largest brewery, and Miller, number two, had been aggressively promoting and discounting their prices in order to boost volume for several of their key products, and in November, Anheuser-Busch joined the price war. Prices for Budweiser, the number one selling brand of beer, were discounted.

Value Line expected the price war "to lead to yet another industry shake-out. The playing field has narrowed considerably in recent years, but we think yet more changes are in the offing." They went on to say, "The most important questions are not who will be the winner and loser, but how long the price war will last and just what exactly do the victors win?" *Value Line* expected prices to continue on a downward trend and thought that the industry players recognized that there were significant long-term benefits at stake. One share point is approximately equal to 1 million barrels of beer.[20]

Most economists saw continuing recession at least through the first quarters of 1992. Historically, beer demand tended to hold up well during periods of downturns or recessions, but combined with the excise tax and inflation, brewers could experience a downturn as well. Anheuser-Busch's pricing strategy varied somewhat by market. Actually, by offering 14 different types of beer there was a product to satisfy each price point.

[20] "Beverage Industry," *Value Line*, November 1989, p. 1528.

DISTRIBUTION CHANNELS

The company distributed its beer in the United States and the Caribbean through a network of 10 company-owned wholesale operations employing approximately 1,600 people and about 950 independently owned wholesale companies (see Exhibit 22.11). The independent wholesalers employed approximately 30,000 people. Canadian and European distribution was achieved through special arrangements with foreign brewing companies.

The Anheuser-Busch Investment Capital Corporation, a subsidiary company, was formed in 1984 to share equity positions with qualified partners in Anheuser-Busch distributorships. This subsidiary provided operating general partners to function as independent wholesalers while increasing their equity and building toward total ownership. Anheuser-Busch Investment Capital Corporation played a key role in strengthening the brewer-wholesaler team.

EXHIBIT 22.11   Distribution Map

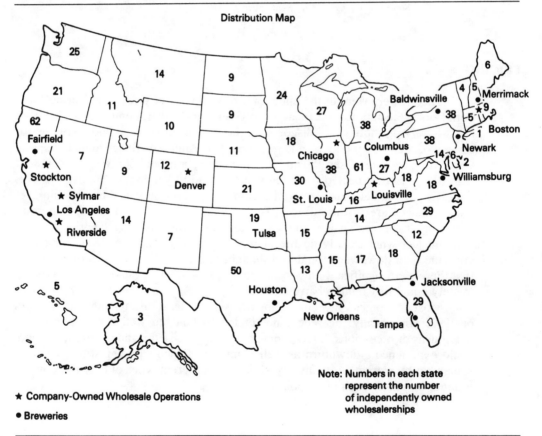

Note: Numbers in each state represent the number of independently owned wholesalerships

★ Company-Owned Wholesale Operations

● Breweries

When Mr. Busch was asked if "strong brewers and beer products make strong wholesalers or strong wholesalers make strong brewers, Busch lays the 'chicken-or-egg theory' to rest, noting succinctly, 'It takes both.'" Henry King, former president of the United States Brewing Association, said, "I've been with August when we've been driving along and he's spotted an A-B distributor's truck." Recalled King, "He pulled up behind it and spoke into his little cassette to dictate a memo to his secretary to send a letter of compliment to the wholesaler because his truck was beautifully cleaned and everything. Had that truck been dirty, there would have been a letter reprimanding him as well."[21]

Busch counts on the wholesalers as "one of our most important assets, who provide critical service to retailers. Personal service is key . . . they are the front-line merchandisers for the entire system and . . . indispensable to the system." "Together with our wholesalers," Busch stated, "we share a commitment to provide the consumer with the highest quality, best tasting, and freshest beer products through the three-tier system, in which the brewer, wholesaler, and retailer each play an important role." He went on to say, "Strong products, suppliers, wholesalers, and service equal retailer profitability. Quality to the consumer and product presentation equal sales success."[22]

THE EXTERNAL ENVIRONMENT

Competition

In 1970, the top five brewers in the United States comprised 33.3 percent of sales. In 1990, this had increased to 89.3 percent share of sales. During this same time period, Anheuser-Busch's market share increased from 18.1 percent to 43.4 percent. Miller Brewing, Stroh's Brewery, G. Heileman, and Adolph Coors increased their market share since 1970 as well. Exhibit 22.12 illustrates the market shares of the leading brewers in the United States.

The big market share shift in the decade of the 1980s was accomplished by Anheuser-Busch, as Miller Brewing remained at approximately the same level. A major part of Stroh Brewery's growth occurred with the acquisition of Joseph Schlitz Brewing Company in 1982, and F&M Schaefer in 1981.

The Market Share Leader.   Anheuser-Busch set a corporate objective of 50 percent market share by the mid-1990s. In 1990, the company's market share was 43.4 percent, compared with 37.1 percent share in 1985, and 28.2 percent a decade ago.

The Market Share Challenger.   Miller Brewing was Anheuser-Busch's prime competitor from the time Philip Morris Company acquired Miller in 1970. Its market

---

[21] Jabbonsky, "What Keeps A-B Hot?" p. 28.
[22] Ibid.

EXHIBIT 22.12   Sales of Leading U.S. Brewers (In thousands of barrels)

	1970		1980		1985		1990	
	Volume	Market Share	Volume	Market Share	Volume	Market Share	Volume	Market Share
Anheuser-Bush	22,202	18.1%	50,160	28.2%	68,000	37.1%	86,400	43.4%
Miller Brewing	5,150	4.2	37,300	21.0	37,100	20.3	43,550	21.9
Adolh Coors Company	7,277	5.9	13,779	7.7	14,738	8.1	19,250	9.7
Stroh Brewery	3,276	2.7	6,161	3.5	23,400	12.8	16,200	8.1
G. Heileman Brewing	3,000	2.4	13,270	7.4	16,200	8.8	12,250	6.2
Top 5 Total	40,905	33.3	120,670	67.8	159,438	87.1	177,650	89.3
Other Domestic	80,995	68.0	52,830	29.6	15,662	8.6	12,246	6.2
Total Domestic	121,900	99.3	173,500	97.4	175,100	95.7	189,896	95.5
Imports	900	0.7	4,600	2.8	7,900	4.3	9,000	4.5
Grand Total	122,800	100.0	177,900	100.0	183,000	100.0	198,896	100.0

Source: *Impact*, Vol. 19, Nos. 16 & 17, August 15 and September 1, 1990, p. 3, *Wall Street Journal*, January 15, 1991, p. B-1.

share in 1970 was 4.2 percent (5.1 million barrels), ranking it as seventh in the industry. The company experienced rapid growth in the 1970s due to the successful introduction of "Lite" beer. Although growth had been rapid during the 1970s, market share remained relatively flat through the 1980s. Offering eight different brands, Miller ranked second in the industry. Anheuser-Busch countered Miller with two separate strategies. First, the company increased its advertising budgets, taking on Miller in head-to-head competition. Second, Anheuser-Busch developed a strategy of flanking each of Miller's products in every beer category with two Anheuser-Busch beer products (e.g., premium beers—Budweiser and Busch flanked Miller High Life).

In December 1989, Miller Brewing introduced a new nonalcoholic beer called Sharp's. At about the same time, Anheuser-Busch delivered its planned O'Doul's brand. The two new brands challenged the industry leader in nonalcoholic beers, Kingsbury, brewed by G. Heileman Brewing, and a host of imported brands such as Cardinal Brewery's Moussy, Binding Brauerei's Clausthaler, and Guinness' Kaliber. Nonalcoholic beer represented less than one-half of 1 percent of domestic beer consumption, but it was growing at a 6 to 15 percent rate yearly.[23] Supposedly, Miller Brewing did not fully test market Sharp's in order to beat Anheuser-Busch into the market place.

Stroh Brewery.   In 1981, the Stroh Brewery purchased F&M Schaefer and closed its Detroit brewery (7.2 million barrel capacity). On April 27, 1982, the Joseph Schlitz Brewing Company was merged into Stroh Brewery, resulting in Stroh becoming the third largest brewer. The company shipped 16.2 million barrels of beer in 1990, representing an 8.1 percent market share, which was a decline from its peak of 12.8 percent share in 1985.

Adolph Coors Company.   The fourth largest brewer, Adolph Coors Company, had an 11.8 percent volume increase in sales in 1990. This increase was the largest of any of the major brewers in the United States. It was enough to move Coors from fifth place to fourth in market share.

In September 1989, Coors proposed the acquisition of Stroh Brewing Company for $425 million. The acquisition was opposed in the federal courts by S&P Company, a privately held company that owned Falstaff, Pabst, Pearl, and General Brewing Companies. S&P Co. alleged that the merger would violate the antitrust laws. In addition, G. Heileman Brewing was considering antitrust action against Coors as a purchaser. (Heileman also had considered making a bid for parts of the Stroh Company.) The merger had to be approved by the U.S. Department of Justice (DOJ). Peter H. Coors, president of Coors Brewery, had commented on why his company was interested in purchasing Stroh's, "You can't survive long term with a nine percent market share." The transaction was supposed to close in early 1990, but Coors eventually withdrew its offer.[24]

---

[23] "This Safe Suds Is For You," *Newsweek*, March 5, 1990, p. 42.

[24] "Insights," *Impact*, Vol. 19, No. 20, October 15, 1989, p. 12; "Coors May Take a Gulp of a Rival Brew," *Business Week*, October 21, 1989, p. 70.

G. Heileman Brewing. The United States' fifth largest brewer, Heileman had been very effective in competing against Anheuser-Busch in regional markets. It successfully developed and implemented a strategy of acquiring struggling local brewers at low cost. After acquiring the new brewery, Heileman reintroduced its brands with an aggressive marketing plan. Anheuser-Busch countered with a strategy focused on heavy price competition from its Busch brand. Although G. Heileman halted its planned expansion into the Southwest market, the company's market share grew from 2.4 percent (3.0 million barrels) in 1970 to 8.8 percent (16.2 million barrels) in 1985. The company's earnings from the brewing industry declined by 11 percent in 1985, and it closed its small Phoenix plant (500,000 barrels.)

In a hostile takeover in 1987, Bond Holding Corporation, an Australian conglomerate involved in the world beer market, acquired G. Heileman Brewing Company. Since the takeover, Heileman faced weakening sales and deteriorating finances. In 1989, Heileman suffered its third year of declining beer shipments. In Chicago, Heileman's largest market, "supermarket sales of Old Style last year slipped to 15 percent market share from 21 percent."[25] In April 1990, Bond announced that Heileman was close to restructuring its bank loans. The banks would write off the debt and take an equity investment in the company. Heileman management had previously announced plans to sell some unneeded breweries and, possibly, some minor brands. However, market share further deteriorated in 1990 to 6.2 percent, which caused Heileman to lose its fourth place position to Coors. A continuation of the price war would cause further deterioration of the weaker beer companies.

Niche Strategies. During the 1980s, many micro-breweries and boutique-type breweries were started. These breweries had a different target market from the national firms. The target market for these breweries was the connoisseur, the moderate beer drinker who is particular and seeks a certain taste. Actually, the select target market for the distinctive taste cuts across the traditional demographic lines and was not limited to any one class.

International Competition. Anheuser-Busch's world market share was approximately 9.5 percent. Miller Brewing, which was in second place, had approximately 5.0 percent of the world market. The top two brewers were American, and the next three (Heineken NV—4 percent, Kerin Brewery Co.—3.1 percent, and Bond Corporation—3.1 percent) were European. These top five brewers had approximately 30 percent of the world market. The annual growth rate for the entire world market was 3 to 4 percent a year.[26] The per capita consumption of beer for the top 20 countries ranged from 38.73 gallons in West Germany to

25 Ira Teinowitz, "Heileman Close to Deal with Banks," *Advertising Age*, April 16, 1990, p. 66.
26 Paul Heme, "King of Beers in Bitter Battle in Britain," *Wall Street Journal*, June 9, 1988, p. 26.

16.03 gallons in Venezuela. The United States was ranked in 12th place with 13.99 gallons. Eight nations exceeded the 30-gallon per capita figure.[27]

Leonard Goldstein, president of Miller Brewing Company, said, "I think U.S. brewers have a long way to go in the overseas markets . . . we're in more than 50 countries . . . they are all very small situations to get our foot in the door . . . [it allows] us [to] see what innovation is around the world."[28]

The international market was estimated to be three and one-half to four times the size of the U.S. market. In the Far East and Europe, the consumption of alcoholic beverages was on the rise. All the U.S. brewers, except Coors, were largely pursuing a share of these markets. *Value Line* "believes overseas sales will play an increasing larger role in the results of brewers . . . with 1990 easing of economic barriers in Europe."[29] The world market for beer, including the U.S. market, was approximately 700 million barrels.

Anheuser-Busch International, the company's international licensing and marketing subsidiary, was formed in 1981 to develop and explore markets outside the United States. Budweiser was introduced into England in 1984 and four years later had eked out only a 1 percent share of the market. It was the same Bud that was sold in the United States. By contrast, Australian Foster's, made by Elder IXL, modified its brew to appeal to British tastes. Foster's had a 6 percent market share after seven years. Norman Strauss, British marketing consultant, said, "Foster got into the British lager drinking culture with the humor of its ads [Paul Hogan of *Crocodile Dundee* is the Foster spokesperson] and an unerring eye for the pub lifestyle." Budweiser's first approach was to sell America without addressing British pub culture. Anheuser-Busch went through three advertising agencies in the past two years. John Dunsmore, a beer analyst, said, "The day Anheuser stops gaining share in the States' beer market, they'll go into overdrive in trying to develop their international business." He went on to say, "They could well be too late."[30]

Mr. Busch states, "As we go along, we are learning how to deal in these international markets from our partners."[31] Budweiser was licensed-brewed in 7 countries and exported to more than 30 others. Additional expansions were planned. Budweiser was marketed in Japan as a superpremium beer and led in the category. Bud had great success in Japan and Korea. Anheuser-Busch's prominent partners around the world included Carlsberg, Guinness, Suntory, and Oriental Brewery.

Robert S. Weinberg, beer analyst and consultant, said, "If you're talking about continuing to license and play the game as they are playing it . . . I think it is a very attractive and worthwhile game." He went on to say, "If you're talking

[27] *Impact Data Bank—1988 Edition*, Table 2-AA, p. 20.
[28] "Miller's Drive to Innovate," *Impact*, Vol. 20, No. 9, May 1, 1990, p. S.
[29] *Value Line*, November 23, 1990, p. 1533.
[30] *Impact Data Bank*, Table 4-AA, p. 43.
[31] Jabbonsky, "What Keeps A-B Hot?" p. 30.

about buying breweries and so forth, I don't think there are any great economies of scale in being an international brewing company."[32]

Social Values and Beer

Anheuser-Busch "is deeply concerned about the abuse of alcohol and the problem of driving while intoxicated. It supports the proposition that anything less than responsible consumption of alcoholic beverages is detrimental to the individual, society, and to the brewing industry."[33] The company was a leader in developing programs that support this position.

Anheuser-Busch designed programs to meet the needs of its employees, its wholesalers, its retailers, and its customers. The programs covered the following areas: (1) consumer education programs—Know When to Say When, The Buddy System, and Pit Stop; (2) training retailers—TIPS (Training for Intervention Procedures by Servers of Alcohol); (3) designated driver programs—Alert Cab and I'm Driving; (4) helping communities fight against alcohol abuse—Operation ALERT (Action and Leadership through Education Responsibility and Training) (5) helping employees deal with alcohol abuse—Employee Assistance Program; (6) company guidelines and policies—Industry Advertising Code and Young Adult Marketing Guidelines; (7) underage drinking—SADD (Students against Driving Drunk); and (8) Alcohol Research Center, UCLA.

Legislation and Litigation

In recent years, Anheuser-Busch became more active in monitoring and taking positions on issues that could have a major impact on the company. The Industry and Government Affairs Division expanded in order to identify and respond to such issues with specific programs.

Trademark Protection. A lawsuit, filed by G. Heileman Brewing and joined by Miller Brewing Company against Anheuser-Busch's use of "LA" (low alcohol) as a brand name, was won by Anheuser-Busch with its claim that LA was a trademark and not a generic term. However, a short time later the company dropped LA from the product line when its O'Doul's brand was introduced.

Exclusive Distribution. The Malt Beverage Interbrand Competition Act of 1985 dealt with the exclusive wholesale distribution rights for distributors within their territories. The state of Indiana was the only state to forbid exclusive distribution contracts, and 27 states required the contracts.

In 1977, a Supreme Court decision ruled such exclusive contracts could be legal if the contracts did not hamper competition, but that a decision would be made on a case-by-case basis. Distributors and brewers said that this court

[32] Ibid.
[33] *Fact Book 1989/90*, p. 33.

decision created lawsuits by inviting competitors, both wholesalers and retailers, to challenge the competitor's exclusive distribution contracts.

A new bill, which was cleared by the Senate Judiciary Committee, would preserve the right to sue for antitrust violations. The 140-member U.S. Brewers Association and the 2,000-member National Beer Wholesaler Association lobbied for the bill, because they felt it would clarify the existing antitrust law. Opponents to the bill, including the Federal Trade Commission, Senator Strom Thurmond, Senator Howard Metzenbaum, and numerous consumer groups, felt that exempting the beer industry from the antitrust laws would increase prices and reduce competition. In fact, the New York attorney-general filed a class action lawsuit against Miller, Stroh, Heileman, and Anheuser-Busch claiming that their exclusive agreements with distributors caused price increases and decreased competition.

Kickbacks. Dennis P. Long, president of Anheuser-Busch, resigned in March 1988 when Joseph E. Martino, vice president of sales, and Michael A. Orloff, vice president for wholesaling, left the company after an internal investigation of kickbacks at Anheuser-Busch. Martino and Orloff were found guilty by a federal grand jury of fraud, conspiracy, and filing false tax returns. Mr. Long "was not accused of any wrongdoing, but stepped down because of what transpired under his nose."[34] With Mr. Long's departure, Mr. Busch became president of Anheuser-Busch, and kept this position until he appointed Mr. Stokes as president.

Minimum Drinking Age. The National Minimum Drinking Age Act of 1984 granted the federal government the authority to withhold federal highway funds from states that failed to raise their legal drinking age to 21 by 1986. Currently, all 50 states have mandated a 21-year-old minimum drinking age.

Anheuser-Busch and Minorities. In 1983, the Reverend Jesse Jackson's campaign PUSH was directed against Anheuser-Busch Companies. PUSH accused the company of discriminating against blacks and encouraged minorities to boycott Anheuser-Busch's products. Using the battle cry "Bud Is a Dud," Jackson claimed the company did not do business with enough minorities, did not hire and promote black employees, did not patronize black-oriented community organizations, and did not have enough black wholesalers in the distribution system. Eventually, Wayman Smith, vice president of corporate affairs, was able to make the Reverend Jackson aware of the company's minority hiring and promotion practices, its support to minorities throughout the country, and the role of minority suppliers.

[34] Jabbonsky, "What Keeps A-B Hot?" p. 26.

Excise Tax. In 1988, Anheuser-Busch paid $781 million in state and federal excise taxes. The company "believes that excise taxes discriminate against both the industries involved and consumers."[35]

Warning Labels. Congress passed legislation that went into effect in November 1989 requiring a warning statement to appear on all alcoholic beverage containers. The two-part statement read: "Government Warning: (1) According to the Surgeon General, women should not drink alcoholic beverages during pregnancy because of the risks of child defects. (2) "Consumption of alcoholic beverages impairs your ability to operate machinery and may cause serious health problems." The legislation required this two-part statement and restricted state governments from requiring any additional statements.

Advertising and Marketing Restrictions. There are proposals to ban beer and wine advertising from radio and television. In addition, some groups are calling for restriction of the brewing industry's ability to advertise or promote beer and wine at sporting events. Anheuser-Busch "strongly opposes such restrictions."[36]

Concentration and Possible Antitrust Review. A knowledgeable beer market analyst has wondered if the Department of Justice would take or propose antitrust action as Anheuser-Busch's market share approached 50 percent. This growth over the past decade from 28.2 percent in 1980 to 43.4 percent in 1990 was accomplished in a maturing industry through internal expansion. If Anheuser-Busch attempted to grow by merger to achieve 50 percent market share, the Justice Department would probably have rejected the mergers based on the Herfindahl Index. Named for Orris Herfindahl, an economist, the index is a calculation based on the premise that market leaders have even greater economic power in an industry than can be assumed by simply looking at market share. A possibility exists that one of the remaining small brewers will ask the Justice Department for protection or relief under the antitrust laws.

FINANCIAL CONDITION

In 1989 Anheuser-Busch completed the company's most successful decade in its 147-year history (see Exhibits 22.13 and 22.14). During the 1980s, net sales increased by 287.7 percent ($3,295,400,000 to $9,481,300,000); net income rose by 346.6 percent ($171,800,000 to $767,200,000); gross profits increased 332.3 percent

[35] *Fact Book 1989/90*, p. 54.
[36] Ibid., pp. 54, 59.

($741,500,800 to $3,205,500,000); and the total assets of the company increased 268.4 percent ($2,449,700,000 to $9,025,700,000). The company paid a stock dividend for 57 consecutive years (see Exhibit 22.15).

During 1989, the company established an employee stock ownership plan (ESOP) for its salaried and hourly employees. The plan borrowed $500 million to buy approximately 11.3 million shares of common stock from the company. The ESOP and other stock ownership plans would eventually lead to approximately 10 percent ownership by the company's employees.[37]

On November 26, 1989, Anheuser-Busch Companies registered more than 8 million shares of common stock with the Securities and Exchange Commission that may be sold periodically by the heirs of August Busch, Jr., who died in September 1989. This secondary share offering represented about 8.4 percent of the company's outstanding common stock. Before Mr. Busch's death, about 23 percent of the company was closely controlled—12 percent by Mr. Busch and 11 percent by Centerre Trust Company of St. Louis, and 1 percent by other directors.[38]

Over the next five years, the capital expenditures were expected to exceed $4.4 billion. The company was not opposed to long-term financing for some of its capital programs, but cash flow from operations would be the principal source of funds to support these programs. For short-term capital requirements, the company had access to a maximum of $500 million from a bank credit-line agreement. In 1992, the company had an AA bond rating. In 1989, the company's long-term debt almost doubled, from $1,615,300,000 in 1988 to $3,307,300,000 in 1989. (The acquisition of Sea World was for $1.1 billion.)

The beer and beer-related segment had sales of $7,405,700,000 (78.1 percent) and operating income of $1,244,700 (93.7 percent) in 1989. The food products segment had sales of $1,803,000,000 (19.0 percent) and operating income of $56,900,000 (4.3 percent), and the entertainment segment had sales of $286,300,000 (3.0 percent) and operating income of $27,100,000 (2.0 percent). The combined sales and operating income for the two nonbeer segments totaled 22.0 percent of sales and 6.3 percent of operating income. A former Anheuser-Busch executive would attribute the performance of the nonbeer segments to the fact that they were managed by "beer guys." He said, "They continue to use 'beer guys' on the diversifications. It's a big mistake."[39]

---

[37] "Directors Approve ESOP, Employees Could Own 10%," *Wall Street Journal*, April 27, 1989, p. C-17; "Heirs' Shares," *St. Petersburg Times*, November 27, 1989, B-1.

[38] "Anheuser-Busch," *Value Line*, August 25, 1989, p. 1531.

[39] Marshall, "The Czar of Beer," p. 30.

EXHIBIT 22.13   10 Year Financial Summary—Balance Sheet and Other Information
(In millions except per share and statistical data)

	1980	1981	1982	1983
Balance Sheet Information				
Working Capital	$ 26.3	$ 41.0	$ 60.2	$ 173.1
Current Ratio	1.1	1.1	1.1	1.2
Plant and Equipment, Net	1,947.4	1,324.5	3,579.8	3,269.8
Long-Term Debt	743.8	862.2	1,029.9	1,003.1
Total Debt to Total Debt Plus				
Equity (%)	43.4	42.5	36.8[a]	32.8[a]
Deferred Income Taxes	261.6	357.7	455.2	574.3
Shareholders' Equity	1,031.4	1,206.8	1,526.6	1,766.5
Return on Shareholders' Equity (%)	17.8	19.3	19.9[a]	18.0[a]
Book Value per Share	3.81	4.43	5.27	6.09
Total Assets	2,449.7	2,938.1	3,965.2	4,386.8
Other Information				
Capital Expenditures	$590.0	$441.5	$380.9	$441.3
Depreciation and Amortization	99.4	110.0	136.9	191.3
Total Payroll Cost	594.1	695.5	864.0	1,361.7
Effective Tax Rate (%)	35.7	33.2	40.0	43.7
Price/Earnings-Ratio	7.3	8.9	11.0	9.6
Percentage of Pretax Profit on				
Gross Sales (%)	7.1	7.3	9.1	9.2
Market Price Range of Common Stock				
High/	5 1/4	7 3/8	11 7/8	12 7/8
Low	3 1/2	4 1/2	6 1/2	9 3/4

Note: All per share information reflects the September 12, 1986 two-for-one stock split and the June 14, 1985, three-for-one stock split. All amounts reflect the acquisition of Campbell-Taggart, as of November 2, 1982, and the acquisitions of Sea World as of December 1, 1989. Financial information prior to 1988 has been restated to reflect the adoption in 1988 of Financial Accounting Standards No. 94, Consolidation of Majority-Owned Subsidiaries.

[a] This percentage has been calculated by including convertible redeemable preferred stock as part of equity because it was convertible into common stock and was trading primarily on its equity characteristics.

Source: *Annual Report 1989*, pp. 62–63.

	1984	1985	1986	1987	1988	1989
	$ 71.5	$ 116.0	$ (3.7)	$ 75.8	$ 15.2	$ (25.7)
	1.1	1.1	1.0	1.1	1.0	1.0
	3,579.5	4,494.9	4,994.8	4,994.8	5,467.7	6,671.3
	879.5	904.7	1,164.0	1,422.6	1,615.3	3,307.3
	28.2[a]	26.9[a]	31.6	33.0	34.2	52.4
	757.9	964.7	1,094.0	1,164.3	1,212.5	1,315.9
	1,951.0	2,173.0	2,313.7	2,892.2	3,102.9	3,099.9
	18.2[a]	18.9[a]	20.5[a]	22.4	23.9	24.7
	6.91	7.84	8.61	9.87	10.95	10.95
	4,592.5	5,192.9	5,898.1	6,547.9	7,109.8	9,025.7
	$532.3	$611.3	$796.2	$841.8	$950.5	$1,076.7
	207.9	240.0	281.2	320.1	359.0	410.3
	1,438.6	1,559.1	1,640.9	1,790.5	1,818.2	1,954.2
	43.5	43.4	45.3	42.2	38.3	37.5
	9.8	14.9	15.5	16.4	12.9	14.4
	9.6	10.1	11.2	11.7	12.0	11.9
	12 3/8	22 7/8	28 5/8	39 3/4	34 1/8	45 7/8
———	8 7/8	8 7/8	20	26 3/8	29 1/8	30 5/8

EXHIBIT 22.14   Consolidated Balance Sheet (In millions)

	December 31	
	1988	1989
Current Assets		
Cash and Marketable Securities	$ 63.9	$ 36.4
Accounts and Notes Receivable, Less Allowance for		
Doubtful Accounts of $4.2 in 1989 and $4.1 in 1988	463.1	527.8
Inventories		
Raw Materials and Supplies	344.6	314.6
Work in Process	84.7	99.0
Finished Goods	82.9	118.1
Total Inventories	512.2	531.7
Other Current Assets	155.1	181.0
Total Current Assets	1,194.3	1,276.9
Investments and Other Assets		
Investments In and Advances to Affiliated Companies	82.3	87.4
Investment Properties	34.9	141.1
Deferred Charges and Other Non-current Assets	225.7	312.2
Excess of Cost Over Net Assets of Acquired Businesses,		
Net	104.9	536.8
	447.8	1,077.5
Plant and Equipment		
Land	126.6	289.6
Buildings	1,085.1	2,683.1
Machinery and Equipment	4,715.0	5,504.2
Construction in Progress	716.3	711.0
	7,643.0	9,187.9
Accumulated Depreciation	(2,175.3)	(2,516.6)
	5,467.7	6,671.3
Total Assets	$7,109.8	$9,025.7

EXHIBIT 22.14   (cont.)

	December 31	
	1988	1989
Liabilities and Shareholders Equity		
Current Liabilities		
Current Portion of Long-Term Debt	$ 0	$ 104.0
Accounts Payable	568.7	608.0
Accrued Salaries, Wages, and Benefits	229.4	212.0
Accrued Interest Payable	49.5	60.2
Due to Customers for Returnable Containers	40.7	42.2
Accrued Taxes, Other Than Income Taxes	60.1	65.4
Estimated Income Taxes	75.2	40.0
Other Current Liabilities	155.5	170.8
Total Current Liabilities	1,179.1	1,302.6
Long-Term Debt	1,615.3	3,307.3
Deferred Income Taxes	1,212.5	1,315.9
Common Stock and Other Shareholders' Equity		
Common Stock, $1.00 Par Value, Authorized 400 Shares	331.0	333.9
Capital in Excesss of Par Value	428.5	507.2
Retained Earnings	3,444.9	3,985.9
Foreign Currency Translation Adjustment	10.9	9.7
	4,215.3	4,836.7
Treasury Stock, at Cost	(1,112.4)	(1,236.8)
Employee Stock Ownership Plan Shares	0	(500.0)
	3,102.9	3,099.9
Total Liabilities and Shareholders' Equity	$7,109.8	$9,025.7

Source: *Anheuser-Busch Annual Report 1989*, pp. 44–45.

EXHIBIT 22.15   Financial Summary—Operations

	1975	1980	1981	1982
Barrels Sold	35.2	50.2	54.5	59.1
Sales	$1,036.7	$3,822.4	$4,435.9	$5,251.2
Federal and State Excise Taxes	391.7	527.0	562.4	609.1
Net Sales	1,645.0	3,295.4	3,873.5	4,642.1
Cost of Products and Services	1,343.8	2,553.9	3,001.9	3,384.3
Gross Profit	301.2	741.5	871.6	1,257.8
Marketing Distribution, and				
Administrative Expenses	126.1	428.6	518.6	758.8
Operating Income	175.1	312.9	353.0	499.0
Interest Expense	(22.6)	(75.6)	(90.7)	(93.2)
Interest Capitalized	0	41.7	64.1	41.2
Interest Income	10.9	2.4	6.2	17.0
Other Income (Expense), Net	1.9	(9.9)	(7.3)	(5.8)
Income before Income Taxes	165.3	271.5	325.3	478.6
Income Taxes	80.6	99.7	107.9	191.3
Net Income	84.7	171.8	217.4	287.3
Per Share—Primary Income				
before Cumulative Effect of				
Change in Accounting Method	.63	.64	.80	1.00
Cumulative Effect of Change in				
Accounting Method	—	—	—	—
Net Income	.63	.64	.80	1.00
Per Share—Fully Diluted	.63	.64	.77	.98
Cash Dividends Paid				
Common Stock	22.8	44.8	51.2	65.8
Per Share	.2133	.165	.188	.23
Average Number of Common				
Shares	135.3	271.2	272.4	288.6

1983	1984	1985	1986	1987	1988	1989
60.5	64.0	68.0	72.3	76.1	78.5	80.7
$6,714.7	$7,218.8	$7,756.7	$8,473.8	$9,110.4	$9,705.1	$10,283.6
624.3	657.0	683.0	724.5	760.7	781.0	802.3
6,090.4	6,561.8	7,073.7	7,754.3	8,349.7	8,924.1	9,481.3
4,161.0	4,464.6	4,729.8	5,026.5	5,374.3	5,825.5	6,275.8
1,929.4	2,097.2	2,343.9	2,727.8	2,975.4	3,098.6	3,205.5
1,226.4	1,338.5	1,498.2	1,709.8	1,826.8	1,834.5	1,876.8
703.0	758.7	845.7	1,018.0	1,148.6	1,264.1	1,328.7
(115.4)	(106.0)	(96.5)	(99.9)	(127.5)	(141.6)	(117.9)
32.9	46.8	37.2	33.2	40.3	44.2	51.5
12.5	22.8	21.8	9.6	12.8	9.8	12.6
(14.8)	(29.6)	(23.3)	(13.6)	(9.9)	(16.4)	11.8
618.2	692.7	784.4	947.3	1,064.3	1,160.1	1,226.7
270.2	301.2	340.7	429.3	449.6	444.2	459.5
348.0	391.5	443.7	518.0	614.7	715.9	767.2
1.08	1.23	1.42	1.69	2.04	2.45	2.68
—	—	—	—	—	—	—
1.08	1.23	1.42	1.69	2.04	2.45	2.68
1.08	1.23	1.42	1.69	2.04	2.45	2.68
78.3	89.7	102.7	120.2	148.4	188.6	226.2
.27	.3133	.3667	.44	.54	.66	.80
321.0	317.4	312.6	306.6	301.5	292.2	286.2

_____ CASE 25 _____

Harley-Davidson

INTRODUCTION

The name's Johnny. You might've heard of me. I run a little business down off of 38th and Main. It's an investments business. You ain't heard of it? Oh, well. . . . Hey, you got a light? Thanks, man. Hey, while you're up, can you grab me a cold one? Thanks. Aaaah. That's more like it. Grab some wood, pal. I've got one helluva story to tell you.

It all started a few months ago. I had just stalled the landlady for another week. So I'm sitting in my office, sipping a Jack and Coke, minding my own business, when this incredible blonde walks in.

"Johnny," she says, "I need a loan."

"Well, beautiful, you came to the right guy."

So for the next few hours I listened to her story. Great girl. Really smart. Her name was Connie. Maybe you know her. But anyway, turns out she had this hot tip on Harley-Davidson. A sure thing, she said. But she needed my money to play the market. So we'd be partners, or something like that.

At first, I thought to myself, this can't miss. Harley's like apple pie. I used to ride around on my HOG back in the '60s. Damn, those were some good times. Then that little voice went off inside my head. Only this time my voice ain't whispering, he's shouting.

"Hey, yo, Johnny! You snapperhead! What're you thinking, huh? Look at the economy. We're heading for a friggin' recession and you want to put your wad in Harley? Geez. And what about Holiday Rambler? Yeah, you forgot about them, you dunce! They're the RV sub that keeps sucking all of Harley's profits! Come on Johnny, pull your head out before it's too late!"

Whew. My little voice never spouted off like that before. So I figured I'd better listen to him. So, I told the dame that before I shelled out my coin, I was gonna have to check out Harley for myself. She gave me a week. And here's what I found out. So light 'em if you've got 'em . . .

This case was prepared by Scott Draper, A. Scott Dundon, Allen North, and Ron Smith under the supervision of Sexton Adams and Adelaide Griffin as a basis for class discussion rather than to illustrate either effective or ineffective handling of an administrative situation. Copyright © 1990 by Sexton Adams and Adelaide Griffin. Used with permission from Sexton Adams.

COMPANY HISTORY

In the Beginning . . .

The year was 1903. Henry Ford introduced the first Model A, the Wright brothers flew over Kitty Hawk, and, in a shack near Milwaukee, Wisconsin, a machine called the Silent Gray Fellow was born. Three brothers—William, Walter, and Arthur Davidson had invented a machine that would exemplify "the American desire for power, speed, and personal freedom"—the Harley-Davidson motorcycle.[1]

The Davidson's first crude machines found a ready market among both individuals and law enforcement agencies,[2] and by 1907, production had reached 150 motorcycles per year.[3] Two years later, a new engine, the V-twin, was introduced and enabled motorcycles to attain top speeds of 60 mph.[4] Motorcycles were fast becoming the primary source of transportation in the United States.

The Harley-Davidson Motorcycle Company took pride in America, and when the United States joined Europe in World War I, Harley-Davidson motorcycles helped the U.S. Army chase the kaiser across Germany.[5] After World War I, however, it was the automobile, not the motorcycle, that gained popularity as the principal means of transportation in the United States. Harley's annual production plunged from 28,000 to 10,000 units immediately after the war. After a decade of struggle, Harley-Davidson again reached prewar production levels, only to be ravaged by the Great Depression. By 1933, only 3,700 motorcycles were produced by Harley-Davidson.[6]

The economic boost provided by World War II and the military's high demand for motorcycles enabled Harley-Davidson to again match its 1920 production level. But after World War II, the motorcycle industry crashed. As America's heroes returned, their focus was on housing and family necessities, not motorcycles.[7] At one time Harley-Davidson was one of 150 U.S. motorcycle manufacturers, but by 1953, the weak motorcycle market had eliminated its final U.S. competitor, Indian Motocycle Company. Harley-Davidson stood alone as the sole manufacturer of motorcycles in the United States.[8]

The AMF Reign

Harley-Davidson made its first public stock offering in 1965, and shortly thereafter, the struggle for control of Harley-Davidson began. In 1968, Bangor

---

[1] Mark Marvel, "The Gentrified HOG," *Esquire*, July 1989, pp. 25–26.
[2] Robert L. Rose, "Vrooming Back," *Wall Street Journal* (southwestern ed.), August 31, 1990, p. 1.
[3] Peter C. Reid, *Well Made in America—Lessons from Harley-Davidson on Being the Best*, (New York; McGraw-Hill, 1990), p. 9.
[4] Marvel, "Gentrified HOG," p. 25.
[5] Ibid.
[6] Reid, *Well Made*, p. 9.
[7] Ibid.
[8] Rose, "Vrooming Back," p. 1.

Punta, an Asian company with roots in the railroad industry, began acquiring large amounts of Harley-Davidson stock. At the same time, AMF, an international leader in the recreational goods market, announced its interest in Harley-Davidson, citing a strong fit between Harley-Davidson's product lines and AMF's leisure lines. Bangor Punta and AMF then entered a bidding war over Harley-Davidson. Harley's stockholders chose AMF's bid of $22 per share over Bangor Punta's bid of $23 per share because of Bangor Punta's reputation for acquiring a company, squeezing it dry, and then scrapping it for salvage. AMF's plans were initially perceived as being more favorable for Harley-Davidson's long-term existence by touting plans for expansion of Harley.[9]

AMF's plans did not, however, correspond with Harley-Davidson's ability to expand. Much of Harley-Davidson's equipment was antiquated and could not keep up with the increase in production. One company official noted that "quality was going down just as fast as production was going up."[10] These events occurred at a time when Japanese motorcycle manufacturers began flooding the U.S. market with high-quality motorcycles that offered many innovative features and cost less.

Many of Harley's employees felt that if AMF had worked *with* the experienced Harley personnel instead of dictating orders for production quotas, many of the problems could have been properly addressed. One Harley senior executive stated that "the bottom line was that quality went to hell because AMF expanded Harley production at the same time that Harleys were getting out of date, and the Japanese were coming to town with new designs and reliable products at a low price."[11] Unlike their Japanese competitors whose motorcycles failed to pass inspection an average of 5 percent of the time, Harley's motorcycles failed to pass the end-of-the-assembly-line inspection at an alarming 50 percent to 60 percent rate.

After a $4.8 million annual operating loss and 11 years under AMF control, Harley-Davidson was put up for sale in 1981. A management team, led by Vaughn Beals, vice president of motorcycle sales, used $81.5 million in financing from Citicorp to complete a leveraged buyout. All ties with AMF were severed and the "new" Harley-Davidson was created.[12]

The Tariff Barrier

Although Harley-Davidson had managed to obliterate its U.S. competition during the 1950s and 1960s, the company took a beating from the Japanese in the 1970s. Japanese competition, and the recession presiding over the nation's economy had taken nearly all of Harley-Davidson's business. The company's meager

[9] Reid, *Well Made in America*, p. 9.
[10] Ibid., p. 25.
[11] Ibid., p. 27.
[12] Rod Willis, "Harley-Davidson Comes Roaring Back," *Management Review*, March 1986, pp. 20–27.

3 percent share of total motorcycle sales led experts to speculate as to whether or not Harley-Davidson would be able to celebrate its 80th birthday. Tariff protection appeared to be Harley-Davidson's only hope. Fortunately, massive lobbying efforts finally paid off in 1983, when Congress passed a huge tariff increase on Japanese motorcycles. Instead of a 4 percent tariff, Japanese motorcycles would now be subject to a 45 percent tariff. The protection was to last for five years.[13]

Slowly, Harley-Davidson began to recover market share as the tariff impacted competitors. Management was able to relinquish their ownership with a public stock offering in 1986. Brimming with confidence, Harley-Davidson asked Congress to remove the tariff barrier in December 1986, more than a year earlier than originally planned. It was time to strap on the helmet and race with the Japanese head to head.[14]

Acquisition and Diversification

Holiday Rambler was purchased in 1986 by Harley-Davidson, a move that nearly doubled the size of the firm. As a wholly owned subsidiary, the manufacturer of recreational and commercial vehicles provided Harley-Davidson with another business unit that could diversify the risks associated with the seasonal motorcycle market. That move gave Harley-Davidson two distinct business segments, Holiday Rambler Corporation, and Harley-Davidson Motorcycle Division. In addition, during the late 1980s Harley-Davidson attempted to capitalize on its manufacturing expertise by competing for both government and contract manufacturing opportunities in an attempt to further increase the proportion of revenues derived from nonmotorcycle sources.

HOLIDAY RAMBLER CORPORATION

Harley-Davidson implemented many new management techniques at Holiday Rambler. The Yadiloh (Holiday spelled backward) program was created in 1989. Yadiloh was an acronym for "Yes Attitude, Deliver, Involvement, Leadership, Opportunity, Harmony." The goal of Yadiloh was to address cost and productivity problems facing Holiday Rambler. The employees of Holiday Rambler seemed to favor the program. "This program will help us solve a lot of problems in the long run. So I think it's a really big step, a positive step," said Raud Estep, a quality control inspector for Holiday Rambler. Another employee, Vickie Hutsell, agreed, "I think that most of the people who've gone through the Yadiloh training session are 'pumped up' about it."[15]

But Holiday Rambler did more than get employees excited. It built a new, centralized facility that was completed in late 1990 to handle all of the compa-

[13] Rose, "Vrooming Back," p. 1.
[14] "Harley Back in High Gear," *Forbes*, April 20, 1987, p. 8.
[15] Harley-Davidson Annual Report 1989, p. 13.

ny's manufacturing needs. They also installed more computer-aided design (CAD) equipment to support the research and development staff, which led to a $1.9 million increase in operating expenses.

Observers, however, felt that the success of Holiday Rambler had been mixed at best. Several strong competitors had entered the recreational vehicle (RV) market in 1988. Holiday Rambler responded by discontinuing its "Trail Seeker" line of recreational vehicles after the line experienced a $30 million sales decline in 1988. Holiday Rambler continued to trim poor performing areas. In October 1989, Parkway Distribution, an RV parts and accessories distributor was sold. A $2.8 million decline in revenues from the business units of Creative Dimensions, Nappanee Wood Products, and B & B Molders was recorded in that same year. Holiday Rambler enacted competitive pricing measures and a lower margin sales mix. The result was a decrease in gross margin percentage from 19.0 percent to 18.2 percent.

Some industry experts recognized a possible recovery for the sluggish RV market in 1990. However, the message of H. Wayne Dahl, Holiday Rambler president, was unclear. "Whether our business is RVs, commercial vehicles, or a related enterprise, we intend to keep it strong and growing by keeping in close touch with its customers."[16]

The Recreational Vehicle Market

In 1986, Harley executives claimed that the acquisition of Holiday Rambler would help to diversify the risks associated with the seasonal motorcycle market. However, some industry experts questioned whether such an acquisition was a wise move for Harley. They pointed out that although the acquisition smoothed seasonal fluctuations in demand, cyclical fluctuations caused by the economy were unaffected. One expert asserted, "Because both items (motorcycles and recreational vehicles) are luxury goods, they are dependent on such key economic factors as interest rates, disposable income, and gasoline prices."[17]

In addition to the economy, the demographics of the RV market presented a challenge to Harley. The main consumer of recreational vehicles in the 1970s was the blue-collar employee who worked a steady 40 hours per week. However, economic trends led to a switch from manufacturing to a more service-oriented economy. The trends left most consumers with little time on their hands for recreational activities. In 1989, statistics revealed that the typical owner of an RV was between 35 and 54 years old with an average income of $39,800. Census projections indicated that the U.S. population was growing older at the end of the 1980s. The high incomes and older ages gave RV manufacturers the opportunity to include extra features that allowed them to raise total vehicle cash prices by $20,000 and more.

---

[16] Ibid., p. 14.
[17] Raymond Serafin, "RV Market Puzzled," *Advertising Age*, July 1988, p. 52.

The RV industry had support from nonconsumer groups that existed specifically to accommodate the RV owner. The Escapees, for instance, offered insurance and cash-handling services to members driving RVs. The Good Sam's Club provided road service to RVs in need of repair. RV owners were even treated to their own television program to watch while on the road—"Wish You Were Here." The show, broadcast via satellite by the Nashville channel, highlighted RV lifestyles through interviews with owners across the country.[18]

MANAGEMENT

Vaughn Beals' outward appearance was far removed from the burly image that many might have expected of a "Harley" chief executive. The middle-aged Ivy Leaguer graduated from MIT's Aeronautical Engineering School and was known in manufacturing circles as a productivity guru.[19] But, on the inside, Vaughn Beals was a HOG (a member of the Harley owners group) in the truest sense of the word. He began working with Harley-Davidson as vice-president of motorcycle sales with AMF.[20] Disgruntled with AMF's declining attention to quality, Beals led a team of 12 others who successfully completed the leveraged buyout from AMF.

But Beals had a difficult mission ahead. Even after receiving protection, Harley-Davidson had to find a way to restore confidence in its products. So Beals decided to hit the road—literally. He drove Harley-Davidson motorcycles to rallies where he met Harley owners. In doing so, Beals was able to learn about product defects and needed improvements directly from the consumer. Industry experts believed that these efforts were vital to the resurgence of the company.

Willie G. Davidson, grandson of the company's founder, rode along with Vaughn Beals on Harley's road to recovery. "Willie G." provided a sharp contrast to Beals. If Vaughn Beals looked more at home in a courtroom, Willie G. might have looked more at home behind the bars of a jail cell. Davidson's appearance was that of a middle-aged man who was a remnant of the 1960s era. A Viking helmet covered his long, stringy hair, and his beard hid the hard features of a wind-parched face. He wore a leather jacket that, like his face, showed the cracks of wear and tear that the miles of passage over U.S. highways had caused. Nonetheless, Willie G. was named the new vice president of design for Harley in 1981. Industry observers believed that he had been instrumental in instigating much needed improvements in the Harley HOG.

Beals stepped down as CEO in 1989, passing the reins to Richard Teerlink, who was then serving as chief operating officer for Harley-Davidson Motorcycle Division. Beals, however, retained his position as chairman of the board. After the transition, Harley-Davidson retained a long list of experienced executives. The organizational chart (Exhibit 25.1) highlights the depth of the Harley-Davidson management team.

[18] Joe Schwartz, "No Fixed Address," *American Demographics*, August 1986, pp. 50–51.
[19] Willis, "Harley-Davidson," pp. 20–27.
[20] John Madock Roberts, "Harley's HOG's," *Forbes*, December 7, 1985, p. 14.

EXHIBIT 25.1   Harley-Davidson Organizational Chart

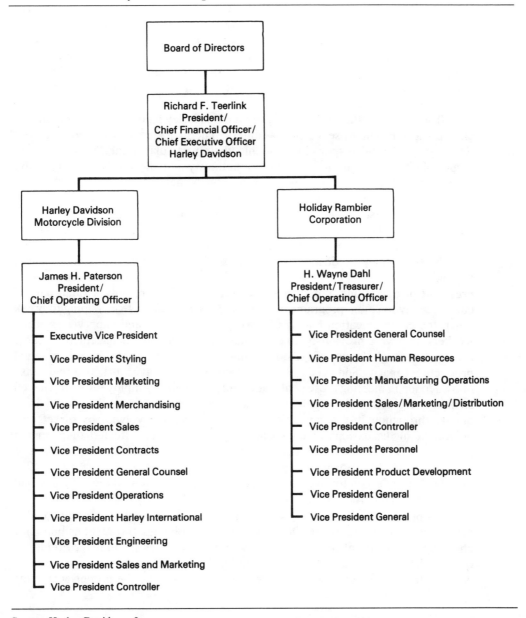

Source: Harley-Davidson, Inc.

In a somewhat ironic turn of events, Beals and other executives of Harley-Davidson had traveled to Japan in 1981 to visit the factories of their competition in an attempt to uncover any secrets. What they found was surprising. The Japanese did not run a low-cost production facility due to sophisticated machinery; instead, they simply used effective management techniques to maximize productivity. Armed with a new management perspective from the Japanese, Harley-Davidson began implementing quality circles (QCs), statistical operations controls, and just-in-time (JIT) inventory.[21]

The first dramatic change implemented by Harley management was to divide each plant into four to seven profit centers. The managers of each profit center were assigned total responsibility within their particular area. The increase in responsibility gave plant managers more authority and allowed Harley-Davidson to greatly reduce the staff functions previously needed to assist production. Harley-Davidson was able to reduce its employee work force by 40 percent after implementing these changes.[22] In 1982, the company adopted a JIT system for control of "in-plant" manufacturing and a materials-as-needed (MAN) system, which dealt with control of *all* inventories both inside and outside of the plants.

Next, Harley-Davidson attempted to increase employee involvement through the formation of quality circles. Thomas Gelb, Harley's executive vice president of operations, noted that even though QCs were only a small part of employee involvement programs, they played a significant role in helping to break down the communication barriers between line workers and supervisors. Line workers who were previously given quotas from high-level management became involved, through the use of QCs, in setting more realistic quotas based on actual production capacity and needs. Employee involvement gave workers a real sense of ownership in meeting these goals, according to Gelb.[23] Employees were viewed as links in a chain, and through employee involvement programs they could drive quality throughout the organization. Employees were involved, by direct participation, in discussions and decisions on changes that affected them in the performance of their own work. Also, management trained employees on ways to recognize and eliminate waste in the production process.[24] According to 1986 figures, Harley's tab for warranty repairs, scrap, and reworking of parts had decreased by 60 percent since 1981.[25]

Employee involvement was further increased through a program called statistical operator control (SOC). SOC gave employees the responsibility for checking the quality of their own work within a predetermined range. Employee quality checks took place on the production floor, and on many occasions, the workers themselves were given the responsibility to make the proper correcting

[21] Willis, "Harley-Davidson," pp. 22–23.

[22] Ibid., p. 26.

[23] Ibid., pp. 22–23.

[24] John A. Saathoff, "Workshop Report: Maintain Excellence through Change," *Target*, Spring 1989, p. 2.

[25] Dexter Hutchins. "Having a Hard Time with Just-in-Time," *Fortune*, June 19, 1986, p. 66.

adjustments. SOC helped to identify errors in the production process on a timely basis and gave line workers more responsibility through making quality checks and correcting adjustments in the production process.[26]

Although employees became more involved at Harley, labor relations remained strained. To correct the problem, management implemented an open-door policy to improve labor relations and increased stock options to include a broader base of employees. Management took a more sensitive stance toward the opinions of all employees. Union relations also improved when management voluntarily agreed to put the union label on all motorcycles produced and by sharing financial information with union leaders. Harley attempted to deal with all employees, even those affected by layoffs, in a humane way. Several employee assistance programs were put into place. Among these were outplacement assistance to cushion the blow of layoffs, early retirement (age 55) or voluntary layoffs, and drug abuse programs administered by the Milwaukee Council on Drug Abuse.[27]

In order for the above changes to work, Harley developed several overall goals. As stated in its annual report, Harley's 1989 management goals included improvement of quality, employee satisfaction, customer satisfaction, and shareholder return. Its long-term focus would address four major areas of concern for the 1990s: (1) quality, (2) productivity, (3) participation, and (4) flexibility.

1. Quality—Management efforts in the late 1980s attempted to overcome its reputation for poor quality. Because most of Harley's upper management believed that quality improvement was an ongoing process, they made a commitment to a long-term goal.
2. and 3. Participation and Productivity—These two areas led to overlapping objectives, according to Harley executives. Because of this, the company emphasized employee involvement programs throughout the firm.
4. Flexibility—The diminishing domestic marketplace and the slowing U.S. economy created the need for flexibility. Harley-Davidson management hoped to explore other options for the firm.

Management hoped to lead rather than follow the competition. In 1990, Harley cultivated the catch phrase "Do the right thing and do that thing right."

PRODUCTION AND OPERATIONS

After the leveraged buyout, manufacturing was still a major problem. According to one Harley executive, "Less than 70 percent of our motorcycles were complete when they reached the end of the assembly line."[28] Motorcycle production schedules were often based on the parts that were available instead of the

[26] Saathoff, "Workshop Report," p. 4.
[27] Willis, "Harley-Davidson," p. 27.
[28] Harley-Davidson Annual Report, 1989, p. 3.

planned master schedule. According to industry experts, "Japanese manufacturing techniques were yielding operating costs 30 percent lower than Harley's."[29] How did the Japanese do it? Though Beals and other managers had visited Japanese plants in 1981, it was not until they got a chance to tour Honda's assembly plant in Marysville, Ohio, after the buyout, that they began to understand Japanese competition. Beals said, "We were being wiped out by the Japanese because they were better *managers*. It wasn't robotics, or culture, or morning calisthenics and company songs—it was professional managers who understood their business and paid attention to detail."[30]

The Just-In-Time Inventory Method

A pilot JIT manufacturing program was quickly introduced in the Milwaukee engine plant. Tom Gelb, senior vice president of operations, called a series of meetings with employees, telling them bluntly, "We have to play the game the way the Japanese play or we're dead."[31]

Gelb was met with extreme skepticism. The York, Pennsylvania, plant, for instance, was already equipped with a computer-based control system that utilized overhead conveyors and high-rise parts storage. In a meeting with the work force of the York facility, Gelb announced that the JIT system would replace these overhead conveyors and storage with pushcarts. The production floor erupted with laughter. Surely, this was a joke. Plant managers mumbled that Harley-Davidson was returning to the 1930s.[32]

Observers noted that the overriding principle of the JIT method was that "parts and raw materials should arrive at the factory just as they are needed in the manufacturing process. This lets the manufacturer eliminate inventories and the costs of carrying them."[33] Anne Thundercloud, the York plant quality circle facilitator, stated, "It is the Harley employees who make JIT work, by having an investment in seeing it work." The same men and women who laughed out loud over the implementation of JIT began to believe in its "exacting discipline." Their belief was justified. Nearly 60,000 square feet of warehouse space was freed.[34] Costs of production plummeted. In 1986, Harley was able to lower its break-even point to 35,000 units—from 53,000 in 1981.[35]

Supplier cooperation was also critical to JIT success, but Harley-Davidson had a poor track record with its vendors. As one industry observer noted, "Harley was notorious for juggling production schedules and was one of the worst customers when it came to last-minute panic calls for parts." Furthermore, suppliers were wary of their role in the JIT picture. Edward J. Hay of Rath &

[29] Saathoff, "Workshop Report," p. 3.
[30] Hutchins, "Having a Hard Time," p. 65.
[31] Hutchins, "Having a Hard Time," p. 64.
[32] *Fortune*, September 25, 1989, p. 161.
[33] Ibid.
[34] Hutchins, "Having a Hard Time," p. 64.
[35] Willis, "Harley-Davidson," p. 14.

Strong, a Lexington, Massachusetts, management consulting firm, stated, "The big problem is that companies treat just-in-time as a way of getting the suppliers to hold the inventories."[36] One expert noted that Harley had to "abandon the security blanket that inventory often represented for them and learn to trust their suppliers."[37]

Critics believed that Harley erred initially by taking a legalistic approach in trying to sign up suppliers for a JIT system. The company insisted on contracts that were 35 pages long, devoted largely to spelling out suppliers' obligations to Harley. This strategy was ambitious and too pretentious. Early results did not meet management's expectations, and the animosity was growing between Harley and its suppliers. One supplier contended, "They're constantly renegotiating contracts, and tinkering with the layout of the plant."[38]

Finally, the company took positive steps to improve vendor relations. Contracts were reduced to two pages. According to one Harley executive, "We need to get out of the office and meet face-to-face." Experts noted, "Teams of buyers and engineers fanned out to visit suppliers: they began simplifying and improving designs and helping suppliers reduce setup time between jobs by modifying equipment to permit quick change of dies. To improve the quality of the parts, Harley gave suppliers courses in statistics to teach workers how to chart small changes in the performance of their equipment. The practice provides early tip-offs when machines are drifting out of tolerance."[39]

Materials-as-Needed

Harley's MAN system was tailored after that of Toyota's production system and was driven by "Kanban" technology—a control system that used circulating cards and standard containers for parts. The system provided real-time production needs information without the use of costly and complex resources which were typically needed for planning and support.[40] Tom Schwarz, general manager of Harley-Davidson Transportation Company, developed a strategically controlled inbound system for dealing with suppliers. As one executive noted, "Harley's ultimate goal is to control all inbound and outbound shipments themselves. They prefer to keep a minimum (number) of carriers involved. That reduces the chance of delays."[41] As an example, Harley-Davidson used its own leased fleet of 26 tractors and 46 trailers for the bulk of its road miles, using contract carriers only to supplement direct point service to its 700 dealers.

Harley-Davidson then began to evaluate its present suppliers based on manufacturing excellence and ability to provide small and frequent deliveries instead of evaluating suppliers strictly on price alone. Harley's trucks made daily,

---

[36] Roberts, "Harley's HOG's," p. 14.
[37] Hutchins, "Having a Hard Time," p. 64.
[38] Ibid.
[39] Ibid.
[40] Ibid., p. 65.
[41] Saathoff, "Workshop Report," pp. 3–4.

timed pickups from five to six suppliers on a predetermined route. Over the course of a week, the truck brought in all inbound shipments from 26 to 30 important vendors within a 200-mile radius of the plant.[42] This type of system also allowed for frequent, small deliveries while helping to reduce freight costs.[43] "From 1981–1986, MAN cut the York plant's inbound freight costs (mostly from vendor billing) by $50,000."[44]

An important element in keeping freight costs down was the elimination of nonproductive travel and Harley's new purchase order system. The company reported in 1986 that only 4 percent of the 2 million miles that the fleet traveled in the past year were empty. Harley changed its purchase order system in 1986 so that the only prices it would acknowledge were FOB vendors' shipping docks. This prevented suppliers from including freight in their prices and, in turn, discouraged them from using their own carriers for shipments to the motorcycle maker's plants.[45]

In 1986, Harley-Davidson began pressing some of its suppliers to start passing up the line more of the cost savings that JIT afforded. "It's time," said Patrick T. Keane, project engineer at Harley's York, Pennsylvania, plant, "to enter an era of negotiated price decreases. And right now we are holding meetings to accomplish that."[46]

After five years of using JIT, reviews poured in. Between 1981 and 1988, the following results were achieved:

1. Inventory had been reduced by 67 percent.
2. Productivity climbed by 50 percent.
3. Scrap and rework were down two-thirds.
4. Defects per unit were down 70 percent.[47]

Some industry experts believed that "the results for Harley and its suppliers have been good, although the company still has not achieved all its goals."[48] "We are very inefficient," said Keane, "but the comparison to where we were five years ago is phenomenal."[49]

Quality

In the 1970s, the running joke among industry experts was, "If you're buying a Harley, you'd better buy two—one for spare parts."[50] After the buyout from AMF, Harley-Davidson was determined to restore consumer confidence by

[42] "At Harley-Davidson JIT Is a Fine Tuned Cycle," *Purchasing*, April 24, 1986, pp. 46–48.
[43] Hutchins, "Having a Hard Time," p. 64.
[44] Saathoff, "Workshop Report," p. 5.
[45] "At Harley-Davidson," p. 48.
[46] Hutchins, "Having a Hard Time," p. 66.
[47] Ibid.
[48] Harley-Davidson News, 1988, p. 1.
[49] Huchins, "Having a Hard Time," p. 66.
[50] Ibid., p. 66.

raising the quality of its motorcycles. Harley-Davidson's quality improvements did not go unnoticed. John Davis, a Harley dealer mechanic, stated, "I've been wrenching on Harley-Davidson motorcycles for 26 years. I think the main key to their success is quality. And since '84 they have been very good."[51] Teerlink boasted in his 1990 letter to shareholders that Harley-Davidson would be competing for the Malcolm Baldridge National Quality Award in 1991. "We will follow the examples established by the 1990 winner (Cadillac)."[52]

Harley's commitment to quality may have led them to opt not to carry any product liability insurance after 1987. One Harley executive commented, "We do not believe that carrying product liability insurance is financially prudent."[53] Instead, Harley created a form of self-insurance through reserves to cover potential liabilities.

Other Production

In 1988, Teerlink proudly stated, "Capitalizing on its reputation as a world class manufacturer, Harley-Davidson is developing a strong contract manufacturing business. In April 1988, the company became the first Army Munitions and Chemical Command (AMCCOM) contractor to be certified under the U.S. Army's Contractor Performance Certification Program. The company achieved the certification for its application of advanced manufacturing techniques in the production of 500-pound casings for the U.S. Army. Additionally, the company is the sole supplier of high-altitude rocket motors for target drones built by Beech Aircraft."[54]

Harley-Davidson formed an agreement with Acustar, a subsidiary of Chrysler Corporation, in early 1988, to produce machined components for its Marine and Industrial Division. Harley also manufactured small engines for Briggs & Stratton. The company planned to further broaden its contract manufacturing business by aggressively marketing its proven and innovative manufacturing efficiencies to the industrial community. For 1990, management placed a goal of nonmotorcycle production to reach between 25 and 30 percent.[55] Teerlink felt strongly that "this goal is actually quite conservative and can be easily accomplished."[56]

International Operations

The international markets of Great Britain, Italy, and other European countries were hardly uncharted territory for Harley-Davidson. Since 1915, Harley-Davidson had been selling its products in these overseas markets. Harley-Davidson's international efforts increased significantly during the mid-1980s. In

[51] Marvel, "Gentrified HOGs," p. 25.
[52] Harley-Davidson Annual Report, 1989, p. 8.
[53] Ibid., p. 4.
[54] Ibid., p. 34.
[55] Harley-Davidson News, 1988, p. 2.
[56] Willis, "Harley-Davidson," p. 27.

1984, it produced 5,000 motorcycles for export; projections for 1990 called for production in the 20,000-unit range.[57]

Several international markets exploded for Harley-Davidson in the late 1980s. In 1989, it expanded its motorcycle sales in France by 92 percent, Great Britain by 91 percent, and Australia by 32 percent.[58] Europeans also bought other Harley products, such as T-shirts and leather jackets. Clyde Fessler, director of trademark licensing for Harley-Davidson, said, "In Europe we're considered Americana."[59]

MARKETING

> When it comes to pleasuring the major senses, no motorcycle on earth can compare to Harley. That's why I've tattooed my Harley's name on the inside of my mouth.
>
> Lou Reed[60]

Probably not every Harley-Davidson owner had Lou Reed's loyalty. Nonetheless, loyalty to Harley-Davidson had almost always been virtually unparalleled. According to the company's research, 92 percent of its customers remained with Harley.[61] Even with strong brand loyalty, however, Harley's marketing division had not reduced its advertising. Harley-Davidson limited its advertising focus to print media, opting not to explore a radio or television campaign. The company used print ads in a variety of magazines, including trade magazines and the company's own trade publication, the *Enthusiast*. The advertising department, headed by Carmichael Lynch, had the benefit of a very well known company name. Unfortunately, the company's name also carried serious image problems.

One major problem that plagued Harley's marketing efforts was that bootleggers were ruining the Harley-Davidson name by placing it on unlicensed, unauthorized goods. This condition might not have been a problem, except that the goods were of poor quality. Furthermore, society was turning away from the attitudes of the 1960s. With antidrug messages becoming a prevalent theme in American society, Harley-Davidson found itself linked to an image of the pot-smoking, beer-drinking, woman-chasing, tattoo-covered, leather-clad biker. One industry expert observed, "When your company's logo is the number one requested in tattoo parlors, it's time to get a licensing program that will return your reputation to the ranks of baseball, hot dogs, and apple pie."[62] This fact was not lost on management. Kathleen Demitros, who became director of marketing in

---

[57] Roberts, "Harley's HOG's," p. 14.
[58] Harley-Davidson Annual Report 1989, p. 9.
[59] "The Harley Priority," *Popular Mechanics*, June 9, 1989, p. 24.
[60] Robert Parola, "High on the HOG," *Daily News Record*, January 23, 1989, p. 74.
[61] Marvel, "Gentrified HOGs," p. 25.
[62] "Thunder Road," *Forbes*, July 18, 1983, p. 32.

1983, stated, "One of our problems was that we had such a hard-core image out there that it was basically turning off a lot of people."[63] Demitros was speaking from experience. The Milwaukee native had been with the company since 1971. Furthermore, like many of the company executives, she owned a Harley. By her own admission, Demitros chose not to ride her HOG to work. She saved it for the weekends.[64]

Harley-Davidson took a proactive approach to solving the image problem. It created a licensing division responsible for eliminating the bootlegged products. This new division was led by John Heiman, who was formerly a mechanical accessories products manager. Goods with the Harley-Davidson logo would have to be sold by licensed dealers to be legal. Using warrants and federal marshals, Heiman went to conventions of motorcycle enthusiasts and began to put an end to the bootleggers.[65]

After accomplishing this, Harley-Davidson was able to sell its own goods. It began to concentrate its efforts on a wide variety of products—ranging from leather jackets to cologne to jewelry—to supplement motorcycle sales.[66] The concept was not new to Harley-Davidson. As far back as the 1920s, Harley had designed and sold leather jackets. The hope was that consumers would buy the other products in order to get comfortable with the Harley name, and then consider purchasing Harley motorcycles. One company executive said, "It helped pull us through the lean years." He continued, "In 1988 we sold 35,000 bikes and over 3 million fashion tops."[67] For Harley-Davidson, these sales were crucial in offsetting the seasonal market of the motorcycle industry. Observers applauded Harley on this marketing strategy. "Historically, the winter months are tough on sales for the motorcycle industry. Harley-Davidson has been successful at selling fashion items." A Harley marketing executive went one step further. "If we can't sell someone a bike in the winter, we'll sell them a leather jacket instead."[68]

Essentially, the licensing division had become an extension of marketing. Heiman said, "If you've got a 6-year-old boy wearing Harley pajamas, sleeping on Harley sheets and bathing with Harley towels, the old man's not going to be bringing home a Suzuki."[69] Additionally, retailers found that the licensed goods were popular. Major retail chains began selling Harley-Davidson products. The logic behind the selection of Harley goods was simple. "Harley is the only motorcycle made in the United States today, and I thought with pride in America high, the time was right for the licensed goods," explained one major retailer.[70]

[63] Marie Spadoni, "Harley-Davidson Revs Up to Improve Image," *Advertising Age*, August 5, 1985, p. 30.

[64] "Thunder Road," p. 32.

[65] Spadoni, "Harley-Davidson Revs Up," p. 30.

[66] Ibid., p. 30.

[67] Parola, "High on the HOG," p. 24.

[68] Ibid.

[69] Marvel, "Gentrified HOGs," p. 25.

[70] Spandoni, "Harley-Davidson Revs Up," p. 30.

However, the hard-core biker image of Harley-Davidson was still a strong influence. For example, when Fifth Avenue Cards decided to sell Harley items, it did so in a satirical manner. According to Ethel Sloan, the card store chain's vice president of merchandising, "We were definitely shooting for tongue-in-cheek, selling this macho, all-black coloration merchandise to bankers in three-piece suits—it was a real hoot!"[71] It may have been this cynical and virtually unexpected market that Vaughn Beals hoped to exploit. Beals predicted the emergence of a new breed of Harley customer. "We're on the road to prosperity in this country, and we'll get there on a Harley."[72]

The customers he spoke of began to buy Harleys in record numbers. The new Harley consumers were a collection of bankers, doctors, lawyers, and entertainers who developed an affection for HOGs.[73] They became known as Rubbies—the rich urban bikers. The Rubbies were not frightened by the high price tags associated with the Harley-Davidson product line. The Sportster 883, which was Harley's trademark motorcycle, and the Nova, which was specifically designed to capture the college student market, sold in a price range of $4,000 to $15,000 in 1987.[74] Harley continued to expand its product line in 1988 with the addition of the Springer Softail, the Ultra Classic Electra Glide, and the Ultra Classic Tour Glide. James Paterson, president and chief operating officer of the motorcycle division, commented, "The Springer goes to the heart of Harley-Davidson, the custom-cruiser type of motorcycle. The Ultra Classics . . . are aimed at the touring market . . . a market we couldn't reach previously."[75] Product line expansion continued in 1989 with a move that several industry observers thought to be a questionable marketing decision. Harley-Davidson introduced the Fat Boy, its largest motorcycle with 80 cubic inches of V-twin engine.

The Rubbies had brought Harley back into the forefront. By 1989, Harley-Davidson was again the leader in the U.S. super heavyweight motorcycle market, with a nearly 60 percent market share (See Exhibit 25.2). One consequence of the Rubbie market was its impact on the demographics of the Harley-Davidson consumer. According to an August 1990 *Wall Street Journal* article, "One in three of today's Harley-Davidson buyers are professionals or managers. About 60 percent have attended college, up from only 45 percent in 1984. Their median age is 35, and their median household income has risen sharply to $45,000 from $36,000 five years earlier."

Even with the growth of the Rubbie market, Harley-Davidson was careful not to lose touch with its grass-roots customers. In 1990, roughly 110,000 members belonged to the HOG, Harley Owners Group.[76] The fact that upper management continued to ride along side of their loyal throng was an important marketing

[71] "Greeting Card Chain Scores Big with Macho 'Biker' Promotion," *Stores*, February 1986, p. 21.
[72] Ibid.
[73] Marvel, "Gentrified HOGs," p. 26.
[74] "Harley Priority," p. 24.
[75] Willis, "Harley-Davidson," p. 14.
[76] Rose, "Vrooming Back," p. 1.

EXHIBIT 25.2   U.S. Market Share of Super Heavyweight Motorcycles, 1989

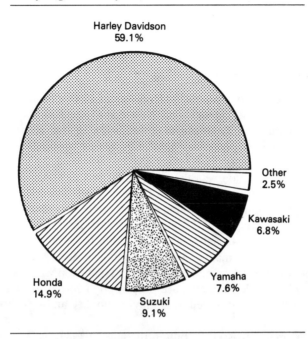

Source: R.L. Polk & Company.

tool. Paterson asserted, "Going to rallies and mixing with our customers has more value than you might initially expect. You begin to understand how important the motorcycle is and how important the Harley-Davidson way of life is to them. . . . At a motorcycle rally, everyone's part of the same family—sharing their love for motorcycling and life in general." Paterson's beliefs were shared by Harley owner Pat Soracino, "It's a family affair. My bike rides better with [wife] Vicki riding next to me. And our daughter has grown up with Harleys. It's more than a motorcycle to us. It's our lives."[77]

HOG and Harley-Davidson combined their efforts often in 1989. One such venture was a series of National Forest improvement projects. The First Annual National Poker Run motorcycle rally received the support of almost 160 Harley dealers nationwide. This rally and others raised about $1.7 million for the Muscular Dystrophy Association, a charity for which Harley-Davidson collected over $6.5 million in the decade of the 1980s.

Although high performance was not a strong selling point for Harley-Davidson motorcycles, the company did enhance its reputation on the racing circuit in 1988 and 1989. In both years, Harley's factory-sponsored rider, Scotty Parker,

[77] Harley-Davidson Annual Report 1989, pp. 5–10.

captured the Grand National and Manufacturer's Championship in the American Motorcyclist Association's Class C racing season.

COMPETITION

Motorcycle Competition

Harley faced stiff competition from Japan's big four motorcycle manufacturers—Honda, Yamaha, Suzuki, and Kawasaki (See Exhibit 25.3). Industry analysts claimed that the Japanese manufacturers held a commanding lead in the world market with 80 percent of total motorcycle production.

Honda.   In 1990, Honda was the world's largest motorcycle manufacturer. The president of the company, Shoichiro Irimaziri, attributed Honda's success to the company's philosophy of producing products of the highest efficiency at a reasonable price. In every aspect of design for both cars and motorcycles, the company's engineers endeavored to achieve a reasonable level of efficiency and obtain the last increment of performance. The president also placed a high value on the early involvement of production and engineering. His vision was one where the marketing and production departments are part of engineering; production departments are part of a bigger unit aimed at achieving quality and efficiency.[78]

Yamaha.   Yamaha grossed $3 billion in sales in 1989, as the second largest producer of motorcycles in the world. For decades, Yamaha remained extremely diversified as the leading producer of outboard motors, sailboats, snowmobiles, and golf carts. At Yamaha Motor, many of the products were developed almost exclusively for overseas markets. Why so much diversification? First, Yamaha executives believed that the motorcycle business in the late 1980s was a shrinking one. Second, as voiced by the president of the company, "Diversification is a hobby of my father's. He gets bored with old businesses."[79]

Suzuki.   Suzuki made its name selling motorcycles, but in 1987 it almost doubled its sales with the introduction of a jeep, the Suzuki Samurai. When first introduced, critics thought it would be a modern-day Edsel. "When these oddball vehicles first came out nobody gave them a nickel's chance of success," said Maryann N. Keller, a vice president and automotive analyst with Furman, Seiz, Mager, Dietz & Birney.[80] But the critics were wrong. Suzuki had a record 48,000 sales in 1986—the best model launch in history of any Japanese auto manufacturer. Despite its success, however, the Samurai was hit with negative publicity in 1988. Specifically, the Consumer Union, a consumer protection organization,

[78] Andrew Tanzer, "Create or Die," *Forbes*, April 6, 1987, pp. 55–59.
[79] Shoichiro Irimaziri, "The Winning Difference," *Vital Speeches*, pp. 650–651.
[80] Tanzer, "Create or Die," pp. 55–59.

EXHIBIT 25.3   Harley-Davidson's Share of the U.S. Super Heavyweight Motorcycle Market

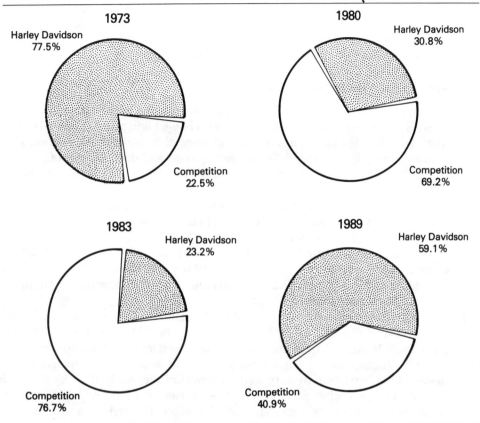

Source: R.L. Polk & Company.

gave the Samurai a "not acceptable" rating and pleaded for the recall of 150,000 Samurai and for full refunds to all owners. The union claimed that the vehicle was unsafe because it rolled over easily when turning corners. Although the negative publicity caused a temporary decline in sales, Suzuki rebounded in the second half of 1988 through utilization of dealer and customer incentives.[81]

Kawasaki.   In 1988, Kawasaki's motorcycle sales increased 5 percent, although the overall motorcycle market shrank 20 percent. Kawasaki's management attributed much of its success to a new service in which dealers could make sales with no-money-down financing. A computer network, Household Finance Corporation, allowed dealers to get nearly instantaneous responses on credit applications.

[81] Rebecca Fannin, "Against All Odds," *Marketing and Media*, March 1988, pp. 45–47.

Kawasaki focused efforts to accommodate its dealers. The K-share program was developed in 1986 to act as a sales support system for dealers. K-share allowed dealers to make payments electronically; as a result, interest expense was reduced and keying errors made by Kawasaki were virtually eliminated because the manual input of checks was no longer necessary.[82]

Recreational Vehicle Competition

With its acquisition of Holiday Rambler, Harley nearly doubled its revenues. However, experts indicated that it also bought into a very troubled industry with declining demand. They further claimed that greater competition in the industry would lead to increasing marketing costs and decreasing profit margins. Harley faced three top competitors in the RV industry—Fleetwood, Winnebago, and Airstream.

Fleetwood Enterprises was the nation's leading manufacturer of recreational vehicles in 1989. Its operations included 21 factories in 17 states and Canada. For 1989, its sales totaled approximately $719 million.[83]

Winnebago was number one in sales with $420 million in 1988. The company experienced financing problems in early 1990 when Norwest Bank canceled a $50 million revolving credit line. This situation caused Winnebago to fall to number two in industry sales in 1990.[84]

Airstream ranked third among the RV manufacturers with sales of approximately $389 million for 1989.[85] Thor Industries bought the failing RV manufacturer from Beatrice Foods in 1980. It made assembly-line improvements and upgraded components to cut warranty costs and help the RV's image. In 1990, thousands of Airstream owners were members of the Wally Bran Caravan Club International. The club was started by Airstream and held regional rallies and caravans throughout the year. This cultlike following provided a loyal customer base, accounting for 60 percent of all Airstreams sold.[86]

THE IMPACT OF THE ECONOMY

Historically, the success of Harley-Davidson hinged significantly on the performance of the U.S. economy. The company suffered along with everyone else during the Great Depression, while the boom periods of both world wars represented times of prosperity for Harley-Davidson. Changing demands of consumers during the postwar years in the 1940s and 1950s had an adverse effect on the motorcycle industry, and, just when Harley was on the road to recovery in the early 1980s, the economy fell into a recession.[87]

---

[82] Jack Bernstein, "Crisis Communications," *Advertising Age*, September 5, 1988, p. 29.
[83] Serafin, "RV Market Puzzled," p. 52.
[84] Fleetwood Annual Report 1989, p. 18.
[85] David Greising, "Unhappy Campers at Winnebago," *Business Week*, May 28, 1990, p. 28.
[86] Airstream Annual Report 1989, p. 17.
[87] David Carey, "Road Runner," *Financial World*, November 1986, pp. 16–17.

Harley-Davidson proved time and again that it was a survivor, having restored peak production levels after each economic downturn. The company had reached its highest levels of output in 1989. But, once again, the threat of recession was looming on the horizon. Standard & Poor's *Industry Surveys* warned that "leading indicators have been roughly flat and pointing to little growth . . . recent financial market activity alternates between fears of recession and inflation. Presently, inflation is a bigger worry for the markets, though recession is the larger worry for the moment."[88]

As the summer of 1990 was reaching its peak, a major international crisis unfolded. On August 2, Iraq invaded Kuwait, unleashing a series of events that seriously impacted the U.S. economy. In the August 16, 1990, *Trends & Projections*, Standard & Poor's discussed some of the effects of the anxiety in the Middle East: "The economy looks a lot more vulnerable than it did only a month ago. That was true before the Iraqi invasion; it is even truer with oil prices climbing. . . . A very slow, sluggish economy is predicted for the second half of 1990."[89]

Valueline offered some further insight into the risks of the Middle East situation to Harley-Davidson: "The chief cause for concern would be curtailment of fuel supply in case of a shooting war. In any event, higher oil prices mean more inflation, which increases the risk of recession and with that, a slump in spending for big-ticket recreational goods."[90] Harley-Davidson's products traditionally carried a reputation of producing less fuel efficient bikes than their Japanese counterparts. "This is no touring bike . . . that will take you nonstop from Tucson to Atlantic City."[91]

Other analysts predicted continued pessimism in the recovery of the RV market: "Consumers are getting nervous about the economy; recent consumer sentiment reports show deteriorating trends . . . . In the consumer durables category, weak auto sales are not likely to be reversed soon . . . the prospect of higher oil prices means more pressure on consumer spending. Because it is difficult to reduce energy consumption in the short run, many consumers react to higher oil prices by reducing their spending on other items."[92]

LEGAL AND SAFETY ISSUES

As of 1988, 21 states had laws that required motorcycles to operate with their headlights on during the daytime as well as nighttime hours. In addition, 20 states required motorcycle riders to wear helmets. Motorcyclists argued that such laws were a violation of their constitutional rights and that helmets actually prevented them from hearing sirens and other important road noises. But such

[88] Reid, *Well Made in America*, p. 9.
[89] Standard & Poor's *Trends & Projections*, August 16, 1990, p. 3.
[90] Ibid., pp. 1, 2.
[91] *Valueline*, p. 1751.
[92] Marvel, "Gentrified HOGs," p. 26.

legislation was not without justification. The number of deaths on motorcycles reached 4,500 in 1987—a rate approximately 16 times higher than that for automobiles. Cycle enthusiasts had a tendency to push the blame on unobservant car drivers. However, statistics from the Insurance Institute for Highway Safety (IIHS) showed that 45 percent of these accidents involved only one vehicle. Of particular concern to the IIHS were the high-speed superbikes that became available to the general public. These bikes accounted for almost twice the number of fatalities as other cycles. Moreover, the IIHS blamed the motorcycle industry for marketing these bikes for their high speed and power. It claimed that this encouraged the reckless use of an already dangerous product.[93] The president of IIHS stated, "The fact is motorcycles as a group have much higher death and injury rates than cars, so the last thing we need is this new breed of cycle with even higher injury rates."[94]

But what did all this mean to Harley? With the high revs of the traditional HOG and the production of lighter-weight race-style cycles like the Nova, industry experts claimed that they were sure to be hit with the same adverse publicity and criticisms as their Japanese counterparts.

The Rubbie Influence

> I love riding the motorcycle. What a shame it nearly throws you into the jaws of death.
>
> Blly Idol[95]

> Every motorcycle rider thinks about the possibility of an accident. But I figured I was sharp enough in my reactions not to have one. . . . But the fact is, on Sunday, December 4, 1988, there I was, sprawled at the feet of a policeman with paramedics on the way.
>
> Gary Busey[96]

Both Idol, the international rock star, and Busey, the Academy Award-nominated actor, suffered near-fatal accidents while riding Harley-Davidson motorcycles. Neither Idol nor Busey were wearing helmets at the time of their accidents. An apparent disdain for the safety of motorcycle riding was condoned by these role models. Busey, in fact, continued to be an opponent of helmet laws

[93] Standard & Poor's *Industry Surveys*, August 16, 1990, p. 4.
[94] Fannin, "Against All Odds," pp. 45–46.
[95] "Billy Idol," *Rolling Stone*, July 1990, p. 174.
[96] "Gary Busey: A Near-Fatal Motorcycle Crash Changes an Actor's Life, But Not His Refusal to Wear a Helmet," *People*, May 15, 1990, p. 65.

even after his ordeal. His stance remained among the throng of enthusiasts that felt "the decision to wear a helmet is a matter of personal freedom."[97]

The Rubbies that helped revive Harley-Davidson were a double-edged sword. Well-known personalities such as comedian Jay Leno, actors Sylvester Stallone, Mickey Rourke, Lorenzo Lamas, Kurt Russell, Daniel Day-Lewis, John Schneider, and Michael Hutchence of the rock group INXS were members of the Rubbie "fraternity." Their high-profile status drew attention to the helmet laws. Many of these celebrities were often seen in paparazzi, mounted on their Harleys, without wearing helmets. Peter DeLuise, star of television's *21 Jumpstreet*, explained, "Biking is like sliding through the air. When you put a helmet on, it takes away part of the feeling."[98] Ironically, DeLuise's show, which catered to an adolescent audience, often depicted teenagers cruising streets and highways without helmets.

Statistics showed that "142,000 Americans are injured in motorcycle accidents each year." In the early 1970s Congress used its power over the states to enact legislation that required all motorcycle riders to wear helmets. U.S. highway funds were cut in those states that did not pass the laws. Forty-seven states complied with the demand, but in the bicentennial year, aggressive lobbying efforts by biking groups succeeded in influencing Congress to revoke the sanctions. By 1980, 25 of the states had removed or weakened their helmet laws. Federal figures reported an increase in motorcycle fatalities of over 40 percent during this three-year period. General Motors did a study in 1986 that revealed that one-fourth of the 4,505 motorcyclists killed that year would have lived had they worn helmets.[99]

With models that can reach top speeds of 150 mph, Harley-Davidsons continued to satisfy the American desire for power, speed, and personal freedom. The company was never in the business of manufacturing helmets, nor did it take a stance on the helmet issue, but while the contention of pro-choice enthusiasts was that the decision was personal, statistics showed that society was absorbing the cost. According to *Time*, a 1985 survey in Seattle found that 105 motorcycle accident victims hospitalized incurred $2.7 million in medical bills, of which 63 percent was paid for from public funds.[100]

FINANCIAL HIGHLIGHTS

Harley-Davidson's financial position had improved greatly from 1986 to 1989 (see Exhibits 25.4 to 25.8). Even after the public stock offering in 1986,

[97] Ibid.
[98] Ibid., p. 66.
[99] Ibid., p. 65.
[100] Ibid.

EXHIBIT 25.4   Harley-Davidson Net Income Comparison

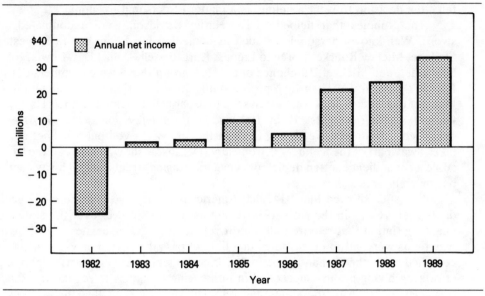

Source: Harley-Davidson, Inc.

insiders continued to maintain some ownership of the company. *Valueline* reported in September 1990 that insiders owned 11.6 percent of Harley-Davidson's stock. Other major shareholders included FMR Corporation (7.2 percent) and Harris Association (6.7 percent). In June 1990, Malcolm Glazer reduced his ownership in Harley-Davidson from 7.29 percent to less than 1 percent, earning a $10 million profit in the process.[101]

Management's concern for employee satisfaction impacted its financial statements, when in April 1989, Harley paid a $1.3 million signing bonus to the Wisconsin labor unions.[102] Harley lowered its debt-equity ratio considerably in 1989, with the repurchase of $37.1 million of debt during the year. This created a decrease in its debt-equity ratio from 55 percent to 40 percent. In 1990, Harley-Davidson's stock was pounded—from a high of $34, to a low of $13, before recovering to $18 as 1990 drew to a close.

[101] *Valueline*, p. 1761.
[102] Rose, "Vrooming Back," p. 6.

EXHIBIT 25.5   Consolidated Balance Sheets (In thousands except per share data)

	1988	1989
Assets		
Current Assets		
Cash and Cash Equivalents	$52,360	$39,076
Accounts Receivable, Net of Allowance for Doubtful Accounts	42,857	45,565
Inventories	89,947	87,540
Deferred Income Taxes	8,844	9,682
Prepaid Expenses	4,795	5,811
Assets of Discontinued Operation	12,488	—
Total Current Assets	211,291	187,674
Property, Plant, and Equipment, Net	107,838	115,700
Goodwill	68,782	66,190
Deferred Financing Costs	4,495	2,356
Other Assets	4,307	7,009
Noncurrent Assets of Discontinued Operation	4,401	—
Total Assets	$401,114	$378,929
Liabilities and Stockholders' Equity		
Current Liabilities		
Notes Payable	$21,041	$22,789
Current Maturities of Long-Term Debt	12,188	4,143
Accounts Payable	36,939	40,095
Accrued Expenses and Other Liabilities	63,047	69,334
Liabilities of Discontinued Operation	3,172	—
Total Current Liabilities	$136,387	$136,361
Long-Term Debt	$135,176	$74,795
Accrued Employee Benefits	3,309	5,273
Deferred Income Taxes	4,594	6,253
Commitments and Contingencies		
Stockholders Equity		
Series A Junior Participating Preferred Stock, 1,000,000 Shares Authorized, None Issued	—	—
Common Stock, 9,155,000 Shares Issued	92	92
Additional Paid-In Capital	76,902	79,681
Retained Earnings	44,410	77,352
Cumulative Foreign Currency Translation Adjustment	374	508
	121,778	157,633
Less		
Treasury Stock (447,091 and 520,000 Shares in 1989 and 1988, Respectively), at Cost	(130)	(112)
Unearned Compensation	—	(1,274)
Total Stockholders' Equity	121,648	156,247
Total Liabilities and Stockholders' Equity	$401,114	$378,929

Source: Harley-Davidson, Inc.

EXHIBIT 25.6   Consolidated Statements of Income (In thousands except per share data)

Years Ended December 31	1987	1988	1989
Net Sales	$645,966	$709,360	$790,967
Operating Costs and Expenses			
Cost of Goods Sold	487,205	533,448	596,940
Selling, Administrative, and Engineering	104,672	111,582	127,606
	591,877	645,030	724,546
Income from Operations	54,089	64,330	66,421
Interest Income	2,658	4,149	3,634
Interest Expense	(23,750)	(22,612)	(17,956)
Other—Net	(21,430)	165	910
Income from Continuing Operations Before Provision for Income Taxes and Extraordinary Items	30,854	46,032	53,009
Provision for Income Taxes	13,181	18,863	20,399
Income from Continuing Operations before Extraordinary Items	17,673	27,169	32,610
Discontinued Operation, Net of Tax			
Income (loss) from Discontinued Operation	—	(13)	154
Gain on Disposal of Discontinued Operation	—	—	3,436
Income before Extraordinary Items	17,673	27,156	36,200
Extraordinary Items			
Loss on Refinancing/Debt Repurchase, Net of Taxes	—	(1,468)	(1,434)
Additional Cost of 1983 AMF Settlement, Net of Taxes	—	(1,776)	(1,824)
Benefit from Utilization of Loss Carry Forward	—	—	—
Net Income	$21,215	$23,912	$32,942
Per Common Share			
Income from Continuing Operations	$2.72	$3.41	$3.78
Discontinued Operation	—	—	.41
Extraordinary Items	.55	(.41)	(.38)
Net Income	$3.27	$3.00	$3.81

Source: Harley-Davidson, Inc.

EXHIBIT 25.7   Consolidated Statements of Cash Flow (In thousands)

Years Ended December 31	1987	1988	1989
Cash Flows from Operating Activities			
Net Income	$21,215	$23,912	$32,942
Adjustments to Reconcile Net Income to Net Cash Provided by Operating Activities			
Depreciation and Amortization	15,643	17,958	20,007
Deferred Income Taxes	(2,875)	(1,375)	821
Long-Term Employee Benefits	(439)	1,037	2,741
Gain on Sale of Discontinued Operation	—	—	(5,513)
Loss on Disposal of Long-Term Assets	1,505	1,451	28
Net Changes in Current Assets and Current Liabilities	12,205	(30,346)	10,051
Total Adjustments	26,039	(11,275)	28,135
Net Cash Provided by Operating Activities	47,254	12,637	61,077
Cash Flows from Investing Activities			
Capital Expenditures	(17,027)	(23,786)	(24,438)
Less Amounts Capitalized under Financing Leases	—	2,877	809
Net Capital Expenditures	(17,027)	(20,909)	(23,619)
Proceeds on Sale of Discontinued Operations and Other Assets	—	—	19,475
Other—Net	901	(1,204)	(2,720)
Net Cash in Investing Activities	(16,126)	(22,113)	(6,864)
Cash Flows from Financing Activities			
Net Increase in Notes Payable	5,891	1,083	1,748
Reductions in Debt	(78,478)	(42,652)	(69,245)
Proceeds from Issuance of Common Stock	18,690	35,179	—
Proceeds from Additional Borrowings	70,000	—	—
Repurchase of Warrants	(3,594)	—	—
Deferred Financing Costs	(3,265)	—	—
Net Cash Provided by (Used in) Financing Activities	9,244	(6,390)	(67,497)
Net Increase (Decrease) in Cash and Cash Equivalents	40,372	(15,866)	(13,284)
Cash and Cash Equivalents:			
At Beginning of Year	$27,854	$68,226	$52,360
At End of Year	$68,226	$52,360	$39,076

Source: Harley-Davidson, Inc.

EXHIBIT 25.8 Consolidated Statements of Changes in Stockholders' Equity, 1987 to 1989 (In thousands except per share data)

	Common Stock		Additional Paid-In Capital	Retained Earnings (Deficit)	Cumulative Foreign Currency Translation Adjustment	Treasury Stock	Unearned Compensation
	Outstanding Shares	Balance					
Balance, December 31, 1986	6,200,000	$62	$26,657	$ (717)	$287	$(130)	$—
Net Income	—	—	—	21,215	—	—	—
Net Proceeds from Common Stock Offering	1,230,000	12	18,678	—	—	—	—
Repurchase of 230,000 Warrants in Connection With Public Debt and Common Stock Offering	—	—	(3,594)	—	—	—	—
Cumulative Foreign Currency Translation Adjustment	—	—	—	—	443	—	—
Balance, December 31, 1987	7,430,000	74	41,741	20,498	730	(130)	—
Net Income	—	—	—	23,912	—	—	—
Net Proceeds from Common Stock Offering	1,725,000	18	35,161	—	—	—	—
Cumulative Foreign Currency Translation Adjustment	—	—	—	—	(356)	—	—
Balance, December 31, 1988	9,155,000	92	76,902	44,410	374	(130)	—
Net Income	—	—	—	32,942	—	—	—
Issuance of 72,909 Treasury Shares of Restricted Stock	—	—	2,779	—	—	18	(1,274)
Cumulative Foreign Currency Translation Adjustment	—	—	—	—	134	—	—
Balance, December 31, 1989	$9,155,000	$92	$79,681	$77,352	$508	$(112)	$(1,274)

EPILOGUE

So at the end of the week I thought I'd go for it. I told Connie that I'd just need a few more days to raise some capital. So I'm hanging out at Bernie's Bank, flipping through a Wall Street Journal, *when I come across this ad* [Exhibit 25.9].

I couldn't believe it myself. Another American-made motorcycle. My little voice had some words of wisdom, but I already knew I was gonna have to break off the deal with Connie. It wasn't easy, but hey—that's why I'm Johnny Callatino. So there you have it. I don't know about you, but I could sure use another cold one.

EXHIBIT 25.9   *Wall Street Journal*, **Wednesday, November 7, 1990**

POSITIONS AVAILABLE   **POSITIONS AVAILABLE**

Indian Motocycle Co., Inc.

The Historic Indian Motocycle Company, Inc. of Spring-field, MA is now accepting resumes for key executive positions in the manufacturing and marketing of the new Indian line of Motorcycles and accessories.

Please forward all resumes to:

Indian Motocycle Co., Inc.

86 Springfield Street
Springfield, MA 01107
Phone: 413-747-7233 Corporate Office
413-746-3766 Final Assembly
CEO. Philip S. Zanghi

—————————————— CASE 29 ——————————————

Rubbermaid

During 1990, we celebrated the 70th anniversary of the founding of the Company. It has progressed through seven decades of successful growth from the results of innovation, diversification, the company's emphasis on quality, and the contributions of extremely dedicated associates. Those same strengths position Rubbermaid to continue its success into the 1990s.

Today, Rubbermaid is a growing and vital enterprise. We have modern manufacturing facilities, aggressive plans for the future and, most importantly, experienced management with over 9,000 skilled and committed associates throughout the organization. We are confident that the Company will continue to perform vigorously and effectively and achieve another successful year in 1991.[1]

Stanley C. Gault

RUBBERMAID TODAY

Rubbermaid, under the highly respected leadership of chairman and chief executive officer Stanley Gault, enjoyed a banner year in 1990. In keeping with its corporate goals of increasing sales and earnings annually, the firm reported record net sales of $1.53 billion, a 6 percent increase over the $1.45 billion of 1989. Record net earnings were $143.5 million, or $1.80 per share, versus $125.0 million net earnings and $1.57 per share in 1989, an increase of 15 percent.

Sales for the fourth quarter of 1990 increased 13 percent to $382 million from the $337 million of 1989's comparable quarter. Earnings were $33.0 million, or 41 cents per share, a 15 percent increase over the $28.7 million, or 36 cents per share of last year. The fourth-quarter results represented the 40th consecutive quarter in which both sales and earnings increased over those of the prior year's period. Since 1980, Rubbermaid's sales quadrupled, and earnings rose sixfold.

This case was prepared by Bernard A. Deitzer, Alan G. Krigline, and Thomas C. Peterson as a basis for class discussion rather than to illustrate either effective or ineffective handling of an administrative situation. Copyright © 1991 by Bernard A. Deitzer. Used with permission from Bernard A. Deitzer.

[1] *Rubbermaid Annual Report*, Rubbermaid Incorporated, Wooster, Ohio, 1990, p. 5.

Consistent with its announced overall growth objectives, Rubbermaid acquired two companies in 1990, and entered into a joint venture with a European housewares company, confirming its plan to expand and diversify its rubber and plastic products in advance of the European Community (EC) markets of 1992.

COMPANY HISTORY

During 1990, Rubbermaid celebrated the 70th anniversary of the founding of the company. It was early May 1920 that the Wooster Rubber Company began manufacturing its first product—the Sunshine brand of toy balloons.

In the mid-1920s, Horatio B. Ebert and Errett M. Grable, executives of the Wear-Ever Division of the Aluminum Company of America, purchased Wooster Rubber as a personal investment. They then engaged Clyde C. Gault, Stanley Gault's father, who had been general manager of Wooster Rubber, to continue managing the business. By 1928, the company had prospered sufficiently to build a new factory and office building. However, the great depression of the 1930s caused sales to plummet.

First Housewares Product—The Rubber Dustpan

Meanwhile, James R. Caldwell of New England, who had developed a rubber dustpan, was forced into selling it door to door, because department store buyers refused to purchase because, they said, "We have no calls for a one dollar rubber dustpan. We can sell metal dustpans for 39 cents." Persistence paid off, and eventually Caldwell, the door-to-door entrepreneur, succeeded in convincing department store buyers to carry rubber dustpans. He adopted the brand name Rubbermaid and developed three other rubber items—a drainboard mat to protect countertops, a soap dish, and a sink stopper.

During this period, Ebert, while calling on New England department stores, saw and became interested in Caldwell's rubber housewares products. Subsequently the two combined businesses, and in July 1934 the manufacture of rubber housewares products began at the Wooster Rubber Company. The lowly dustpan had arrived.

The War Years

During World War II, civilian use of rubber was frozen by the government. The company's consumer business became in effect nonexistent. Survival came in the form of subcontracts to produce components for self-sealing fuel tanks for military aircraft in addition to life jackets and medical tourniquets.

The New Beginning

Following the war, Rubbermaid resumed the production and sale of rubber housewares products. Because coloring materials were not yet available, all products were produced in black. In 1950, the company established an operation in Canada and in 1955 issued its first public offering of stock, trading in the over-the-counter market.

The first plastic product, a dishpan, was introduced in 1956. In 1958, a salesman was assigned to call on hotels and motels to sell doormats and bathtub mats. Thus was the beginning of today's successful institutional business, established as Rubbermaid Commercial Products in 1967.

Wooster Rubber to Rubbermaid

In 1957, the firm officially changed its corporate name to Rubbermaid to capitalize on an already widely accepted brand name. When Caldwell retired as president in 1958, Donald E. Noble, who had joined Rubbermaid in 1941, was elected chief executive officer, serving first as president and later as chairman of the board. During Noble's 39 years of service, new businesses were entered, physical facilities were expanded, and an operation in West Germany was established. Rubbermaid's rite of passage from a small, rural Ohio company to a multinational firm with one of America's best-known brand names was underway.[2]

THE BUSINESS

Rubbermaid operated in a single line of business: the manufacture and sale of plastic and rubber products for the consumer and institutional markets. It manufactured and marketed over 3,000 products worldwide, including kitchenware; laundry and bath accessories; microwave ovenware; toys; and home horticulture, office, foodservice, health care, and industrial maintenance products.

Rubbermaid owned one of the largest plastic and rubber housewares production facilities in the world: some 1.6 million square feet spread over a single floor. Half a million housewares products of all sizes, shapes, and colors were processed daily from plastic resin. With products as ordinary as Rubbermaid's, it was critical that the line always appeared up to date.

Corporate headquarters as well as the housewares products and specialty products divisions remained in Wooster, Ohio. Wooster's population was approximately 21,000 and it was located some 50 miles from downtown Cleveland.

Redesigned versions of the early and ordinary dustpan along with drainboard mats, sink mats, and soap dishes remained in the company's extended portfolio of rubber and plastic products. However, ordinary, colorless kitchen utensils were transformed into appealing, colorful, upscale housewares.

By 1990, with a brand name highly recognized and associated with quality household products, the maker of toy balloons, and later, dustpans had grown to over a billion-dollar firm with international ranking and acclaim for its spectacular

[2] *Rubbermaid Annual Report*, 1989, pp. 10–11.

successes by industry analysts. Stanley Gault was regularly hailed by the media for his stunningly superior leadership, as Rubbermaid was second only to Merck as one of *Fortune*'s most admired U.S. corporations.

RUBBERMAID'S MANAGEMENT

Stanley Carleton Gault, 65, chairman of the board, chief executive officer, and director, joined Rubbermaid in 1980. He had just ended an illustrious 31-year career at General Electric (GE), where he served as senior vice president and sector executive of the industrial products and components sector. He decided to leave GE when he realized that he was being passed over in the process of determining GE's next CEO.[3]

Walter W. Williams, 57, director, president, and chief operating officer, joined Rubbermaid in 1987. Similar to Gault, Williams left a 31-year career at General Electric, where he was senior vice president of corporate marketing. Williams' strong marketing skills were considered by Gault to be critical to Rubbermaid's future success.

Wolfgang R. Schmitt, 47, executive vice president, began his Rubbermaid career in 1966 as a management trainee after graduating from Otterbein College in Westerville, Ohio. He held numerous top marketing and management assignments before assuming his current position.

RUBBERMAID'S CORPORATE GOALS

Over the years Rubbermaid was widely recognized as an innovative company. The corporatewide drive for innovation apparently mirrored Gault's efforts to implement corporate growth objectives and to expand the corporation's markets. Rubbermaid's new product goal was to have 30 percent of sales each year come from products not in the line five years earlier. In confirmation of this, over 1,000 new products were introduced between 1985 and 1990.

Another Rubbermaid goal was to continue to be the lowest-cost, highest-quality producer in the household products industry. During the period from 1981–90, over $612 million was invested in the business' facilities to increase productivity, develop new products, and achieve world-class manufacturing status.

In 1989, Gault set a challenging goal of achieving $2 billion in annual sales by 1992, just five years after Rubbermaid had reached sales of $1 billion. Gault at that time predicted:

---

[3] Actually this was a return home for Gault, a graduate of the College of Wooster. His father Clyde was one of the founders of the Wooster Rubber Company. After six years, however, the elder Gault sold his ownership and remained until his retirement as general manager.

With a growth rate of 15 percent a year we can reach that goal. We have entered 1989 with existing product offerings supported by operating plans and merchandising programs designed to produce another record year. We expect to record favorable sales and earnings comparisons through 1989.[4]

Rubbermaid was expected to reach the $2 billion mark by the last quarter of 1992. Gault believed it could do so simply by following its present course. "We project our growth to come from a combination of areas. We'll see growth occur in the core product lines of Rubbermaid's domestic business, the effort under way to grow business internationally, from new product development in all our businesses, new product categories being added to existing businesses, and growth through a selective acquisitions program."[5]

Essentially Rubbermaid summarized its mission as an attempt to offer exceptional value to its customers with high-quality and cost-competitive products, excellent distribution, and a highly focused customer mentality. It was a business, according to management, whose fundamental corporate strengths served it effectively over the years with widely recognized and respected brand names, high-quality innovative products, strategic marketing direction, efficient modern manufacturing facilities, an enviable financial performance record, dedicated associates, and a focused direction for growth and profitability.[6]

RUBBERMAID'S OBJECTIVES FOR THE 1990s

1. The corporate objective was to increase sales, earnings, and earnings per share 15 percent per year, while achieving a 20 percent return on shareholders' equity.

2. It was also the company's objective to pay approximately 30 percent of current year's earnings as dividends to shareholders while using the remainder to fund future growth opportunities.

3. Each year, 30 percent of its sales was projected to come from new products introduced over the previous five years. It planned to enter an entirely new market every 12 to 18 months.

4. The objective for customers and consumers was to offer the best value possible. It intended to provide the highest-quality products that were reasonably priced, a continuous flow of new products, and exceptional service to its customers.

5. The company aimed to treat all constituents fairly and consider the interests of associates as individuals.

6. The company aimed to be an environmentally responsible corporate citizen.[7]

Rubbermaid had a number of fundamental strengths that would benefit the organization in achieving its objectives. Those strengths are outlined in Exhibit 29.1.

[4] *Rubbermaid Annual Report*, 1990, p. 9.
[5] *Rubbermaid Annual Report*, 1986, pp. 4–6.
[6] *Wall Street Transcript*, March 23, 1987, p. 84964.
[7] *Rubbermaid Annual Report*, 1990, p. 10.

EXHIBIT 29.1   Rubbermaid's Fundamental Strengths

Rubbermaid's growth is the result of seven fundamental strengths:

1. A focused direction to maximize the value of Rubbermaid for its shareholders. Each operating unit is well-positioned in attractive markets with quality products, has a strong organization and a well-defined mission for growth.
2. The strength of its franchise with customers and consumers. Its brand names are recognized and respected within each market segment it serves.
3. A reputation for quality products. All of its brand names connote quality and value within their respective markets.
4. An emphasis on new products. Its goal is to have 30 percent of sales each year come from products which were not in the line five years earlier.
5. Marketing, sales, and manufacturing capabilities. These organizations are among the strongest, best qualified in each of the industries it serves.
6. Financial performance and strength. Rubbermaid enjoys a strong financial position with very little debt. It has the capability to pursue its business objectives successfully.
7. Human resources. Capable and dedicated people throughout the organization have demonstrated their ability to perform impressively and consistently.

Source: Rubbermaid *Annual Report*, 1987, p. 9.

GAULT'S INITIAL STRATEGY

When Stanley C. Gault became CEO of Rubbermaid in 1980, revenues were climbing steadily, and, although sales totaled $341 million, earnings had dipped to $21 million. The company was facing the severe pressures and challenges of the 1980s.[8]

Prior to Gault's arrival, Rubbermaid employed a strategy of efficiency. The company was in a slow-growth business with increasing overhead and a declining rate of productivity and whose personnel, according to management, apparently had grown comfortable and unaccustomed to change. "Our product development lagged, our retail customers claimed we were arrogant, and our profit margins had fallen," summarized the new CEO.[9]

Accepting the challenge, Gault immediately restructured the firm and its in-place management. "You have to set the tone and pace, define objectives and strategies and demonstrate through personal example what you expect from others," advised Gault.[10] He reshuffled, hired, and fired. Ten percent of all salaried personnel were abruptly dismissed. Some two years later, only 2 of 172 Rubbermaid managers still held their original jobs.

[8] Kenneth Labich, "The Seven Keys to Business Leadership," *Fortune*, October 24, 1988, p. 60.
[9] Patricia Sellers, "Does the CEO Really Matter?" *Fortune*, April 22, 1991, p. 86.
[10] Labich, "Seven Keys to Business Leadership."

The housewares and commercial products divisions generated over 96 percent of total corporate income; the remaining units were "six weak soldiers." All operations were subsequently and rigorously evaluated to determine their strengths, weaknesses, and opportunities. Early on, Gault dramatically informed the organization that he was aiming for a 15 percent average annual growth in sales, profits, and earnings per share, plus $1 billion in sales revenues by 1990.[11]

Rubbermaid Restructured

The CEO's first strategic step in restructuring was to review Rubbermaid's eight lines of business and to excise half of them. One casualty was its in-home party plan company. Gault perceived that current demographics and the changing lifestyles of today's working women allowed little time for after-hours housewares parties. Furthermore, Rubbermaid did not have a presence commensurate with its competitive archrival, Tupperware.

In addition, Rubbermaid subsequently sold its domestic car mat and auto accessories business. Gault judged auto accessories to be a commodity business with stiff price and volume elastic competition where automakers tended to pressure suppliers.[12]

Rubbermaid's Acquisition Strategy

Gault's relentless and unyielding commitment to controlled growth earmarked the firm's approach to expansion. Rubbermaid consistently demonstrated an ability to expand its existing businesses. Both new product flow and new market entries thrived via opportunistic and related acquisitions. Gault deliberately looked for small companies that fit, that were number one or number two in their product category, and that could benefit from Rubbermaid's manufacturing and marketing expertise.

Acquisition-minded Gault's first target was Carlan, maker of Con-Tact Brand self-adhesive decorative shelf covering. Later came a vigorous expansion into entirely new markets. In 1982, Rubbermaid's commercial products company entered the burgeoning health care field. Next, Gault expanded into the horticulture and agriculture markets. In 1983, the firm entered the then $300 million microwave cookware business with an intense marketing drive.[13] In 1984, Gault acquired Little Tikes, which allowed the company to enter the preschool toy market. Rubbermaid entered the microcomputer accessories business by acquiring Micro-Computer Accessories Inc., and in 1990 entered the office molded products business by acquiring Elson Industries.

As Gault emphasized, "We are definitely receptive to good acquisition opportunities. We have made numerous acquisitions; they have all been top-notch

---

[11] Ibid.
[12] James Braham, "The Billion Dollar Dustpan," *Industry Week*, Penton Publishing Company, August 1, 1988, p. 47.
[13] "Special Citations," *Sales and Marketing Magazine*, January 16, 1984, p. 14.

EXHIBIT 29.2   Rubbermaid's Acquisitions and Joint Ventures

1981	Con-Tact Brand self-adhesive decorative coverings
1984	Little Tikes Company—leading quality manufacturer of preschool children's toys
1985	Gott Corporation—high-quality consumer recreational products
1986	SECO Industries—leading manufacturers of maintenance products
1986	MicroComputer Accessories—accessories for the microcomputer market
1987	Viking Brush Limited—household brushes
1987	Little Tikes Company (Ireland) Limited
1987	MicroComputer Accessories Europe S.A.—computer-related accessories
1987	Reynolds Compression—molding facilities of Polymer Engineering
1989	Rubbermaid Allibert (joint venture)—manufactures casual resin furniture for the North American market
1990	Curver Rubbermaid Group, Breda, the Netherlands—(joint venture) manufactures plastics and rubber housewares and resin furniture
1990	EWU AG, Switzerland—producer of floor care supplies and equipment
1990	Eldon Industries—distributor of molded plastic office products and equipment

companies. We want them to be companies that are well managed and where the management will want to stay and be part of the growing Rubbermaid family."[14] Exhibit 29.2 summarizes Rubbermaid's acquisitions and joint-venture activities.

RUBBERMAID'S GROWTH STRATEGY

Gault strongly believed in developing strategies to control and direct new product activities to meet two types of ambitious growth objectives. The first was incremental growth, which concentrated on doing what Rubbermaid did best— only better. It focused on growth within the company's businesses that was responsive to customer's needs and in turn, provided value to Rubbermaid's customers.

Gault's second approach was leap growth, which involved a higher degree of risk because it created high visibility on the one hand yet high vulnerability on the other. The company won big or lost big. Within these two major classifications, there were eight strategic elements. Four of these applied to incremental growth and four were leap approaches.

Rubbermaid's Incremental Growth Strategies

- To increase the volume of Rubbermaid's existing products. The key to this growth area was in providing value to dealers, distributors, and consumers. The key to value is providing quality, low cost, and service.

[14] *Wall Street Transcript*, April 18, 1988, p. 9116.

- To upscale existing products to meet today's consumer and new design preferences. Upscaling includes introducing new colors to existing lines.
- To extend existing lines to capitalize on product successes, increase retail shelf space, and boost sales volume.
- To expand Rubbermaid's international business as a significant growth opportunity during the 1990s.[15]

Rubbermaid's Leap Growth Strategies

- To develop new products. Rubbermaid's goal is to have at least 30 percent of annual sales coming from new products introduced during the past five years.
- To hone product lines and optimize the number of stock units retained to keep the lines manageable and provide proper customer service levels.
- To enter entirely new markets. This is consistent with a corporate objective to enter a new market every 18 to 24 months.
- To engage in joint ventures or acquisitions to enter new markets by combining the capabilities of a strong outside partner with the many strengths of Rubbermaid.[16]

RUBBERMAID'S STRATEGIES FOR THE 1990s

1. The Company will continue its market-driven approach to product development and marketing, to listen to customers and consumers and effectively respond to the changes in needs, demographics, and lifestyles. This outside-in strategy will help develop new markets and create unique, proprietary products, and programs.

2. To continue to grow using both incremental and leap growth strategies. Incremental growth comes from continuous improvement in all aspects of the business such as line extensions, international expansion, and innovative marketing and sales programs. The leap approach involves new technologies, new market entries, acquisitions, and joint ventures.

3. To continue to invest for future growth and to keep facilities modern and efficient. It is the company's intention to continue to be the lowest cost, highest quality producer in its industry.

4. To continue to build partnerships with customers, suppliers, associates, and communities to enhance the value of Rubbermaid for shareholders and other constituencies.

5. To increase the use of technology in manufacturing and communications, both internally and externally.

6. To continue to pursue world-class status and compete on a global basis.[17]

---

[15] Adapted from remarks by Stanley C. Gault, chairman of the board and chief executive officer, Rubbermaid, before the Conference Board of Canada's 15th Annual Marketing Conference, Hilton International, Toronto, Canada, March 29, 1990.

[16] Ibid.

[17] Ibid., p. 10.

Focus on Quality

Rubbermaid was regularly honored as one of America's most admired corporations. Gault, recognized as among the nation's top 1,000 elite corporate executives, transformed Rubbermaid, a moderately successful firm, into a giant superstar using quality as its hallmark.[18]

The quality and consistency of Rubbermaid's products were aptly matched by the quality and consistency of its management. This could be seen from Rubbermaid's selection to the *Fortune* magazine's annual survey of "America's Most Admired Corporations." The poll, taken from more than 8,000 senior executives, outside directors, and financial analysts, placed Rubbermaid in the number two position. The year 1990 was the sixth consecutive year that the company was selected to be among the top 10, occupying second place in 1987, 1988, and 1990. Rubbermaid was the smallest company ever named to this list. The only other company to appear as consistently on the list was aforementioned Merck, the giant pharmaceutical company.

Indefatigable, Gault did not hesitate to personally phone and placate disgruntled dealers. He never stopped acting as Rubbermaid's top quality controller. Precise and methodical, the hands-on manager visited several stores a week to see how Rubbermaid products were displayed and to inspect the quality of workmanship. If he found an ill fitting lid or wrinkled label, Gault bought the offending goods and then later summoned his senior manager for a lecture. "He gets livid about defects," said Walter W. Williams, the chief operating officer.

When responding to the hint that plastic was once synonymous with junk, Gault launched into an energetic speech on the mixture of his polyethylene and the intricacies of his injection molding. Irrepressible Gault, when comparing his enormously popular garbage cans to flimsier competing versions remarked, "On quality I'm a sonofabitch. No one surpasses our quality." Gault declared of products that do not seem to ever break or wear out, "We use more and better resin. We don't buy any scrap resin. And we use a thicker gauge."[19]

Gault, viewed as a brilliant strategist, paid as much attention to how even simple products looked as he did to the ultraviolent inhibitors in their resins. Sales of big garbage cans jumped 20 percent when he suggested that his design engineer come up with a specific shade of blue instead of chocolate brown.[20]

Management Environment

Stanley Gault's leadership philosophy simply stated that a leader has to be a living example, has to inspire the organization, and has to be a part of the team yet

---

[18] Brian O'Reilly, "Leaders of the Most Admired Corporations," *Fortune*, January 29, 1990, p. 42.

[19] Ibid., p. 43.

[20] Ibid.

still be the manager. Gault judged that leaders must be supportive and, when sensing the need for change, must genuinely communicate the need for it. Highly interactive and strong on interpersonal communications, he regularly strolled through Rubbermaid factories to talk one on one with managers and workers alike. Looking to the future, Gault, who ran a lean and flat organization, believed, "Any incoming chief executive will need to be able to run a flatter organization. As companies continue to cut costs further, middle managers will be eliminated and the CEO will have more people reporting directly to him."[21]

Gault was recognized as a tireless, energetic leader who expected and rewarded hard work from his subordinates. He was a dynamic and affable person who was well liked by his staff even though he demanded a lot from them. His personal schedule often included 12- to 14-hour workdays six days a week. Furthermore, his relentless spirit was emulated at all levels of the firm. Hard driving, Gault was described by his associates as being a very involved manager who wanted to know everything that was going on in each of Rubbermaid's businesses.

Rubbermaid rigorously sought out managers with a strong work ethic who were entrepreneurial types, enthusiastic, competent, and ambitious. They were also good team players, hard-working managers, willing to enhance shareholder wealth, and whose bonuses were based on both increase in profit and increase in the firm's book value.

Gault believed successful CEO's should set strategic direction, align employees behind that strategy so they will carry it out, and groom a successor. "I am very demanding and I know it. But I'm demanding of myself, first. I set high standards and I expect people to meet them. I want all the business we can get, provided we get it fairly. If people can't meet my standards after training and counseling then a change has to be made. That's not saying they aren't good people but they are not cut out for the particular job."[22]

Hourly workers also generally reflected the feeling that the Rubbermaid family comes first and that there was no other way. Regularly enjoying profit sharing since 1944, workers offered over 12,000 cost-cutting suggestions in housewares alone. In 1987, the Housewares and Specialty Products Division saved $24.7 million and in late 1988, $30.8 million.

Although doubling sales, Rubbermaid increased its work force by only 50 percent and has halved its number of sales representatives. It held the line on prices, and all gains came from increased volume and productivity improvement. Relations with the United Rubber Workers were good. In 1987's negotiations, a new contract froze wages for three years in return for the company's pledge to maintain existing jobs.[23]

[21] Jennifer Reese, "CEO's: More Churn at the Top," *Fortune*, March 11, 1991, p. 13.
[22] Braham, "Billion Dollar Dustpan," p. 48.
[23] Ibid.

RUBBERMAID'S MARKETING STRATEGY

One of Gault's first moves upon assuming leadership in 1980 was to revamp Rubbermaid's sales and marketing strategy. The key, according to Gault, was strict adherence to fundamentals. At the time, Rubbermaid's sales force traditionally sold every product category such as sinkware, household containers, and space organizers to all customers.

Gault split off the field sales function from marketing and put sales strategies in place to cover each market segment. As Gault explained it, "A distribution channel that would serve supermarkets and drug stores would not necessarily work for mass merchants or hardware stores or catalog showrooms." Accordingly, he decentralized marketing into product categories and installed the product manager system. This allowed effective specialization and permitted a "more intense level of management involvement with customers."[24]

Consumer Research

Although the firm employed demographic and lifestyle analysis techniques to identify trends, the core of product development at Rubbermaid lay in the use of consumer research. Qualitative and quantitative research allowed by-passing of test marketing and still revealed shopper preferences.

Rubbermaid never test marketed its products. Instead, it tested color preferences year round through fact-finding consumer focus groups in five different cities, and it regularly quizzed people in shopping malls. To avoid tipping off competitors, it generated flows of consumer research through user panels, brand awareness studies, and diaries that consumers filled with notations about product use.[25]

Rubbermaid had some 150 competitors in home products alone but no one competed across its entire product li.ie. Rubbermaid was regularly the only brand name with recognition, because competitor's products often carried no name. Frequently, with 95 percent brand recognition, the company received complaints about some other manufacturer's product. Gault took advantage of this. "We're the only name they can think of so they write us their complaint letters." Gault responded, "Please make certain that every time you buy a plastic product you look for our name. If we make it, our name is on it. But because you did mean to buy ours and made a mistake and will not do so in the future, here, have one on us."[26]

Rubbermaid's Promotion Strategy

Gault's meticulously honed growth strategy, a combination of market positioning, careful expansion, and emphasis on quality, achieved stunning sales and

[24] Christy Marshall, "Rubbermaid, Yes, Plastic," *Business Month*, December 1988, p. 38.
[25] Alex Taylor III, "Why the Bounce at Rubbermaid?" *Fortune*, April 13, 1987, p. 78.
[26] Ibid.

earnings growth and thoroughly dominated competition. Indeed, it was argued by analysts, Rubbermaid's proliferation of innovative, well-crafted, and colorful housewares virtually created a whole new market.[27]

The company, furthermore, supported its products with national television and radio commercials and magazine advertisements along with allowances for promotion and coop advertising. Such focus boosted Rubbermaid's outlets from 60,000 in 1980 to over 100,000 in 1988. Although Rubbermaid's prices might have been higher than those of competitors, it offered a wider range of promotable products that commanded more shelf space.[28] Industry analysts estimated that Rubbermaid's advertising and promotion budget for 1989 was about 3.6 percent of sales or about $5 million.[29]

New Product Development

Rubbermaid single-mindedly pursued its mission to introduce new products with almost fanatic fervor. It was adept at searching out ways to grow. Designers continually tweaked mature products to provide incremental sales.[30] Gault's recipe for success was simple and uncomplicated. "Our formula for success is very open. We absolutely watch the market and we work at it 24 hours a day."[31] Gault saw the business as being a disciple of demographics in lock step with current trends, forever listening to customers' stated and perceived needs.

Team Development at Rubbermaid

Rubbermaid practiced the team development approach, which it considered the productivity breakthrough of the 1990s. For example, in 1987 the firm considered developing the so-called auto office, a portable plastic device that straps onto a car seat. It holds files, pens, and other articles and provides a writing surface. Simultaneously, a cross-functional team composed of, among others, engineers, designers, and marketers was assembled. The team then entered the field to determine what features customers desired. With considerations from several different functions, Rubbermaid brought the new product to the market in 1990. Sales at last count were running 50 percent beyond projections.[32]

Keeping its many products flowing took a deep commitment to research and development. Each of Rubbermaid's operating divisions had its own R&D team, and some divisions were required to enter a new market segment every 18 to 24 months.[33] Rubbermaid's CEO oversaw the launch of more than 250 new products in each of the past two years.[34] The firm boasted a success rate, according to

[27] Marshall, "Rubbermaid, Yes, Plastic," p. 38.
[28] Ibid.
[29] Taylor, "Why the Bounce at Rubbermaid?", p. 78.
[30] Ibid.
[31] Ibid.
[32] Brian Dunmaine, "Who Needs a Boss?" *Fortune*, May 7, 1990, p. 53.
[33] Marshall, "Rubbermaid, Yes, Plastic," p. 38.
[34] Sellers, "Does the CEO Really Matter?" p. 86.

Gault, of 90 percent. The company's goal of 30 percent of sales each year coming from products less than five years old was consistently met and often exceeded.[35]

Rubbermaid looked for fresh design ideas anywhere: from trying to apply the Ford Taurus style soft look to garbage cans to successfully introducing stackable plastic chairs.[36] As Gault explained it, "We just keep bringing these new categories out while expanding categories we're already in, like bathware, sinkware, trash, and refuse collection, and gadgets."[37]

According to industry analysts, new product development appeared to be the single most important reason for Rubbermaid's rise to a billion-dollar multinational firm. Stanley Gault assigned top strategic importance to product development, and that was where he allocated capital. "I have this vision," he said, "that when you look down the aisle of a store you see nothing except Rubbermaid products."[38]

Rubbermaid was considered one of America's most innovative and fastest-growing companies. Since 1934, when Rubbermaid, then the Wooster Rubber Company, made the dust pan a radical addition to its line of balloons, product innovation has been the firm's signature. The humble dust pan spawned more than 2,000 mostly utilitarian products. Those new products kept both sales and earnings at Rubbermaid growing by at least 15 percent a year.[39]

In summarizing Rubbermaid's R&D strategy, Gault once disclosed, "The primary reason for developing so many new products is to identify and develop entirely new categories that permit us to enter new areas and new sections within a retail store. New lines keep the products fresh, up to date and highly salable."[40]

RUBBERMAID'S DIVISIONS

To stay close to its customers, Rubbermaid's eight businesses operated as autonomous companies. In addition to the Housewares Product Division, the firm had a Specialty Products Division, the Little Tikes Company, Rubbermaid Commercial Products, the Rubbermaid Office Products Group, Rubbermaid-Allibert, the international division, Rubbermaid Canada, and Curver Rubbermaid Group. All were expected to embrace the new product thrust of the core household business.

Rubbermaid's philosophy was that of a market-driven organization whose goal was to offer the best value by providing the highest-quality products plus a continuous flow of new products at reasonable prices with exceptional service to

---

[35] "Special Citations," *Sales and Marketing Management*, January 16, 1984, p. 14.
[36] "Masters of Innovation," *Business Week*, McGraw Hill, April 10, 1989, p. 10.
[37] Braham, "Billion-Dollar Dustpan," p. 46.
[38] Sellers, "Does the CEO Really Matter?" p. 86.
[39] Maria Mallory, "Profits on Everything but the Kitchen Sink," Innovations in America, *Business Week*, McGraw-Hill, 1989, p. 22.
[40] Marshall, "Rubbermaid, Yes, Plastic," p. 38.

all customers. Each operating company established and executed strategic plans to support this overarching corporate philosophy.

Housewares Products Division

Formerly the Home Product Division, the Housewares Product Division was renamed to define more clearly its mission of serving the housewares industry. It manufactured and marketed sinkware, space organizers, household and refuse containers, food preparation utensils and gadgets, microwave cookware, food storage products, bathware, rubber gloves, casual dinnerware and drinkware, workshop organizers, Con-Tact brand decorative coverings, shelf liners, and vacuum cleaner bags.

Rubbermaid entered the consumer recycling market with containers to separate and collect recyclable materials in the home. Containers themselves were manufactured using recycled post-consumer plastics such as milk and soft drink containers.

Specialty Products Division

This division was responsible for aggressively innovating, manufacturing, and marketing three major product categories having seasonality and outdoor leisure activity as common bonds. Categories included insulated products, home horticulture products, and outdoor casual resin furniture. Specialty Products made and marketed insulated chests, thermal jugs, water coolers, fuel containers, storage containers, Blue Ice refreezable ice substitute, planters, and bird feeders.

The Little Tikes Company

Many new products were introduced and added to the company's product lines in 1989, including three new categories—trucks, infant products, and a doll house. The doll house category included Little Tikes Place and miniature accessories of such highly popular items as the Cozy Coupe, Party Kitchen, and Play Slide. The infant product category offered 11 items including Stacking Clown, Baby Roller, Baby Mirror, and a variety of tub toys. The third new category, trucks, featured the Big Dump Truck and Big Loader.

The quality and integrity of Little Tikes products received favorable recognition as three products—Little Tikes Place, Little Tug, and Toddle Tots' child care center—were named first, second, and ninth among the top 10 nonvideo new toys for 1989 by the Consumer Affairs Committee of Americans for Democratic Action.[41]

Rubbermaid's market share in preschool and infant toys and furnishings gained steadily in the past three years.[42]

---

[41] *Rubbermaid Annual Report*, 1989, pp. 16–17.
[42] *Akron Beacon Journal*, March 15, 1989, p. 1.

	Market Share	
	1987	1990
Fisher Price	64%	44%
Rubbermaid (Little Tikes)	13%	22%
Hasbro (Playschool)	23%	22%
Mattel (Disney)	—	11%
Combined Sales	$1.2 billion	$1.4 billion

Little Tikes enjoyed a 40 percent annual growth and, since its founding in 1970, doubled sales every three years to about $300 million, although it spent less than $2 million for advertising. Little Tikes' fanatical attention to quality seemed to be gaining popularity with parents selecting larger toys such as plastic jungle gyms and slides.

Rubbermaid Commercial Products

Rubbermaid Commercial Products was established in 1967 to design and manufacture lines of products for the commercial, industrial, and institutional markets. It sold a wide variety of products to the sanitary maintenance, foodservice, industrial, and agricultural markets. In June 1990, Rubbermaid acquired EWU AG, a Swiss-based manufacturer of mopping equipment and cleaning tools, to gain increased commercial distribution throughout Europe.

The municipal recycling market offered many growth opportunities for Commercial Products. The operation pioneered the use of recycled plastics in many of its containers and participated in national efforts to help raise awareness that containers manufactured with post-consumer resin are used widely in municipal curbside recycling programs.

Office Products Group

Located in Inglewood, California, this business was established in January 1991 to focus on the office products industry, which was growing at a rate in excess of the gross national product. The acquisition of Eldon Industries enhanced Rubbermaid's position in the office products market as Eldon was the leading manufacturer of office accessories and offered a wide range of products for the desk. Rubbermaid was the leader in chair mats and MicroComputer Accessories led in computer-related accessories for personal computer, word processor, and data terminal users.

Davson produced communication boards, building directories, signage, and furniture such as lecterns and wall cabinets. Ungar served the electronics industry by supplying tools for the assembly and repair of electronic circuits.

Rubbermaid-Allibert

During 1989, this operation was established as a joint venture with Allibert S.A. of Paris, France, to manufacture and market resin casual furniture for the

North American market. Rubbermaid had 50 percent ownership and management control of the venture. Allibert was a leading European manufacturer of casual furniture and participated in international markets for years. It had extensive experience in materials technology, processing technologies, and furniture design.

Curver Rubbermaid

The Curver Rubbermaid Group became operational in January 1990 as a joint venture between Rubbermaid and the Dutch chemical conglomerate, DSM. The group manufactured and marketed plastic and rubber housewares and resin furniture for Europe, the Middle East, and North Africa.

As its venture share, Rubbermaid contributed its European housewares manufacturing facilities and distribution centers in Germany, France, Austria, the Netherlands, and Switzerland. DSM contributed its Curver Housewares Group, which included its manufacturing and marketing subsidiaries scattered throughout the European continent.

The integration of the two organizations, Rubbermaid and Curver, with their respective product lines, sales and marketing organizations, and manufacturing and distribution facilities, positioned Rubbermaid for a leadership role in the European Community of 1992 and the emerging Eastern Bloc markets.

International Operations

Rubbermaid's international businesses achieved record sales and earnings growth in 1990, particularly in Europe, Latin America, Mexico, the Far East, and Canada. With the exception of the Far East, the management of Rubbermaid businesses around the world plus the coordination of sales and marketing in foreign markets were the responsibility of the respective U.S. operating companies.

To maximize return on existing investments, Rubbermaid emphasized exporting from existing manufacturing facilities primarily in the United States and Europe. Where market size and economies justifed it, local manufacturing facilities were established. Licensing agreements were employed in those markets where the costs of importing were prohibitive and where local company-owned manufacturing was not economically justified.[43]

European Market.   The Curver Rubbermaid Group, the European joint venture, experienced exceptional growth in 1990. Little Tikes continued to enjoy substantial success in the European market. Its expanded facility in Dublin, Ireland, increased its product offering and established a more competitive cost base to serve the growing EC market.

Rubbermaid Commercial Products increased its presence with the acquisition of EWU AG, Switzerland. Eldon's presence in Europe expanded the opportunities for Rubbermaid Office Products Group.

[43] *Rubbermaid Annual Report,* 1990, p. 5.

Latin American Market.   Rubbermaid's approach in Latin America was a mixture of exports from North America and licensing of local companies. In 1990, significant gains were achieved in all product lines in the Caribbean markets, and substantial growth was achieved in Mexico for consumer product lines.

Middle East Market.   Middle East sales suffered a setback during the fourth quarter because of the Persian Gulf crisis, yet the Middle East remained an attractive market for exports from Europe and the United States, particularly for Specialty Products' insulated line and Little Tikes toys. Rubbermaid's position in the insulated product segment was strong, with insulated coolers holding a major market share in key markets.

Far East Market.   All product categories registered gains in Asia during 1990. Far East activities were managed from Rubbermaid's Hong Kong office, which also served as a sourcing location. A sourcing office also opened in Taiwan. Substantial progress was made in broadening distribution for commercial products and Little Tikes toys.

   The Japanese housewares license, Iwasaki Kogyo, experienced continued growth of sales and products featuring the Rubbermaid name. An expanded line of Rubbermaid products was developed by Iwasaki to position the company in the upscale Japanese market.

PRODUCTION STRATEGY

   The skill of Rubbermaid's product planners was matched by the know-how of its production engineers. In 1990, the firm spent $104 million or 6.8 percent of net sales for capital expenditures (in an industry where the average was under 5 percent) in order to update and expand production equipment processes and facilities. By upgrading plants, worker productivity increased from 300 units per day in 1952 to 500 in 1980 and under Gault accelerated beyond 900 units.[44]

   During 1988, Rubbermaid witnessed the largest increase ever in material costs. Beginning in late 1987, volatile resin costs escalated at a double-digit rate, which required extremely fast response with cost-containment efforts and selling price increases to protect its required margin. Total resin costs increased over 50 percent from those of the prior year. Rubbermaid incurred some $100 million of increased expenses for resin in its 1988 product cost structure. Resin shortages, moreover, adversely affected production schedules, causing service and delivery problems during peak sales periods. Correspondingly, all operating companies moved aggressively and effectively. Expenditures were closely controlled, pro-

---

[44] Taylor, "Why the Bounce at Rubbermaid?" p. 78.

ductivity improvements were accelerated, and price increases were implemented.[45]

During 1986, Rubbermaid invested $68 million to expand manufacturing
capacity, increase asset utilizations, improve productivity, and develop new
products. In 1989, over $85 million was invested in capital expenditures, again to
expand manufacturing and distribution facilities, to modernize equipment, to
install process control systems and automatic packaging systems, to purchase
new tooling for new products, and to increase capacity for existing ones. Overall,
from 1981 to 1990, over $612 million was invested in the business's facilities to
increase productivity, develop new products, and achieve world-class manufacturing status.[46]

FINANCIAL MANAGEMENT

Not only did Gault keep the firm's 9,000 plus employees informed through
regular facility visits "to promote the genuine Rubbermaid family atmosphere,"
but he also made sure that the financial community knew the company's story as
well. He personally made at least 20 to 25 formal presentations a year to financial
analysts responsible for recommending Rubbermaid shares, all in the pursuit of
satisfying the firm's overall financial objective of maximizing the shareholders'
investment,[47] an objective realized in the firm's 32.5 percent increase in annual
return to investors between 1980 and 1990.[48] Rubbermaid's financial statements
are included in Exhibits 29.3 through 29.7.

Investment analysts saw Rubbermaid as a big-capitalization company whose
very bigness should inspire investor confidence. Although rumored at times as a
takeover candidate, Rubbermaid was considered a solid firm with an excellent
long-term outlook, superior management, and sound position. Rubbermaid, said
analysts, enjoyed little debt, and the company's many low-price "necessity products" made it relatively recession resistant. Its marketing and distribution system
was enviable, and its product name was synonymous with quality, a value useful
in horizontal integration.[49]

Gault, however, pointed out that a high price/earnings ratio not only gave
shareholders a good return but also made the company less vulnerable to takeover attempts. Rubbermaid's daily stock price, posted prominently at corporate
headquarters, rose about 900 percent during his tenure. According to company
sources, had one invested $1,000 in Rubbermaid shares in 1980 and reinvested

[45] *Rubbermaid Annual Report*, 1988, p. 2.
[46] *Rubbermaid Annual Report*, 1990, pp. 9–10.
[47] Braham, "Billion-Dollar Dustpan," p. 48.
[48] Yalinda Rhoden, "Rubbermaid Profits up 10%," *Akron Beacon Journal*, April 11, 1990,
p. B7.
[49] Ann C. Brown, "Big Plays," *Forbes*, January 23, 1989, p. 116.

EXHIBIT 29.3   Consolidated Statement of Earnings (In thousands except per share data)

	Year Ended December 31,		
	1988	1989	1990
Net Sales	$1,291,584	$1,452,365	$1,534,013
Expenses			
Cost of Sales	886,850	967,563	1,014,526
Selling, General, and Administrative	221,497	268,148	286,647
	1,108,347	1,235,711	1,301,173
Operating Earnings	183,237	216,654	232,840
Other Charges (Credits), Net			
Interest Expense	7,987	8,810	8,627
Interest Income	(1,531)	(5,650)	(5,363)
Miscellaneous, Net	4,951	8,814	1,571
	11,407	11,974	1,693
Earnings before Income Taxes	171,830	204,680	231,269
Income Taxes	64,972	79,696	87,749
Net Earnings	$ 106,858	$ 124,984	$ 143,520
Net Earnings per Common Share	$1.34	$1.57	$1.80

Source: Rubbermaid Incorporated, *1990 Annual Report.*

dividends, the investment would be worth over $25,000 at the close of the first quarter 1991.

Rubbermaid was in an industry whose products were likely to be purchased during either good or bad economic times; therefore, a consistent and steady growth in sales was to be expected rather than not. In downturns consumers were likely to continue buying the relatively inexpensive and needed houseware-type products. However, in economic upturns consumers would not buy additional products simply because they had additional income. Accordingly, Rubbermaid's sales led market indexes in hard times and lagged behind them in good times. Thus, Rubbermaid was a nearly recession-proof company.

Although 1990 sales only increased by 6 percent over 1989 sales from $1,452,365 to $1,534,013, the annual growth of sales compounded from 1980 to 1990 was 15.1 percent for the 10-year period. Unit volume increased by 12 percent; prices were lower by 3 percentage points due to promotional discounts implemented to stimulate sales to overcome the sluggish economy in 1990. The improved sales performance for the year was due to increased sales of product and not price increases.

Similarly for net earnings, Rubbermaid's 10-year annually compounded growth rate was 20.2 percent; for earnings per share the annually compounded rate for the 10-year period was 19.6 percent. Return on average shareholders' equity increased from 15.0 percent in 1980 to a high of 20.8 percent in 1987, to 20.6

EXHIBIT 29.4   Consolidated Statement of Cash Flows (In thousands)

	Year Ended December 31,		
	1988	1989	1990
Cash Flows from Operating Activities			
Net Earnings	$106,858	$124,984	$ 143,520
Adjustments to Reconcile Net Earnings to Net Cash from Operating Activities			
Depreciation	46,134	57,341	55,346
Employee Benefits	7,411	12,409	16,484
Provision for Losses on Accounts Receivable	3,837	11,822	11,777
Other	4,933	8,556	515
Changes In			
Accounts Receivable	(37,794)	(41,084)	(64,292)
Inventories	(18,237)	(19,786)	(26,453)
Prepaid Expenses and Other Assets	3,443	(5,276)	(6,521)
Payables	(10,784)	17,864	10,926
Accrued Liabilities	(4,752)	4,166	20,904
Deferred Income Taxes and Credits	680	2,676	(5,153)
Net Cash from Operating Activities	$101,729	$173,672	$157,053
Cash Flow from Investing Activities			
Additions to Property, Plant and Equipment	$ (87,333)	$ (89,787)	$(103,720)
Other, Net	3,630	2,255	(32,199)
Net Cash from Investing Activities	$ (83,703)	$ (87,532)	$(135,949)
Cash Flows from Financing Activities			
Net Change in Short-Term Debt	$ (3,581)	$ (5,479)	$ 4,572
Proceeds from Long-Term Debt	9,003	16,870	—
Repayment of Long-Term Debt	(9,332)	(5,404)	(9,330)
Cash Dividends Paid	(29,520)	(35,975)	(42,621)
Other, Net	(21)	6,527	1,768
Net Cash from Financing Activities	$ (33,451)	$ (23,461)	$ (45,611)
Net Change in Cash and Cash Equivalents	(15,425)	62,679	(24,477)
Cash and Cash Equivalents			
At Beginning of Year	$ 54,721	$ 39,296	$ 101,975
At End of Year	$ 39,296	$101,975	$ 77,498
Supplemental Cash Flow Information			
Income Taxes Paid	$ 68,733	$ 94,791	$ 88,992
Interest Paid	$ 8,006	$ 8,507	$ 8,765

( ) Denotes decrease in cash and cash equivalents.
Source: Rubbermaid Incorporated, *1990 Annual Report.*

in 1988, 20.6 in 1989, and 20.2 in 1990. Return on average shareholders' equity was above 20 percent from 1983 to 1990. With the payment of $0.54 per share in 1990, dividends per share increased for the 36th consecutive year.

An important factor in the outstanding financial results achieved was Rubbermaid's handling of long-term debt. Although very low in comparison to its industry, the company used long-term debt and internal funding of acquisitions

EXHIBIT 29.5   Consolidated Balance Sheet (In thousands except per share data)

	Year Ended December 31,		
	1988	1989	1990
Assets			
Current Assets			
Cash and Cash Equivalents	$ 39,296	$ 101,975	$ 77,498
Receivables, Less Allowance for Doubtful			
Accounts of $15,426 in 1990, 9,629 in 1989	a	259,878	302,271
Inventories	a	199,525	216,808
Prepaid Expenses	a	5,929	6,120
Total Current Assets	452,639	567,307	602,697
Property, Plant, and Equipment, Net	347,677	3,797,107	405,520
Intangible and Other Assets, Net	42,389	38,591	106,033
Total Assets	$842,705	$ 985,005	$1,114,250
Liabilities and Shareholders' Equity			
Current Liabilities			
Notes Payable	a	$ 12,302	$ 16,866
Long-Term Debt, Current	a	3,376	1,908
Payables	a	96,696	101,089
Accrued Liabilities	a	102,747	115,437
Total Current Liabilities	197,431	215,121	235,300
Deferred Income Taxes and Credits	0	36,390	29,751
Other Deferred Liabilities	47,471	30,724	41,804
Long-Term Debt, Noncurrent	39,023	50,294	39,191
Shareholders' Equity			
Preferred Stock, No Par Value Authorized			
20,000 Shares None Issued	—	—	—
Common Shares, $1 Par Value Authorized			
200,000 Shares 79,992,610 Issued in 1990			
79,556,748 Issued in 1989 and 79,381,000 Issued			
in 1988	79,381	79,557	79,993
Paid-In Capital	21,138	24,715	37,857
Retained Earnings	453,009	541,042	638,551
Foreign Currency Translation Adjustment	5,252	7,162	11,803
Total Shareholders' Equity	558,780	652,476	768,204
Total Liabilities and Shareholders' Equity	$842,705	$ 985,005	$1,114,250

a Figure does not appear in 1990 annual report.

Source: Rubbermaid Incorporated, *1990 Annual Report.*

with cash from operations that allowed great flexibility in timing. The company arranged for a line of credit that increased from $27 million in 1986 to $115 million in 1990, to compensate for fluctuations in working capital and operations that allowed for the selection of proper timing and negotiation for the best possible long-term financing. In 1990, long-term debt ($39,191,000) as a percentage of total capitalization fell from 15 percent to 5 percent.

EXHIBIT 29.6 Consolidated Financial Summary (In thousands except per share data)

	1986	1987	1988	1989	1990
Operating Results					
Net Sales	$864,721	$1,096,055	$1,291,584	$1,452,365	$1,534,013
Cost of Sales	554,421	727,927	886,850	967,563	1,014,526
Selling, General, and Administrative Expenses	166,954	199,145	221,497	268,148	286,647
Other Charges (Credits), Net	684	10,761	11,407	11,974	1,571
Earnings before Income Taxes	142,662	158,222	171,830	204,680	231,269
Income Taxes	67,658	67,499	64,972	79,696	87,749
Net Earnings	$ 75,004	$ 90,723	$ 106,858	$ 124,984	$ 143,520
Per Common Share	$ .95	$ 1.15	$ 1.34	$ 1.57	$ 1.80
Percentage of Sales.	8.7%	8.3%	8.3%	8.6%	9.4%
Financial Position					
Current Assets	322,655	418,563	452,639	567,307	602,697
Property, Plant, and Equipment, Net	248,224	310,017	347,677	379,107	405,520
Intangible and Other Assets, Net	45,780	45,748	42,389	38,591	106,033
Total Assets	$626,659	$774,328	$ 842,705	$ 985,005	$1,114,250
Current Liabilities	$156,456	$ 209,771	$ 197,431	$ 215,121	$ 235,300
Deferred Taxes, Credits, and Other Liabilities	40,013	47,585	47,471	67,114	71,555
Long-Term Debt	35,668	40,042	39,023	50,294	39,191
Shareholders' Equity	394,522	476,930	558,780	652,476	768,204
Total Liabilities and Shareholders' Equity	$626,659	$ 774,328	$ 842,705	$ 985,005	$1,114,250
Long-Term Debt to Total Capitalization	9%	8%	7%	8%	5%
Working Capital	$176,199	$ 208,792	$ 255,208	$ 352,186	$ 367,397
Current Ratio	2.13	2.00	2.29	2.64	2.56
Other Data					
Average Common Shares Outstanding (000)	79,032	79,234	79,464	79,625	79,844
Return on Average Shareholders' Equity	20.5%	20.8%	20.6%	20.6%	20.2%
Cash Dividends Paid	$ 19,771	$ 24,581	$ 29,520	$ 35,975	$ 42,621
Cash Dividends Paid Per Common Share	.26	.32	.38	.46	.54
Shareholders' Equity Per Common Share	5.00	6.02	7.04	8.20	9.60
NYSE Stock Price Range, High-Low	29–17	35–19	27–21	38–25	45–31
Additions to Property, Plant, and Equipment	71,587	104,429	87,333	89,787	103,720
Depreciation Expense	34,135	44,155	46,134	57,341	55,346
Number of Shareholders' at Year End	8,379	10,104	10,482	11,225	13,305
Average Number of Associates	6,509	7,512	8,643	9,098	9,304

EXHIBIT 29.7 Statement of Shareholders' Equity (In thousands except per share data)

	Common Shares	Paid-In Capital	Retained Earnings	Foreign Currency Translation Adjustment	Total Shareholders' Equity
Balance at December 31, 1987	$79,249	$17,790	$376,307	$ 3,584	$476,930
Transactions for 1988					
Net Earnings	—	—	106,858	—	106,858
Cash Dividends, $.38 per Share	—	—	(29,520)	—	(29,520)
Employee Stock Plans	132	3,348	(497)	—	2,983
Foreign Currency Translation Adjustment	—	—	—	1,668	1,668
Other, Net	—	—	(139)	—	(139)
Balance at December 31, 1988	79,381	21,138	453,009	5,252	558,780
Transactions for 1989					
Net Earnings	—	—	124,984	—	124,984
Cash Dividends, $.46 per Share	—	—	(35,975)	—	(35,975)
Employee Stock Plans	176	3,577	(670)	—	3,083
Foreign Currency Translation Adjustment	—	—	—	1,910	1,910
Other, Net	—	—	(306)	—	(306)
Balance at December 31, 1989	79,557	24,715	541,042	7,162	652,476
Transactions for 1990					
Net Earnings	—	—	143,520	—	143,520
Cash Dividends, $.54 per Share	—	—	(42,621)	—	(42,621)
Employee Stock Plans	436	13,142	(3,313)	—	10,265
Foreign Currency Translation Adjustment	—	—	—	4,641	4,641
Other, Net	—	—	(77)	—	(77)
Balance at December 31, 1990	$79,993	$37,857	$638,551	$11,803	$768,204

Source: Rubbermaid Incorporated, *1990 Annual Report.*

Actually, long-term debt at Rubbermaid slowly increased from $25 million in 1980 to $39 million in 1990. The percentage of this debt to total capitalization fell due largely to the 489 percent increase in shareholders' equity over the years. The soundness of Rubbermaid's management was demonstrated not only by the low and falling percentage of long-term debt over the past 10 years, but also by rapid reduction of excess (by Rubbermaid's standards) long-term debt that appeared in 1989.

RUBBERMAID IN 1991

Assessing the impact of the Persian Gulf crisis on the company, Gault felt guardedly optimistic: "For the year ahead, we anticipate great uncertainty and slow economic growth. We have also experienced mounting apprehension and caution within the retail, institutional, and industrial sectors. However, each operating company has developed comprehensive contingency action plans for aggressive promotional programs and consumer advertising to assist our customers in selling Rubbermaid products. We have faced similar challenges in the past and are confident we can continue to produce record performances in the future."[50]

MANAGEMENT IN THE COMING DECADE

On May 1, 1991, Stanley Carleton Gault retired from Rubbermaid as chairman of the board and chief executive officer. The Board of Directors, meanwhile, confirmed a new management team to replace Gault. Walter W. Williams became chairman and chief executive officer, Wolfgang R. Schmitt became president and chief operating officer, and Charles A. Carroll became president and general manager of Rubbermaid's Housewares Products Division, the firm's oldest and largest consumer business. The company, in looking to the future, concluded that management transition as well as the entire management structure were well planned and successfully implemented over the past several years.[51]

Gault, who planned to maintain his association with Rubbermaid, promised, "I'm going to take some time and do some of the things I enjoy but just haven't had time to do."[52] "I certainly won't be running the company anymore, but I'll be around to talk about it."[53] Gault, who had a two-year consulting contract, was to maintain an office at Rubbermaid headquarters and be a member of the board of directors until he turned 70 years of age.[54]

[50] Yalinda Rhoden, "Gault Stepping Down as Rubbermaid Chief," *Akron Beacon Journal*, January 11, 1991, pp. B8, B12.

[51] Ibid., p. B8.

[52] Ibid.

[53] Alecia Swasy, *Wall Street Journal*, April 2, 1990, p. 26.

[54] Yalinda Rhoden, "Sans Gault," *Akron Beacon Journal*, April 22, 1991, p. D2.

————————— CASE 33 —————————

Sun Microsystems:
Competing in a High-Tech Industry

INTRODUCTION

In 1982, four individuals who were 27 years old combined forces to found Sun Microsystems, with the objective of producing and marketing computer workstations to scientists and engineers. Two of the four were Stanford MBA graduates—Michigan-born Scott McNealy and Vinod Khosla, a native of India. They were joined by Andreas Bechtolsheim, a Stanford engineering graduate who had constructed a computer workstation with spare parts in order to perform

This case was prepared by William C. House and Walter E. Greene as a basis for class discussion rather than to illustrate either effective or ineffective handling of an administrative situation. Used with permission from William C. House.

numerical analysis, and UNIX software expert William Joy from the Berkeley campus. Sun's founders believed there was demand for a desktop computer workstation costing between $10,000 and $20,000 in a market niche ignored by minicomputer makers IBM, Data General, DEC, and Hewlett-Packard.

Sun Microsystems was the market leader in the fast-growing workstation industry, expecting sales revenue growth of 90 percent annually during the next five years compared to the projected industry average of 5 to 10 percent for personal computers. Workstations can be used in stand-alone fashion or as part of networked configurations. The product lines produced range from low-priced diskless units to the top- of-the-line, higher-powered graphics-oriented stations.

In contrast to personal computers, workstations are characterized by 32-bit versus 16-bit microprocessors, a strong tendency to use the UNIX operating system instead of MS/DOS, more sophisticated software and graphics capabilities, large storage capacities, faster processing speeds, and the ability to function effectively in a networking environment. The principal users of workstations have been engineers and scientists. However, price reductions and technological improvements broadened the appeal of workstations so that they were being used in financial trading, desktop publishing, animation, mapping, and medical imaging applications.

Sun, the fastest-growing company in the computer hardware industry, had revenues that were increasing at a five-year compounded rate of 85 percent and income increasing at a 67 percent rate from 1985 to 1990.[1] For fiscal 1991, Sun's revenues were $3.2 billion and net income was $190 million.[2] The company's rapid growth rate severely drained its cash resources.

CHAIRMAN AND CEO OF SUN MICROSYSTEMS

In 1992, Scott McNealy was the chairman of Sun. He was a native of Detroit and grew up on the fringes of the U.S. automobile industry. Originally rejected by both Harvard and Stanford Business Schools, he graduated from Harvard with a major in economics. In between his Harvard and Stanford academic careers, he accepted a job as a foreman at Rockwell's International truck plant. After two months of hectic workplace activity, he was hospitalized with hepatitis. He entered Stanford University in 1978 on his third try.

In 1981, at the age of 26, McNealy became manufacturing director at Onyx Systems, a small microcomputer maker. The company was faced with serious quality problems. In two months, the operation showed drastic improvement as McNealy probed work rules and production bottlenecks, encouraging workers to identify problems and to overcome obstacles on the way toward improving workplace efficiency.

[1] John Markoff, "The Smart Alecs at Sun Are Regrouping," *New York Times*, April 28, 1991.
[2] G. Paschal Zachary, "Sun Challenges Microsoft's Hold Over Software," *Wall Street Journal*, September 4, 1991.

In 1982, former Stanford classmates Andy Bechtolsheim and Vinod Khosla asked him to join them as director of operations in a new company to be called Sun Microsystems. Two years later, McNealy was chosen by the board of directors to be CEO over Paul Ely, who became executive vice president of Unisys. During the first month after McNealy became CEO one of the three co-founders resigned, the company lost $500,000 on $2 million in sales, and two-thirds of its computers did not work.

McNealy was a workaholic, working from daylight to dark, seven days a week, rarely finding time for recreational activities. The frantic pace he brought to Sun was sometimes referred to as "sunburn." There was a tendency for Sun executives to take on too many projects at once, thereby creating tremendous internal pressure and organizational chaos.

McNealy's philosophy can be capsuled in these company sayings.[3]

1. On decision making—Consensus if possible, but participation for sure.

2. On management cooperation—Agree and commit, disagree and commit, or just get the hell out of the way.

3. On market response—The right answer is the best answer. The wrong answer is second best. No answer is worst.

4. On individual initiative—To ask permission is to seek denial.

He stated that the company was trying to achieve four goals—significant increases in revenue and book value, improved product acceptance, and higher profit margins.

CHIEF COMPUTER DESIGNER

Andreas Bechtolsheim, chief computer designer, was one of Sun's co-founders. At the age of 35, he had the title of vice president of technology. A native of West Germany, Bechtolsheim designed his first computer in 1980 while still a graduate student at Stanford University. It was a workstation designed for scientists and engineers. However, he was unable to sell the idea to any computer company at the time. Shortly thereafter, he joined Joy, Khosla, and McNealy in founding Sun Microsystems, and the company's first product was based on his machine.

Initially, Bechtolsheim persuaded Sun to use off-the-shelf products to develop its workstations instead of following the usual industry practice of utilizing proprietary components. This meant that company products would be easy for competitors to copy, but it also allowed quick entry into the marketplace. As nonproprietary open systems came to be more widely accepted, competitors such

[3] "Sun Microsystems Turns on the Afterburners," *Business Week*, July 18, 1988.

as Apollo, Digital Equipment Corporation (DEC), and IBM encountered problems in keeping pace with product lines that lacked the flexibility and performance of Sun's products. When Steve Jobs formed NeXT and announced the development of a desktop workstation, Bechtolsheim urged Sun officials to build a truly desktop computer. There was considerable resistance to the project, and he almost left the company at that point.

Almost at once, he began working on the new computer on his own. He spent $200,000 of his own funds on the project without official company backing. He also formed a small company called Unisun to provide the vehicle for marketing his new computer and persuaded Khosla, a member of Sun's board of directors to become president of Unisun. Khosla offered Sun the right to invest in or purchase the smaller company outright. Sun seriously considered both possibilities, but McNealy was fearful that the new venture might be considered a competitor of Sun.

In view of the possible negatives of a smaller company selling an identical clone of Sun, the larger company finally agreed to build the new computer and called it Sparcstation I. Initially, restrictions were placed on the project, and only engineers who had indicated they would resign to work on the new computer were allowed to join the team. Because the company had a culture based on building bigger boxes, the Sparcstation was widely criticized within the company as being too small. However, Bechtolsheim stubbornly refused to change the specifications and eventually prevailed.[4]

FIELD OPERATIONS DIRECTOR

Carol Bartz, national sales director and the number two executive at Sun Microsystems, had about half of the company's 12,000 employees reporting to her. Although many outsiders felt that she would soon be named chief operating officer, she abruptly dismissed the idea, observing that she did not believe the company needed a COO. At 42, the hard-driving and aggressive female seemed to be reaching new heights in her career.

Bartz attended the University of Wisconsin, receiving a Bachelor of Computer Science degree in 1971. After that, she spent seven years with DEC. Since joining Sun in 1983, she became intimately involved in marketing operations, including supervising field support activities and a subdivision that sold to federal government agencies. Bartz indicated that her relationship with McNealy permitted her to tell him what he was doing wrong as well as what he was doing right. According to Bob Herwick, an investment analyst, Bartz was a very effective problem solver, turning around a sluggish service organization and ensuring that the company fully exploited the market potential in the government market.[5]

[4] G. Paschal Zachary, "Sparc-Station's Success Is Doubly Sweet for Sun Microsystem's Bechtolsheim," *Wall Street Journal*, May 29, 1990.
[5] Andrew Ould, "Carol Bartz: Star Is Still Rising for Hard Driving Executive," *PC Week*, September 3, 1990.

TEAM AND CONSENSUS MANAGEMENT AT SUN

McNealy attended Cranbrook, a North Detroit prep school. While there, he excelled in a variety of activities including music, tennis, golf, and ice hockey. According to Alan De Clerk, a high school classmate, McNealy developed a strong self-image and competitive spirit as a result of participating in sports activities and competing with two brothers and a sister. Through the years he approached all activities as if they were team sports.

McNealy's father was the vice chairman of American Motors (AMC). Scott followed his dad on the golf course, listened to automobile industry discussions, and found himself pouring over internal company memos along with his father who was heavily involved in AMC's battle to stay alive. The elder McNealy ruled his household with an iron hand. Scott's strong commitment to consensus management may be a reaction to the type of environment in which they were raised, according to his brother who is an architect in St. Louis.[6]

McNealy's efforts to build consensus among executives before a decision was made became famous throughout the company. As he stated, "Give me a draw and I'll make the decision but I won't issue an edict if a large majority is in favor of an alternative proposal."[7] A frequently quoted example occurred in 1988 when he stubbornly resisted changing prices at a time when rapidly increasing memory costs were reducing profit margins. With a consensus arrayed against him, he finally agreed to some product price increases that were enacted without reducing sales. In fact, he had a hard time saying no to any project pushed by one or more company groups. He demanded loyalty within his concept of teamwork and became very angry if he believed that individuals or teams had let him down.[8]

PRODUCT LINE FOCUS

Sparcstation I was introduced in April 1989 at a stripped down price of $9,000. A lower-priced version was introduced in May 1990 at a price of $5,000. The machine processed data at 12 mips (about twice as fast as most personal computers). Sun expected the lower price to facilitate sales to large companies that often based computer purchases on quantity discounts. However, the low-end Sparcstation did not have disk drives, color monitors, or add-in slots. Therefore, it had to be networked and could not be used as a stand-alone unit.

An improved version of Sparc I was introduced in the summer of 1990 with a better graphics interface, a color monitor, and a sales price of $10,000. Sun asserted that a personal computer with the same characteristics as the Sparcstation I personal computer (IPC) would cost $15,000 to $20,000 and would have only about one-third the processing power of this workstation model. By 1991 Sparc-

---

[6] Jonathan B. Levine, "High Noon for Sun," *Business Week*, July 24, 1989, pp. 71, 74.
[7] "Sun Turns on the Afterburners," p. 32.
[8] Ibid.

EXHIBIT 33.1   A Comparison of Performance Measures for Major Workstation Makers

Manufacturer/Model	Price	Specmarks	Price per Specmark
Hewlett-Packard 9000	$11,990	55.5	$216.00
Sun Sparcstation ELC	4,995	20.1	248.50
IBM RS/6000	13,992	32.8	426.50
Sun Sparcstation IPX	13,495	24.2	557.60

Source: J. A. Savage, "Price Takes a Backseat with Users," *Computerworld*, September 2, 1991, p. 4.

station was Sun's top seller among all its product lines and Sparcstation products produced 80 to 90 percent of total company revenues.

Exhibit 33.1 illustrates prices and specmarks (a measure of processing power and speed) for two Sun models as well as for the latest Hewlett-Packard and IBM workstation models. The relative performance of Sun's products in terms of computing power per dollar compared favorably against the company's major competitors.

COMPANY STRATEGY

Early on, Sun executives believed that they only had a short time to focus on growing demand for computer workstations from scientists and engineers before large companies such as IBM, DEC, and Hewlett-Packard would aggressively move into that market niche. Therefore, company strategy was designed to emphasize gaining market share and concentrated on sales growth, no matter what the cost. At one point, the organization was adding more than 300 employees and a new sales office each month. Company engineers developed a steady stream of innovative but sometimes impractical prototypes. Products were sold largely by word of mouth with virtually no formal sales promotion programs.

In the mid-1980s, as part of the focus on market share, the company began creating autonomous divisions to develop and market its products. This policy allowed rapid movement into such market areas as sales to government agencies, universities, and financial institutions. A special team was created in 1986 to successfully counter the threat posed by Apollo. "Sun can win market share battles in such cases," noted F. H. Moss, formerly vice president for software development at Apollo, "because it has no strong preconceptions about what can or cannot be done."[9] The autonomous groups did create unnecessary duplication and contributed to developmental costs that were almost twice the industry average. When attempts were made to consolidate functions, fierce turf battles resulted and top executives were forced to step in and referee the conflicts.

[9] Michael Alexander, "PC Workstation Firms Prepare for Price War," *Computerworld*, September 20, 1989.

The market share/sales growth emphasis created many unexpected problems. Needed investments in customer service and data processing activities were postponed. The existence of independent, autonomous divisions caused numerous difficulties for both sales and manufacturing activities. At one point, the company had more than 10,000 computer and option combinations to track. Three different product lines based on three different microprocessors—Sparc, Motorola 68000, and Intel 386—required excessive investment and extensive coordination to ensure that they all operated on the same network. Overlaps and duplications in marketing and finance made forecasting all but impossible. At its increased size the company could no longer scramble madly to meet shipping deadlines at the last minute.

By summer 1989, the company was experiencing production bottlenecks as discounted sales of older products mushroomed. At the same time, demand for newer products increased faster than expected. Large backlogs of sales orders were not being entered into the inventory control system, preventing the company from knowing how many or what kinds of products it needed to produce.

In the last quarter of 1989, Sun experienced a $20 million loss due to misjudgments concerning consumer demand for its new Sparcstation as well as parts requirements. A new management information system produced inaccurate parts forecasts that contributed to order snafus and lower earnings. However, the company posted a $5 million profit in the first quarter of 1990. Sun produced revenues of $2.5 billion in fiscal 1990 and expected to achieve revenues of $3.3 billion in 1991.[10] Sun changed its approach to place more emphasis on profitability and less on growth, expanding its customer service and hiring fewer employees. McNealy tied executive pay to before-tax return on investment. In the 1989 annual report he stated that he desired performance to be judged on the basis of significant increases in revenues, acceptance of new products, improvements in profit margins, and increases in book value.

McNealy was one of the early pioneers pushing open systems that allowed computers of many different manufacturers to be linked together into networks. In fact, Sun actually encouraged competition through its focus on open systems development and invited the industry to build Sparc-based clones in order to expand the position of the workstation industry. As the percentage of totally Sparc-based computers sold by Sun began to decline, Sun changed its position on clones. Recently, it told its own dealers they would incur Sun's displeasure if they sold clones along with Sun workstations. Many of these dealers were angry at what they perceived to be Sun's arrogance.

Sun intentionally maintained a narrow product line. It gradually phased out all microprocessors except Sparc and concentrated on low-end workstations with the greatest market share growth possibilities. The company avoided entering markets for higher-priced lines and the personal computer segment with emphasis

---

[10] Kathy Rebello, "Sun Microsystems on the Rise Again," *USA Today*, April 20, 1990; "Workstations Makers Try to Reboot Sales," and "Sun to Market Workstation with PC Price," *USA Today*, May 14, 1990; "Sun Targets PCs with Workstation," *USA Today*, July 26, 1990; "H-P to Rattle Workstation Market," *USA Today*, March 18, 1991.

on low price and compactness. However, recently Sun announced plans to move into high-end workstation markets where processing speed and power requirements necessitated linking a series of microprocessors and using sophisticated software. Sun might encounter problems in this market, similar to those it experienced in product upgrades of its lower level models, because it did not have a good record in managing product introductions.

As workstations became more powerful and less expensive, manufacturers faced a serious challenge in maintaining profit margins. Newer models combined high functionality with high volume, in contrast to an earlier focus on producing highly functional units in small quantities. Extensive use of application-specific integrated circuits with fewer components reduced system sizes, increased reliability, and lowered product costs. Sun and other companies increasingly followed the practice of involving manufacturing representatives in the design process as early as possible in order to minimize manufacturing problems. Increased attention was also being paid to maintaining product quality and improved product testing before systems were shipped.

In past years, Sun's strategies included focusing on lower prices, well-developed marketing programs, and third-party software development. From 1,500 to 2,000 applications were available for the Sun Sparcstation compared to approximately 1,000 for Hewlett-Packard and DEC. The company was licensing its sparc chip to third-party clone companies with the intent of expanding the installed RISC computer base. The overall company goal was to deliver a complete processing solution, including graphics, input/output, software, and networking.

DISTRIBUTION CHANNELS AND CUSTOMER SERVICE

Workstation makers traditionally sold their units using manufacturers' sales representatives and specialized hardware resellers, who repackaged specialized software with other companies' workstations. Sun had about 300 value-added resellers (VARs) compared to more than 500 for Hewlett-Packard; DEC and IBM had between 300 and 500 each. Some experts thought the majority of VARs were not capable of selling workstations.[11] Sun then considered the possibility of selling some of its models through retailers such as MicroAge in a manner similar to personal computer distribution used by other manufacturers such as IBM, COMPAQ, and Apple. Management felt that the change would reduce selling and inventory costs but was having difficulty convincing dealers who were unaccustomed to handling complex workstation models.

Sun sold a large number of workstations through its 1,000-person sales force. In July 1990, Sun selected 200 dealers from three retail chains and provided

[11] Susan E. Fisher, "Vendors Court Resellers as Workstations Go Mainstream," *PC Week*, July 30, 1990.

them training for selling workstations. The company expected sales of workstations to reach $30 million through retail dealers in fiscal 1990, but it appeared that a full-fledged dealer network was going to require several years to develop. Because of the higher average selling prices and greater product differentiation of workstations compared to personal computers, many PC vendors have expressed interest in handling workstations despite the small volumes generated.

One area of concern was Sun's service organization which had not been very effective in supporting customer software. Bartz stated that the company wanted to improve customer service but without making large monetary expenditures or building a dinosaur service group.[12] In line with this, Sun announced plans to start using company-trained, third-party service personnel who could be dispatched to customer locations on demand.

CUSTOMER CATEGORIES

The workstation market for engineers and scientists rapidly became saturated. About one-third of Sun's customers came from the commercial side, up from only 10 percent several years ago. The company concentrated more of its efforts on airlines, banks, insurance and finance companies, trying to persuade them to utilize Sun workstations to solve new problems. Eric Schmidt, Sun vice president, said that Sun tended to get early adopters of new technology.[13] Often, by starting with a pilot program that proved to be successful, workstations could be expanded to other areas in a customer's operations. Eastman Kodak began using Sun workstations in engineering design and soon expanded their use to marketing data bases and mail room operations.

Sun machines were used by Wall Street firms such as Merrill Lynch, Shearson, Lehman, Hutton and Bear, Stearns on the trading floor. Northwest Airlines used 500 workstations in Minneapolis to monitor ticket usage, checking the correctness of airfare charges as well as the impact of flight delays or cancellations on revenues and profits. To increase customer satisfaction, Sun changed product designs to make its machines easier to install and improved understandability of product manuals. Sun discovered that commercial customers needed more help than engineers.

Dataquest predicted that by 1994, 29.1 percent of workstation sales would be made to commercial users as opposed to scientific or engineering users in a market expected to reach $22 billion.[14] Workstation manufacturers encroached into the personal computer market by offering UNIX versions that would run on both workstations and on personal computers. Workstations provided much greater computing power at a lower cost than would be available by upgrading a personal computer so that it possessed the equivalent capability of a typical

[12] "High Noon for Sun," p. 74.
[13] Julie Pitts, "The Trojan Horse Approach," *Forbes*, April 15, 1991.
[14] "Getting Down to Business," *Information Week*, January 14, 1991.

workstation. Workstations seemed to be making the biggest inroads into CPU-intensive applications previously performed on mainframes (e.g., stock transactions, airline reservations).

Sun's first major TV advertising effort occurred in April 1991 and took the form of a 30-second commercial seen on CNN, ESPN, and the three major TV networks. The commercial was not directed specifically at the consumer audience, but instead was an attempt to get broad exposure for a new message targeted to the business market. Sun expected the advertisement to reach 59 percent of U.S. households and 42 percent of the target market of senior-level corporate and computer executives. The campaign also included an eight-page insert in the *Wall Street Journal*.

Sun's advertising budget of approximately $4.6 million in 1990 was spent on computer and general interest business publications. Sun's advertising budget was only about 0.25 percent of sales revenues compared to 1.0 to 1.5 percent by its major competitors. Some observers questioned the cost-effectiveness of a high-priced TV advertisement by a company that sells high-priced computers to a limited group of customers.

SOFTWARE DEVELOPMENTS

Availability of software remained a major problem in expanding sales of workstations. Only about 5 to 10 percent of UNIX-based software was designed for business and commercial applications. Sun tried to sign up software developers to produce UNIX-based versions of many common personal computer products. UNIX-based versions of some popular PC software, including Lotus 1-2-3 and dBASE IV were available. The company expected that the increased availability of software plus the narrowing cost gap between low-end workstations and high-end personal computers would help it penetrate the personal computer market. However, it had to sell users on the benefit/cost performance of workstations compared to personal computers as well as expand its existing base of software developers.

The type of software to be run was often the determining factor in deciding between a personal computer or workstation. For productivity and business applications, PCs could be more cost-efficient. For technical and graphics applications, workstations were more appropriate. Price was no longer a major differentiating factor.

An entrenched personal computer MS/DOS-based operating system and lack of commercial workstation software hampered a switch from high-end personal computers to workstations. MS/DOS-based computers appeared adequate for a majority of user needs, especially with the advent of the Windows operating environment. PC users were more likely to change if complex applications such as multimedia, integrated data base, or windowing became desirable rather than on the basis of price alone. Workstations were likely to become less attractive if 80846-based personal computers with considerably more computing power than today's systems became more widely available.

Because product/price performance was no longer as important a differentiating factor as it once was, and software availability/usability had increased in importance, Sun formed two software subsidiaries—one for development of application software and one to concentrate on improvements in the UNIX operating system. The Open Look Graphical Interface had been added to make Sun Products more user friendly. The key to maintaining market position seemed to be improving software and convincing software developers and users on the benefits of workstations over other hardware options.

Sun announced that it would release a new version of its operating system designed to run on Intel-based personal computers. Some analysts said that Sun faced a stiff test in competing with Microsoft's DOS/Windows combination. They considered the introduction of the new operating system to be a defensive move, made because Sun could no longer generate enough revenue from its own machines to meet growth goals. McNealy denied that the Sun announcement was defensive, saying that high-powered PC owners would move to Sun's operating systems to take advantage of advanced capabilities (e.g., running multiple programs simultaneously), which was something that was only vaguely promised by Microsoft's new Windows NT version.[15] McNealy sharply criticized Windows NT, referring to it as illusionary or not there.

Sun's Solaris operating system was available in mid-1991 and worked on both Intel's X86 series and Sun's Sparc processors. The new operating system made it easier for Sun's customers to link Sun workstations with other computers in a network and increase the number of Sun users. Sun hoped that this would encourage independent software houses to write new programs for the Sun operating system. Thus far, approximately 3,500 application programs were available for Sun operating systems compared with more than 20,000 for IBM-compatible personal computers.[16]

COMPETITION IN THE WORKSTATION MARKET

Although still the workstation market leader, Sun faced increased competition from much larger computer companies. Sun shipped 146,000 workstations in 1990 out of a total of 376,000 (39 percent of the units sold). The company expected to ship 200,000 units in 1991.[17] Having fully absorbed Apollo into its

---

[15] "Sun Challenges Microsoft," p. B1.

[16] Robert D. Hof, "Why Sun Can't Afford to Shine Alone," *Business Week*, September 9, 1991.

[17] Andrew Ould, "IBM Challenges Sun in Workstation Market," *PC Week*, February 28, 1991.

organization, Hewlett-Packard was selling about two-thirds as many workstations as Sun, with about 20 percent of the market; DEC, which completely reworked its product lines, had about 17 percent of the workstation market. Hewlett-Packard introduced a new workstation model, comparable in price to the Sparcstation, that ran about twice as fast as Sun's current model.[18] Exhibit 33.2 indicates the 1989 and 1990 market shares for the major firms in the workstation market.

IBM made a significant comeback in the workstation market with the RS/6000, after its workstation model proved to be a slow seller. In 1990, IBM shipped more than 25,000 workstations, producing revenue of $1 billion and attaining a market share of 6.6 percent, or more than double its 1989 market share.[19] In 1991, some analysts estimated that IBM would sell between $2 and $3 billion in workstations. IBM had a stated goal of overtaking Sun by 1993, achieving a 30 percent market share. Some experts predicted IBM was more likely to achieve a 15 percent market share by that date.[20] Its late entry, the entrenched positions of competitors in the market, lack of a low-priced entry-level model, and the use of nonstandard operating and graphics environments were likely to hamper IBM's efforts to achieve a market share much above 15 percent.[21] IBM's service and sales reputation, its large reseller base, and strong position in commercial markets should give the company leverage to enter the fast-growing markets for network servers and small or branch office multiuser

EXHIBIT 33.2 Computer Workstation Market Shares (In percent)

Company	1989	1990
Sun Microsystems	30.4	38.8
Hewlett-Packard	26.1	20.1
DEC	26.6	17.0
Intergraph	7.0	3.8
IBM	1.2	4.5
Silicon Graphics	5.1	2.6
SONY	—	3.3
NeXT	—	2.6
Other	3.6	7.0
Total	100.0	100.0

[18] Lawrence Curran, "HP Speeds Up Workstation Race," *Electronics*, April 1991.
[19] "IBM Challenges Sun," p. 134.
[20] Bob Francis, "Big Blue's Red Hot Workstation," *Datamation*, October 15, 1990.
[21] Andrew Ould, "What's Behind Lower Workstation Prices," *UNIX World*, July 1990.

systems. However, if IBM focused its efforts on penetrating these markets with its RS/6000, it ran a serious risk of undercutting sales of its AS/400.

FINANCIAL ANALYSIS

Exhibit 33.3 illustrates revenues, expenses, and income for the five-year period 1986 to 1990. Revenues increased at a more rapid rate than net income. Return on sales declined significantly to 4.5 percent from the peak of almost 7 percent in 1987. In addition, revenue per shipment declined in 1990 compared to the two previous years. Book value per share and unit shipments increased significantly during the five years.

Exhibit 33.4 indicates that Sun's sales, income, and asset growth were higher than the industry average in 1989 and 1990 with market value to equity above the industry average as well. However, the net income to sales figure was below the industry average in 1989 and slightly above the industry average in 1990. As Exhibit 33.5 indicates, Sun appeared to be very close to the industry average in terms of two common productivity measures, sales to assets and sales per employee. In reviewing the common leverage measures, Sun was well above the industry average for R&D expenses to revenues and R&D expenses per employee.

EXHIBIT 33.3   Revenues, Expenses, and Income for Five Years (In billions)

	1986	1987	1988	1989	1990
Net Revenues	$210	$538	$1,052	$1,765	$2,466
Cost of Sales	102	273	550	1,010	1,399
Gross Profit	108	265	502	755	1,067
R&D Outlays	31	70	140	234	302
Selling, Administrative, and General Expenses	57	127	250	433	588
Total	88	197	390	667	890
Operating Income	20	68	111	88	177
Interest Income	369	834	(302)	(10)	23)
Income Taxes	9	33	44	17	43
Net Income	$11	$36	$66	$61	$111
Net Income/Sales	5.3%	6.8%	6.3%	3.4%	4.5%
Net Income/Share	$0.21	$0.55	$0.89	$0.76	$1.21
Book Value/Share	$2.04	$3.57	$4.75	$7.77	$9.82
Unit Shipments (000s)	9.9	24.6	48.4	80.7	118.3
Revenue/Unit Shipped (000s)	$21.2	$21.8	$21.7	$21.9	$20.8

Source: Adapted from 1990 annual report.

EXHIBIT 33.4 Computer Industry Data, 1989 and 1990

Company	Sales Growth		Income Growth		Asset Growth		Net Income/Sales		Market Value/Equity	
	1989	1990	1989	1990	1989	1990	1989	1990	1989	1990
Apple	1.21	1.07	1.05	1.14	1.24	1.12	8.2	8.7	3.21	4.81
COMPAQ	1.39	1.25	1.31	1.36	1.31	1.30	11.6	12.6	3.31	3.26
DEC	1.05	1.01	0.72	0.00	1.10	1.03	6.8	-.72	1.13	1.21
Hewlett-Packard	1.20	1.10	0.97	0.95	1.31	1.09	6.6	5.7	1.98	1.83
Intergraph	1.07	1.21	0.80	0.79	0.97	1.06	9.2	6.0	1.73	1.79
IBM	1.05	1.10	0.68	1.60	1.06	1.30	6.0	8.7	1.62	1.75
NCR	0.99	1.06	0.94	0.90	0.95	1.01	6.9	5.9	3.40	3.54
Silicon Graphics	1.73	1.41	1.94	1.97	0.94	1.37	5.9	8.3	4.30	3.57
Sun Microsystems	1.41	1.34	0.40	318.00	1.50	1.49	1.8	5.5	1.41	2.72
Wang	0.90	0.87	0.00	0.00	0.87	0.72	-13.9	-6.7	0.87	1.27
Average	1.20	1.14	0.88	32.7	1.12	1.15	4.9	5.4	2.37	2.58

Read as "1989 sales growth was 1.21 times 1988 sales."
Source: *Business Week 1000 Companies, 1990, 1991.*

EXHIBIT 33.5 Computer Industry Data, 1988 and 1989

	Sales/ Assets[a]		Sales/ Employee[b]		Advertising Expenses/Sales[c]		R&D Expenses/ Sales[d]		R&D Expenses/ Employee[e]	
	1988	1989	1988	1989	1988	1989	1988	1989	1988	1989
Apple	1.91	1.82	377	364	8.30	7.34	6.7	8.0	25,233	28,937
COMPAQ	1.38	1.32	289	303	2.87	1.75	3.6	4.6	10,849	13,945
DEC	1.15	1.13	94	101	1.01	1.38	11.4	12.0	10,753	12,123
Hewlett-Packard	1.21	1.22	113	125	2.35	2.69	10.4	10.7	11,713	13,358
Intergraph	1.07	1.20	110	105	1.00	1.00	11.1	10.6	12,216	11,157
IBM	0.81	0.79	154	164	0.44	1.17	7.4	8.3	11,415	13,572
NCR	1.32	1.38	100	106	0.53	1.06	7.0	7.5	6,940	7,964
Silicon Graphics	1.19	1.22	105	180	1.00	1.00	15.8	11.9	21,908	21,150
Sun Microsystems	1.41	1.27	148	172	0.74	1.00	13.3	13.3	19,733	22,934
Wang	1.12	1.35	97	109	1.02	1.00	8.7	9.8	8,510	10,543
Average	1.26	1.27	159	173	1.93	2.64	9.5	9.7	14,027	15,568

[a] Read as "$1.91 in sales for every $1 in assets for Apple in 1988."

[b] Read as "$3.77 in sales per Apple employee in 1988."

[c] Read as "advertising was 8.3 percent of sales in 1988 for Apple."

[d] Read as "R&D expense was 6.7 percent of sales in 1988 for Apple."

[e] Read as "$25,233 in R&D per Apple employee in 1988."

Source: *Business Week 1000–1991*, 1991; *Innovation in America*, Special Business Week Issues, 1990, 1989.

REFERENCES

ABBOTT, LAWRENCE. "Good Buys Abound in RISC Workstation." *Datamation*, April 15, 1991.

BRANDELL, WILLIAM. "Manager's Find RISC Not Worth Gamble." *Computerworld*, March 5, 1990.

BRENNAN, LAURA. "Resilient Sun Is on the Rise in PCs Turf." *PC Week*, September 3, 1990.

BULKELEY, WILLIAM L. "DEC's New Workstations May Shake Up Hot Market." *Wall Street Journal*, January 11, 1989.

BULKELEY, WILLIAM L. "Digital Unveils New Workstations: Cuts Some Prices." *Wall Street Journal*, April 4, 1990.

BUSH, PAUL. "Dangerous Liaisons." *Prepared Foods*, August 1990.

CARROLL, PETER B. "New Workstation Line Aims for Credibility." *Wall Street Journal*, February 12, 1990.

COFFEE, PETER. "Desktop Sizzlers." *Computerworld* , December 25–January 1, 1990.

COFFEE, PETER. "Japan Eyes Workstation Market." *Computerworld*, December 25–January 1, 1990.

COFFEE, PETER. "Price, Support, and Integration Are Key in Evaluating Software." *PC Week*, April 2, 1990, p. 25.

COFFEE, PETER. "RISC Software Has Turned the Corner." *PC Week*, April 16, 1990, pp. 18, 20.

DALEY, JAMES. "Can Sun Ride Out Stormy Weather." *Computerworld*, July 24, 1989.

DALEY, JAMES. "Sun Users Staying Loyal for Now." *Computerworld*, March 5, 1990.

DALEY, JAMES. "Workstation Market Leaving PC's Far Behind." *Computerworld*, February 5, 1990.

FISHER, SUSAN E. "Vendors Court Reseller Partners as Workstations Go Mainstream." *PC Week*, July 30, 1990.

FOLEY, MARY JO. "Microcomputers: High-End PC's vs. Workstations." *Systems Integration*, April 1990.

FRANCETT, BARBARA. "Workstations Dust Off after Rough Year's Ride." *Computerworld*, September 25, 1989.

FRANCIS, BOB. "Big Blue's Red Hot Workstation." *Datamation*, October 15, 1990.

FRANCIS, BOB. "Sun Compatibles: Who's Putting the Sizzle in Sparc." *Datamation*, May 1, 1991.

FREIBURN, RICHARD, and RONALD E. ROADES. "The Workstation Revolution," *Information Executive*, Winter 1991.

GANTZ, JOHN. "PC vs. Workstation Dominance Looms Near." *Infoworld*, May 14, 1990.

"Get It While It's Hot: Slicing Up the Worldwide Workstation Market." *PC Week*, January 29, 1990.

GROSS, NEAL. "Why Sun Is Losing Its Heat in the East." *Business Week*, September 10, 1989.

HILKIRK, JOHN. "Workstations, PCs Gain Popularity." *USA Today*, April 26, 1989.

HURLEY, KATHLEEN, and CARL FLOCK. "PCs vs. Workstations: The Battle Revisited." *Computer Graphics Review*, June 1990.

HOF, ROBERT D. "Where Sun Means to Be a Bigger Fireball." *Business Week*, April 15, 1991.

HOF, ROBERT D. "Will Sun Also Rise in the Office Market." *Business Week*, May 21, 1990.

KUCHARVY, THOMAS. "Can IBM Catch Up with the Workstation Market." *Computer Graphics Review*, June 1990.

LEIBOWITZ, MICHAEL R. "UNIX Workstations Arrive." *Datamation,* June 1, 1990.

LEWIS, PETER H. "Can Old Processing Technology Beat Back New Challenge." *New York Times*, February 25, 1990.

LEWIS, PETER H. "With Both Feet, IBM Jumps into Workstations." *New York Times*, February 18, 1990.

LEVINE, JONATHAN B. "Can Sun Stand the Heat in the PC Market." *Business Week*, April 24, 1989.

LEVINE, JONATHAN B. "Hewlett Packard's Screeching Turn toward Desktops." *Business Week*, September 11, 1989.

LEVINE, JONATHAN B. "High Noon for Sun." *Business Week*, July 24, 1989.

LUBERNOW, GERALD. "An Upstart's Rite of Passage." *Business Month*, May 1990.

MARKOFF, JOHN. "The Niche That IBM Can't Ignore." *New York Times*, April 25, 1989.

MARKOFF, JOHN. "A Prescription for Troubled IBM." *New York Times*, December 10, 1989.

MARKOFF, JOHN. "The Smart Alecs at Sun are Regrouping." *New York Times*, April 28, 1991.

MCCROSSEN, MELANIE. "Workstations: A Market Niche Raises Eyebrows." *Standard and Poor's Industry Surveys*, April 1990, pp. 81–82.

OULD, ANDREW. "IBM Challenges Sun in Workstation Market." *PC Week*, February 28, 1991.

OULD, ANDREW. "Carol Bartz: Star Is Still Rising for Hard Driving Executive." *PC Week*, September 3, 1990.

OULD, ANDREW. "Sun's Color Workstation Bridges UNIX, High End PC's." *PC Week*, July 30, 1990.

MCWILLIAMS, GARY. "DEC Is Changing with the Times—A Little Late." *Business Week*, April 9, 1990.

METHVIN, DAVE. "RISC-Based Systems Find Strength in Simplicity." *PC Week*, April 2, 1990.

SAVAGE, J. A. "HP/Apollo Duet Not Yet In Tune." *Computerworld*, September 2, 1991.

SEXTON, TARA. "IBM Raises the Ante in High Stakes RISC Arena." *PC Week*, April 2, 1990, pp. 8, 9.

SPIEGELMAN, LAURA. "RISC Buyers Turn Eyes toward IBM." *PC Week*, March 19, 1990.

SPIEGELMAN, LAURA. "Sun Focuses on SPARC to Fend Off Growing Competition." *PC Week*, March 19, 1990.

SCHNEIDAWAIND, JOHN. "DEC Launches Workstation Attack." *USA Today*, April 12, 1990.

SCHNEIDAWAIND, JOHN. "Sun Expected to Win Place in Fortune 1000." *PC Week*, October 8, 1990.

"Sun Microsystems Turn on the Afterburners." *Business Week*, July 18, 1988.

"Trends: Technical Workstations." *Computerworld*, February 26, 1990.

VERITY, JOHN W. "IBM Is Finally Saying in UNIX We Trust." *Business Week*, February 12, 1990.

"The Versatility of the New Workstations." *I/S Analyzer*, January 1989.

WELTON, THERESE R. "Workstations: Prophecies Coming to Pass." *Industry Week*, January 2, 1989.

WRIGHT, JETHRO. "What Is a Workstation?" *MIS Week*, February 15, 1990.

YODER, STEPHAN K., et al. "Rivals Take Aim at IBM's Workstations." *Wall Street Journal*, February 15, 1990.

YODER, STEPHAN K., et al., "Workstation Options Expanding." *Wall Street Journal*, May 9, 1990.

ZACHARY, G. PASCAL and STEPHAN K. YODER. "A Line Dividing Workstations and PC's Blurs." *Wall Street Journal*, March 20, 1990.